SUMAN KALYANPUR

SONGS' WESTERN NOTES

A rare collection of Songs Lyrics and its Sargam
sung by Suman Kalyanpur
having fresh clean natural waterfall like voice

SUMAN KALYANPUR

Notation writer: Vinod Kumar

Notion Press

Vinod Kumar

NOTION PRESS

India. Singapore. Malaysia.

ISBN xxx-x-xxxxx-xx-x

DEDICATION

This book is dedicated to my Parents.

-Vinod Kumar

CONTENTS

SINGER SUMAN KALYANPUR BIOGRAPHY

Suman Kalyanpur

Birth- 28 January 1937

Age- 85 Years (in Jan 2022)

Parents- Sita Hemmadi, Shankar Rao Hemmadi

Suman Kalyanpur (born as Suman Hemmadi; 28 January 1937) is an Indian playback singer, one of the best-known and most respected playback singers in India.

Her voice was often mistaken to be that of Lata Mangeshkar. Suman Kalyanpur's career started in 1954 and was very popular singer in the 1960s and 1970s. She recorded songs for movies in several languages besides Hindi, Marathi, Assamese, Gujarati, Kannada, Maithili, Bhojpuri, Rajasthani, Bengali, Odia and Punjabi. She is considered among the popular singers of her prime time and golden era of Hindi film music.

Early life

Suman Kalyanpur was born as Suman Hemmadi on 28 January 1937 in Dhaka (now in Bangladesh). Suman Kalyanpur's father

Shankar Rao Hemmadi hailed from a Saraswat Brahmin family belonging to Mangalore. Hemmadi is a village in Kundapur Taluk of Udupi District, Karnataka. He served on a top post in the Central Bank of India and was posted to Dhaka for a very long period. Apart from father and mother Seeta Hemmadi, there were 5 daughters and one son in the family with Suman being the eldest among her siblings. In 1943, her family moved to Mumbai, where she started learning music.

Suman had always been interested in painting and music. After completing schooling from Mumbai's famed St. Columba High School, she got admission in the prestigious Sir J. J. School of Arts for further studies in painting. Simultaneously, she started learning classical vocal from Pune's Prabhat Films' music director and a close family friend, Pandit Keshav Rao Bhole. According to Suman, initially singing was just hobby to her but gradually her interest in music increased and she started learning it professionally from Ustad Khan, Abdul Rehman Khan and Guruji Master Navrang. Suman's younger sister Shyama Hemmady was also a singer.

Married life

Suman Hemmady married a Mumbai-based businessman Ramanand Kalyanpur in the 1958 and thus, became Suman Kalyanpur from Suman Hemmady. He accompanied her for every recording session after her marriage. She has a daughter named Charul Agni who is settled in the United States after marriage. Her grand daughter Aaishanni Agny returned to India and opened an NGO in Mumbai in her grand mother's name.

Career

According to Suman, "Everybody at home had an inclination towards arts and music but public performances were strictly prohibited. Still, I could not say 'no' to an offer to sing for the All India Radio in 1952. This was my first public performance after which I got a chance to sing for the Marathi film Shukrachi Chandni released in the year 1953. At that time, Sheikh Mukhtar was making the film 'Mangu' whose composer was Mohammed Shafi. Sheikh Mukhtar was so impressed with my "Shukrachi Chandni" songs, that he got me to sing 3 songs for the film 'Mangu'. However, due to some unknown reasons, later O. P. Nayyar replaced Mohammed Shafi and only one of my three songs, a lullaby "Koi Pukare Dheere Se Tujhe" was retained in the film. Thus, I entered Hindi cinema with the 1954 release "Mangu".

Immediately, after the film "'Mangu'", Suman sang 5 songs under the baton of composer Naushad for the film Darwaza (1954), which was produced by Ismat Chugtai and directed by Shahid Lateef. Since "Darwaza" released first, it is generally believed to be Suman Kalyanpur's first Hindi film. In the same year (1954), Suman sang the film version of O.P.Nayyar's hit ensemble song "Mohabbat Kar Lo Ji Bhar Lo Aji Kisne Roka Hai" with Mohammed Rafi and Geeta Dutt for the film Aar Paar. According to Suman, she had a couple of solo lines to sing and her services were used, more, as a chorus singer in this song. This proved to be the only song she ever sang for O. P. Nayyar.

Suman Kalyanpur's first film song was a duet with Talat Mahmood in Darwaza (1954). Talat Mahmood heard Kalyanpur singing in a musical concert and was highly impressed by her singing. A rank newcomer, her career hit the big league when Talat agreed to sing the duet with her, making the film industry sit up and take notice of her.

She sang for the movie, Mangu (1954), Koi Pukare Dheere Se Tujhe. Kalyanpur provided playback singing for Miyan Bibi Razi

(1960), Baat Ek Raat Ki (1962), Dil Ek Mandir (1963), Dil Hi To Hai (1963), Shagoon (1964), Jahan Ara (1964), Sanjh Aur Savera (1964), Noor Jehan (1967), Saathi (1968) and Pakeezah (1971). She sang for composers Shankar Jaikishan, Roshan, Madan Mohan, S. D. Burman, N Datta, Hemant Kumar, Chitragupta, Naushad, S. N. Tripathi, Ghulam Mohammed, Kalyanji Anandji and Laxmikant–Pyarelal singing the most songs for the first two in the list. She has sung over 740 movie and non-movie songs. She sang over 140 duets with Rafi in the 1960s.

Suman's first song in Marathi was the super-hit "Bhaatuklichaa Khel Maandila" for Vasant Prabhu, for the film Pasant Aahe Mulgi. After that she never looked back for over 20 years. Putra Vhawa Aisaa, Ekti, Manini and Annapoorna were but a few of her memorable films. But even outside films, her hits are legion and include over 50 timeless gems of Marathi films, bhavgeet and bhaktigeet.

She recorded some popular duets with male singers Mohammed Rafi, Manna Dey, Mukesh, Talat Mahmood, and Hemant Kumar. Some of her memorable duets with Rafi are "Aajkal Tere Mere Pyaar Ke Charche", "Na Na Karte Pyaar", "Tumse O Hasina", "Rahen Na Rahen Hum", "Parbaton Ke Pedon Par Shaam Ka Basera He", "Ajahu na Aye Balama", "Tumane Pukara Aur Hum Chale Aye", "Bad Muddat Ke Yeh Ghadi Ayee", "Mujhe Yeh Bhool Na", "Dil Ne Phir Yaad Kiya", "Tujhko Dilbari Ki Kasam" and "Chand Takata Hai Idhar". With Manna Dey, she sang the popular duet "Na Jane Kahan Ham The" under the music direction of Dattaram. With Mukesh she has sung many popular duets like `Yeh Kisne Geet Chheda', "Akhiyon ka noor hai tu", "Mera Pyar Bhi Tu Hai", "Dil Ne Phir Yaad Kiya", "Shama Se Koi Kehde", etc.

Kalyanpur also recorded some memorable songs with a classical base, including "Manamohan Man Mein Ho Tumhi", "Mere Sang Ga Gunguna" and "Gir Gayi Re More Mathe Ki Bindiya".

Similarity of voice with Lata Mangeshkar

Suman Kalyanpur's voice was very similar to the singer, Lata Mangeshkar and some times people can not differ her voice with Lata's voice and think of Lata's song.

When Lata was not available for recording, or if the producers could not afford her rate of per song, the song used to be sung by Suman Kalyanpur. During the similar period, Lata had refused to sing with Rafi over royalty issues and those songs of Md. Rafi were recorded with Suman Kalyanpur and a great voice came in front of the music listeners. She sang over 140 duets with Rafi in this period.

Notable songs

Hindi songs

- "Sathi Mere Sathi" (Veerana)
- "Na Tum Hamen Jano" (Baat Ek Raat Ki)
- "Chhodo, Chhodo Mori Baiyann" (Miya Biwi Razi)
- "Dil Gham Se Jal Raha" (Shama)
- "Yun Hi Dil Ne Chaha Tha" (Dil Hi To Hai)
- "Bujha Diye Hain" (Shagoon)
- "Mere Sang Ga" (Janwar)
- "Mere Mehboob Na Ja" (Noor Mahal)
- "Tum Agar Aa Sako To"' and
- "Zindagi Doob Gai Dard Ke Toofano Mein" (Ek Sal Pehle)
- "Zindagi imtehan leti hai " (Naseeb)
- "Jo Ham Pe Guzarti Hai" (Mohabbat Isko Kehten Hain)

- "Sharabi Sharabi Yeh Sawan Ka Mausam" (Noor Jehan)
- "Behena Ne Bhai Ki Kalai Main" (Resham Ki Dori), for which she was nominated for the Filmfare Best Female Playback Award in 1975.
- "Dil Ek Mandir Hai" (Dil Ek Mandir)
- "Aajkal Tere Mere Pyaar Ke Charche" from Brahmachari, which was one of her most famous songs, is usually thought to be sung by Lata Mangeshkar but it was in fact sung by her. (The confusion results from the fact that the quality of her voice is similar to Lata Mangeshkar's at times).
- "Aansoo ki ek boond hoon main" (Ek Paheli)
- "Mera Pyar Bhi Tu Hai Yeh Bahar Bhi Tu Hai" (Saathi)
- "Na Na Karte Pyar" (Jab Jab Phool Khile)
- "Zindagi zulm sahi" (shagun)

Marathi songs

- "Rimjhhim Jharati Shrāwan Dhara"
- "Shabda Shabda Japun Thhewa"
- "Re Kshanichya Sangateene Mi Ashi Bharawale"
- "Keshava Madhava Tuzya Namat Re Godawa"
- "Omkar Pradhan Roop Ganeshache"
- "Jethe Sagara Dharanee Milate"
- "Bhaktichya Phulancha Goad To Suwas"
- "Navika Re Vara Vahe Re"
- "Ketakichya Banee Tethe Nachala Ga Mor"
- "Yaa Laadkya Mulino".
- "Samadhi Gheun jayee dnyandev".
- "Mrudul Karani Chhedit Tara".
- "Savalya Vitthala Tujhya Dari Aale".
- "Saang kadhi kalnar tula bhav majhya manat la"
- "Nimbonichya zada mage"

Bengali songs

- "Ronger Basore"
- "Ei Chadro Mollikate"
- "Durashar Baluchare"
- "Mone Karo Aami Nei"
- "Sudhu Swapno Niye"
- "Kande Keno Mon"
- "Tomar Aakash Theke"
- "Badoler Madol Baje Guruguru"
- "Aamar Swapno Dekhar Duti Nayon"
- "Aakash Ajana Tobu"
- "Payer Chinho Niye"
- "Dulchere Mon"
- "Byatha Hoye Keno Phire Ele Bondhua"
- "Bhabis Ne Re Kandhchi Bosey"
- "Ekhane Okhane Jekhane Sekhane"
- "Dure theko na aaro aaro kache eso"

Kannada songs

- "Odanadi Bekendu"
- "Hani Hani Heeri Thani Hareya"
- "Thallana Nooru bage"

Awards

1. Received three times the prestigious "Sur Sringar Samsad" award for the best classical song in a Hindi movie.
2. Lata Mangeshkar Award 2009 by the Maharashtra government
3. Ga Di Ma Award by Ga Di Ma Pratishthan

PREFACE

My hearty greetings and Namaste to Readers. I have written 51 Songs' Sargam books of Mukesh-1,2, Kishor-1,2, Lata, Asha, Manna dey, Yesudas, Kumar Shanu, Rafi-1,2,3,4 and SD Burman's composed song book in Hindi Language and translated many books in English SARGAM and Western CDEFG. Bhajan Swarlipi 1,2,3 and one Gazal Sargam book is also published in Hindi, English and Western notes. All these books are available online. Now I have translated the Suman Kalyanpur ke 51 Geeton ki Sargam book in English as Suman Kalyanpur Songs' Western Notes. It is in English with notes in CDEF style, so that music lovers can play and sing songs and get enjoyed. A person having basic knowledge of music can play the songs on any instrument.

Mostly song's notations are written in original scale but somewhere you have to transpose +1 or − 1 or ±2 to get original scale. Sa taken is also mentioned in each song's detail. Person who knows western notations can understand as given below:

.नी	.नी	सा	रे̲	रे	ग̲	ग	म
.N̲	.N	S	R̲	R	G̲	G	M
.B^b	.B	C	D^b	D	E^b	E	F
.A$^\#$	.B	C	C$^\#$	D	D$^\#$	E	F

मे	प	ध̲	ध	नी̲	नी	सां	रें̲
M*	P	D̲	D	N̲	N	S'	R'̲
G^b	G	A^b	A	B^b	B	C'	D$^{b'}$
F$^\#$	G	G$^\#$	A	A$^\#$	B	C'	C$^{\#'}$

In this book some symbols are given as (G-) it means you have to play G for two beats duration or matra similarly you have to play for the beats for more number of – if there are more dashes. When two notes are written adjacending to each other it means you have to play the notes in one beat or matra as MP mapa is played in one beat.

Notations at the beginning of the song are prelude and notations in the middle of the song are interlude. These notations are written by me by my experience. Hope readers shall understand, like and enjoy it.

One has to practice sargam daily and its palte also so that one can become expert in playing difficult notes sequence. People can enjoy your playing instruments and then only your success will be counted. Care has been taken to provide accuracy still there is no liability of correctness and accuracy of notes and writer, printer, publisher and editor is not respoinsible for any error or ommissions or mistakes. If any mistake is found kindly inform.

For purchasing the books in India, one can visit notionpress.com or flipkart.com and amazon.in. Kindly review my books at amazon and flipkart and give proper stars after purchasing my books from the above sites. For any query, email to me.

- Vinod Kumar (vinod66vk@gmail.com)

Vinod Kumar

SARGAM

SARGAM swars/sound are derived from voice of animals and birds. C scale is as follows:-

Note Name	Swar	स्वर नाम	Swar full name	स्वर का पूरा नाम हिंदी में	यह स्वर किस पशु पछी की आवाज से लिया गया है.
C=	Sa=	सा	Shadaj	षडज	Peacock/ मोर की आवाज़
D=	Re=	रे	Rishabh	रिषभ	Papiha /पपीहा की आवाज़
E=	Ga=	ग	Gandhar	गन्धार	Goat/ बकरा की आवाज़
F=	Ma=	म	Madhyam	मध्यम	Crane/ बगुला की आवाज़
G=	Pa=	प	Pancham	पंचम	Koccoo/Koyal/ कोयल की आवाज़
A=	Dha=	ध	Dhaiwat	धैवत	Frog/ दादुर या मेंढक की आवाज़
B=	Ni=	नी	Nishad	निषाद	Elephant हाथी की आवाज़
C'=	Sa'=	सां	(Higher Sa)		

C#=Re=रे (रे कोमल), D#=Ga=ग (ग कोमल), F#=Ma*=मे (म तीव्र), G#=Dha=ध (ध कोमल), A#=Ni=नी (नी कोमल)

We can write as S R R G G M M* P D D N N S'

All notes underlined are called Komal Swar as Komal Re Komal Ga Komal Dha Komal Ni. One note Ma* is called Tivra Ma Sequence of the notes are-

S	R	R	G	G	M	M*
सा	रे	रे	ग	ग	म	मे
C	D^b	D	E^b	E	F	G^b
C	$C^\#$	D	$D^\#$	E	F	$F^\#$

P	D	D	N	N	S'
प	ध	ध	नी	नी	सां
G	A^b	A	B^b	B	C'
G	$G^\#$	A	$A^\#$	B	C'

Sa and Pa are Shudha Swar they do not have any Komal or Tivra. They are fixed notes as per North Indian music tradition.

OCTAVE

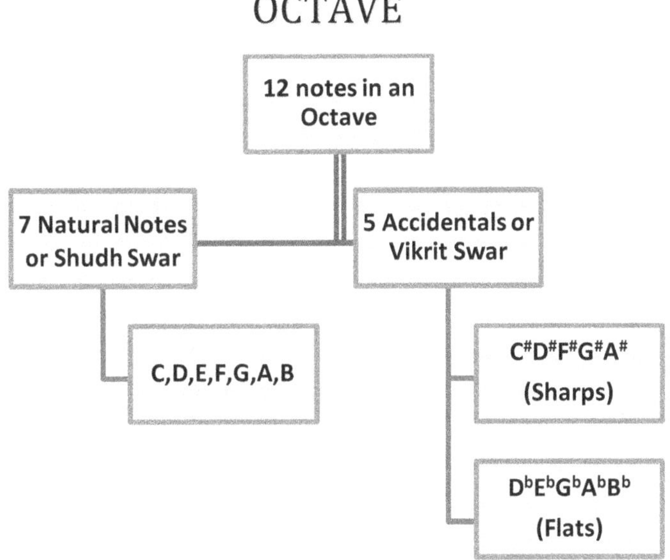

Sequence of the notes on any instrument are:

.B^b .B C D^b D E^b E F G^b G A^b A B^b B C' D$^{b'}$ D' so on…

.A$^\#$ .B C C$^\#$ D D$^\#$ E F F$^\#$ G G$^\#$ A A$^\#$ B C' C$^{\#'}$ D' D$^{\#'}$

C Scale is given as: **C D E F G A B C'**

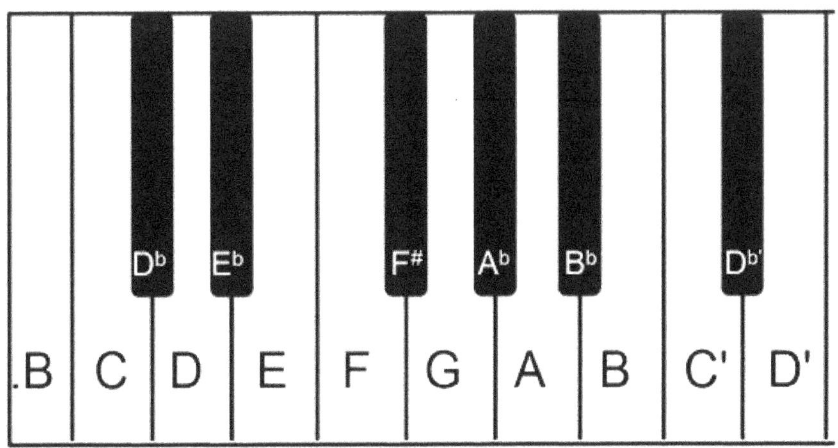

Vinod Kumar

C$^\#$ Scale is given as:

C$^\#$ D$^\#$ F F$^\#$ G$^\#$ A$^\#$ C′ C$^\#$′

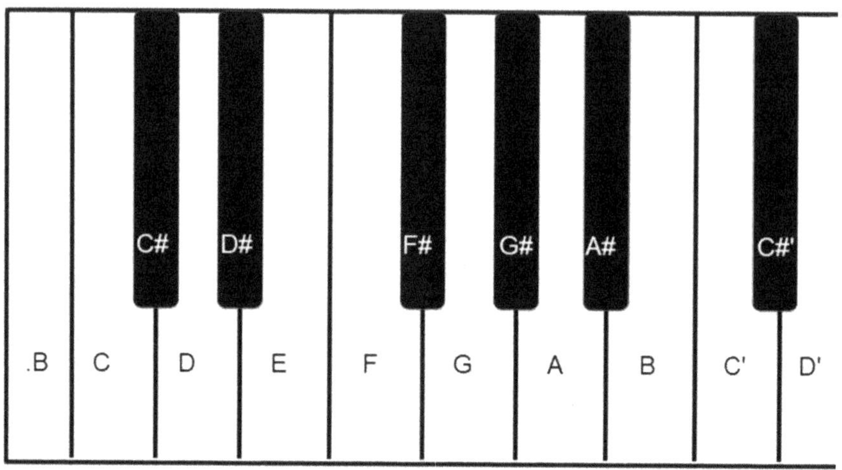

1. ANKHIYON KA NOOR HAI TU

Film: Jauhar Mahmood in Goa (1965)
Lyrics: Qamar Jalalabadi
Taal: Kaharwa
Transpose +2 and play from C Scale
or play as D scale song

Music: Kalyanji Anandji
Singer: Mukesh, Suman K.
Chord: FA^{b}C' S=D

ankhiyon ka nur hai tu, ankhiyon se dur hai tu
fir bhi pukaare chale jaayenge, tu aye na aye
fir bhi pukaare chale jaayenge

dil men payaam tera lab pe hai naam tera
ho ke diwaane tere pyaar men lo aye ji aye
ho ke diwaane tere pyaar men

o mere hamaraaz kahaan hai, mujh ko de awaaz kahaan hai
pyaar ki ankhon se tum dekho, <u>ishq wahin hai husn jahaan hai</u> -2
chhup chhup ke anewaale, dil ko jalaane waale
chupake se aa ja mere saamne
tu aja re a ja, chupake se a ja mere saamne

isalie aya hun main chhupake, dekh ke hamako duniya jale na
pyaar ki mahafil kitani anokhi, <u>nur hai lekin dip jale na</u>-2
yaadon ke daag le ke, dil ke chiraag le ke
kab se khada hun tere saamne
tu maane na maane kab se khada hun tere saamne

ANKHIYON KA NOOR HAI TU

dha	ge	n	ti	n	ke	dhi	n	dha	ge	n	ti	n	ke	dhi	n
1	2	3	4	5	6	7	8	1	2	3	4	5	6	7	8
		C	D	-	D	F	F	F	G	-	A♭	A♭	-	A♭	-
		an	khi	-	yon	-	ka	nu	-	-	r	hai	-	tu	-
-	-	G	A♭	-	G	-	F	F	G	-	A♭	A♭	-	A♭	-
-	-	an	khi	-	yon	-	se	du	-	-	r	hai	-	tu	-
-	-	G	A♭	-	G	-	F	F	G	G	A♭	-	G	G	-
-	-	fi	r	-	bhi	-	pu	ka	-	re	-	-	ch	le	-
F	-	-	F	F	-	F	-	F	G	G	B♭	B♭	-	A♭	-
ja	-	-	yen	ge	-	tu	-	aa	-	ye	n	aa	-	ye	-
-	-	G	A♭	-	G	-	F	F	G	G	A♭	-	G	G	-
-	-	fi	r	-	bhi	-	pu	ka	-	re	-	-	ch	le	-
F	-	-	F	F	-	-	-	A♭	G	A♭	-	G	F	F	-
ja	-	-	yen	ge	-	-	-	-	-	-	-	-	-	-	-
-	-	C	D	-	D	F	F	F	G	-	-	A♭	A♭	A♭	-
-	-	di	l	-	me	-	p	ya	-	-	-	m	te	ra	-
-	-	A♭	A♭	-	G	F	-	F	G	-	-	A♭	A♭	A♭	-
-	-	l	b	-	pe	hai	-	na	-	-	-	m	te	ra	-
-	-	A♭	-	-	G	-	F	F	G	G	A♭	-	G	-	F
-	-	ho	-	-	ke	-	di	va	-	ne	-	-	te	-	re
F	-	-	F	F	-	F	-	F	G	G	B♭	B♭	-	A♭	-
pya	-	-	r	me	-	lo	-	aa	-	ye	ji	aa	-	ye	-
-	-	A♭	-	-	G	-	F	F	G	G	A♭	-	G	-	F
-	-	ho	-	-	ke	-	di	va	-	ne	-	-	te	-	re
F	-	-	F	F	-										
pya	-	-	r	me	-										

interlude:

F' B♭ C' D♭'- F'E♭'D♭'F'- C'B♭ B♭A♭ A♭B♭-
F'E♭'D♭'F'- C'B♭ B♭A♭ A♭B♭-
D♭'C' C'B♭ B♭A♭ A♭B♭-A♭ GA♭-G F
F- FE♭- E♭D♭- D♭C-
F'—E♭'F'G'C'D♭'—B♭C'D♭'A♭B♭
B♭ A♭G GF G F (FA♭C')

| C' | - | | - | B♭ | - | - | B♭ | - | - | - | B♭ | C' | D♭' | - |
| o | - | | - | me | - | - | re | - | - | - | hm | - | - | - |

| - | - | C' | - | - | B♭ | - | B♭ | B♭ | - | - | - | B♭ | - | - | - |
| - | - | ra | - | - | z | - | k | ha | - | - | - | hai | - | - | - |

| - | - | C' | B♭ | - | B♭ | - | - | B♭ | - | - | - | GA♭ GA♭ | - | - |
| - | - | mu | jh | - | ko | - | - | de | - | - | - | aa- | - | - |

| - | - | A♭ | G | - | G | - | F | F | - | - | - | F | - | - |
| - | - | va | - | - | z | - | k | ha | - | - | - | hai | - | - |

| - | - | C' | - | - | B♭ | - | B♭ | B♭ | - | - | - | B♭ | C' | D♭' | - |
| - | - | pya | - | - | r | - | ki | aan | - | - | - | khon | - | - | - |

| - | - | C' | - | - | B♭ | - | B♭ | B♭ | - | - | - | B♭ | - | - | - |
| - | - | se | - | - | tu | - | m | de | - | - | - | kho | - | - | - |

| - | - | C' | - | - | B♭ | - | A♭ | A♭ | - | - | - | GA♭ GA♭ | - | - |
| - | - | i | - | sh | q | - | v | hin | - | - | - | hai- | - | - |

| - | - | B♭ | A♭ | - | G | - | F | F | - | - | - | F | - | F | G |
| - | - | hu | s | - | n | - | j | ha | - | - | - | hai | - | - | - |

| A | - | A | - | - | B♭ | - | C' | B♭ | - | - | - | F | E♭ | - | - |
| - | - | i | - | sh | k | - | v | hin | - | - | - | hai | - | - | - |

| - | - | A♭ | A♭ | - | G | - | F | F | - | - | - | F | - | - |
| - | - | hu | s | - | n | - | j | ha | - | - | - | hai | - | - |

| - | - | C | - | D | - | F | - | F | - | G | A♭ | A♭ | - | A♭ | - |
| - | - | chhu | p | chhu | p | ke | - | aa | - | ne | - | va | - | le | - |

| - | - | G | A♭ | - | G | - | F | F | - | G | A♭ | A♭ | - | A♭ | - |
| - | - | di | l | - | ko | - | j | la | - | ne | - | va | - | le | - |

-	-	G	A^b	G	-	F	-	F	-	G	A^b	-	G	G	-
-	-	chu	p	ke	-	se	-	aa	-	ja	-	-	me	re	-
F	-	-	F	F	-	-	F	F	G	G	B^b	B^b	-	A^b	-
sa	-	-	m	ne	-	-	tu	aa	-	ja	re	aa	-	ja	-
-	-	G	A^b	G	F	F	-	F	G	G	A^b	-	G	-	G
-	-	chu	p	ke	-	se	-	aa	-	ja	-	-	me	-	re
F	-	-	F	F	-	-	-	A^b	G	A^b	-	G	F	F	-
sa	-	-	m	ne	-	-	-	-	-	-	-	-	-	-	-
-	-	C	D	-	F	-	F	F	G	-	-	A^b	A^b	A^b	-
-	-	di	l	-	me	-	p	ya	-	-	-	m	te	ra	-
-	-	A^b	A^b	-	G	F	-	F	G	-	-	A^b	A^b	A^b	-
-	-	l	b	-	pe	hai	-	na	-	-	-	m	te	ra	-
-	-	A^b	-	-	G	-	F	F	G	G	A^b	-	G	-	F
-	-	ho	-	-	ke	-	di	va	-	ne	-	-	te	-	re
F	-	-	F	F	-	F	-	F	G	G	B^b	B^b	-	A^b	-
pya	-	-	r	me	-	lo	-	aa	-	ye	ji	aa	-	ye	-
-	-	G	A^b	-	G	-	F	F	G	G	A^b	-	G	G	-
-	-	ho	-	-	ke	-	di	va	-	ne	-	-	te	re	-
F	-	-	F	F	-										
pya	-	-	r	me	-										

$C'B^bB^bB^b$ $B^bB^bC'D^{b'}$ C' B^b $B^bB^bB^b$
islie   aaya   hu main   chhupke,

$C'B^b$ B^b A^b GA^b GGA^b GF F
dekh ke   hmko-   duniya   jle   na

$C'B^b$ B^b B^b $B^bC'D^{b'}$ $C'B^bB^b$ $B^bB^bB^b$
pyar ki   mhfil-   kitni   anokhi,

$C'B^b$ A^b A^bGA^b B^bA^b GF F
nur hai   lekin   dip   jle   na

music: F G A-

AB^b C'   B^b FE^{b}A^b A^{b}G   FF   F
nur   hai lekin--   dip   jle na

CD   F   FGA^b A^b A^b GA^b G FFGA^b A^b A^b
yado ke da-g le ke, dil   ke chira-g le ke

GA^b G FF   GA^b GF FFF
kb   se khda hu- tere samne

F FG   B^b B^{b}A^b GA^{b}G FF   GA^b GF FFF   A^{b}GA^b- GFF-
tu mane na mane kb se khda hu-tere samne (music)

	C	D	-	D	F	F	F	G	-	A^b	A^b	-	A^b	-
	an	khi	-	yon	-	ka	nu	-	-	r	hai	-	tu	-
-	-	G	A^b	-	G	-	F	F	G	-	A^b	A^b	-	A^b	-
-	-	an	khi	-	yon	-	se	du	-	-	r	hai	-	tu	-
-	-	G	A^b	-	G	-	F	F	G	G	A^b	-	G	G	-
-	-	fi	r	-	bhi	-	pu	ka	-	re	-	-	ch	le	-
F	-	-	F	F	-	F	-	F	G	G	B^b	B^b	-	A^b	-
ja	-	-	yen	ge	-	tu	-	aa	-	ye	n	aa	-	ye	-
-	-	G	A^b	-	G	-	F	F	G	G	A^b	-	G	G	-
-	-	fi	r	-	bhi	-	pu	ka	-	re	-	-	ch	le	-
F	-	-	F	F	-	-	-								
ja	-	-	yen	ge	-	-	-								

2.   AGAR TERI JALWANUMAI NA HOTI

Film: Beti Bete (1964)
Lyrics: Hasrat Jaipuri
Taal: Kaharwa
Transpose +2 and play from C Scale
or play as D scale song

Music: Shanker Jaikishan
Singer: Md. Rafi, Suman K.
Chord: DGB   S=D

Rafi: agar teri jalwa numai na hoti,
            khuda ki kasam ye khudayi na hoti
Suman: agar aankh tumse milayi na hoti
            meri zindagi muskurayi na hoti
Rafi: baharo ka mausam na hota suhana -2
            tere dam kadam se hua aashikana -2
            nazaaro me ye dil rubai na hoti
            khuda ki kasam ye khudayi na hoti
            agar aankh tumse milayi na hoti
            meri jindagi muskurayi na hoti
Suman: tere pyar ne mujh par ahsaan kiya hai -2
            mere dil liya hai mujhe dil diya hai -2
            agar tune ulfat nibhayi na hoti
            meri zindagi muskurayi na hoti
            agar teri jalwa numai na hoti
            khuda ki kasam ye khudayi na hoti
Rafi: agar noor tera na aata jaha me -2
            to rakha hi kaya tha zamii aasma me -2
            ke malik ne dunia banayi na hoti
            khuda ki kasam ye khudayi na hoti
agar aankh tumse milayi na hoti, meri zindagi muskurayi na hoti
agar teri jalwa numai na hoti, khuda ki kasam ye khudayi na hoti.

AGAR TERI JALWANUMAI NA HOTI

dha	ge	n	ti	n	ke	dhi	n	dha	ge	n	ti	n	ke	dhi	n
1	2	3	4	5	6	7	8	1	2	3	4	5	6	7	8

prelude:
GB G'-- F#'-- BG E'—D'— E'D'E'D' E'D'E'D'
AGAG ABAG AGAG ABAG
GF#ED GBAG G-

dha	ge	n	ti	n	ke	dhi	n	dha	ge	n	ti	n	ke	dhi	n
		D	D	B	A	-	G	G	-	-	-	G	-	-	-
		a	g	r	te	-	ri	j	l	-	-	va	-	-	-
-	-	C'	B	-	A	-	G	A	-	-	-	A	-	-	-
-	-	nu	ma	-	ii	-	n	ho	-	-	-	ti	-	-	-
-	-	D'	D'	-	C'	-	B	C'	-	-	-	B	-	-	G
-	-	khu	da	-	ki	-	k	sm	-	-	-	ye	-	-	khu
B	-	-	-	A	-	-	G	G	-	-	-	G	-	-	-
da	-	-	-	yi	-	-	n	ho	-	-	-	ti	-	-	-
-	-	D	D	B	A	-	G	G	-	-	-	G	-	-	-
-	-	a	g	r	aan	-	kh	tum	-	-	-	se	-	-	-
-	-	C'	B	-	A	-	G	A	-	-	-	A	-	-	-
-	-	mi	la	-	ii	-	n	ho	-	-	-	ti	-	-	-
-	-	D'	D'	-	C'	-	B	C'	-	-	-	B	-	-	G
-	-	me	ri	-	zin	-	d	gi	-	-	-	mu	-	-	sku
B	-	-	-	A	-	-	G	G	-	-	-	G	-	-	-
ra	-	-	-	yi	-	-	n	ho	-	-	-	ti	-	-	-

interlude: 1
C'---- D' BBAG ABBAGG—
C'---- D' BBAG ABBAGG—
E'—G' [D]E' [C]D' [B]C' [A]B
AG BA C'--- BAG--

dha	ge	n	ti	n	ke	dhi	n	dha	ge	n	ti	n	ke	dhi	n
		D'	D'	-	D'	-	D'	E'	-	-	-	C'	B	A	-
		b	ha	-	ro	-	ka	mau	-	-	-	sm	-	-	-
-	-	C'	C'	-	C'	-	C'	D'	-	-	-	B	A	G	-
-	-	n	ho	-	ta	-	su	ha	-	-	-	na	-	-	-

-	-	E	E	-	E	-	F	G	-	-	-	B	-	-	B
-	-	te	re	-	dm	-	k	dm	-	-	-	se	-	-	hu
C'	-	-	-	B	-	-	A	G	-	-	-	G	B	A	G
aa	-	-	-	aa	-	-	shi	ka	-	-	-	na	-	-	-
-	-	D	D	B	A	-	G	G	-	-	-	G	-	-	-
-	-	n	za	-	ro	-	me	ye	-	-	-	dil	-	-	-
-	-	C'	B	-	A	-	G	A	-	-	-	A	-	-	-
-	-	ru	ba	-	ii	-	n	ho	-	-	-	ti	-	-	-
-	-	D'	D'	-	C'	-	B	C'	-	-	-	B	-	-	G
-	-	khu	da	-	ki	-	k	sm	-	-	-	ye	-	-	khu
B	-	-	-	A	-	-	G	G	-	-	-	G	-	-	-
da	-	-	-	ii	-	-	n	ho	-	-	-	ti	-	-	-

interlude: 2

G'---- F'E' E'-F'-E'-F'-

D'-E'-D'-E'-D'-

BD'F'E'D' B AA G-

B-G-B-G- B-G-G- GABC'D'--

-	-	D'	D'	-	D'	-	D'	E'	-	-	-	C'	B	A	-
-	-	te	re	-	pya	-	r	ne	-	-	-	mu	jh	pe	-
-	-	C'	C'	-	C'	-	C'	D'	-	-	-	B	A	G	-
-	-	e	h	-	san	-	ki	ya	-	-	-	hai	-	-	-
-	-	E	E	-	E	-	F	G	-	-	-	B	-	-	B
-	-	me	ra	-	dil	-	li	ya	-	-	-	hai	-	-	mu
C'	-	-	-	B	-	-	A	G	-	-	-	G	B	A	G
jhe	-	-	-	dil	-	-	di	ya	-	-	-	hai	-	-	-
-	-	D	D	B	A	-	G	G	-	-	-	G	-	-	-
-	-	a	g	r	tu	-	ne	ul	-	-	-	f	-	-	t
-	-	C'	B	-	A	-	G	A	-	-	-	A	-	-	-
-	-	ni	bha	-	ii	-	n	ho	-	-	-	ti	-	-	-
-	-	D'	D'	-	C'	-	B	C'	-	-	-	B	-	-	G
-	-	me	ri	-	zin	-	d	gi	-	-	-	mu	-	-	sku

B	-	-	-	A	-	-	G	G	-	-	-	G	-	-	-
ra	-	-	-	yi	-	-	n	ho	-	-	-	ti	-	-	-

3. AJAHUN NA AAYE BAALMA

Film: Sanjh aur Savera (1964)
Lyrics: Hasrat Jaipuri
Taal: Kaharwa
Transpose +1 and play from C Scale
or play as C# scale song

Music: Shanker Jaikishan
Singer: Md. Rafi, Suman K.
Chord: CE^{b}G   S=C#

aa aa aa aa aa
ajahun n ae baalama
saawan bita jaae,
haae re saawan bita jaae

nind bhi ankhiyan dwaar na
ae
tose milan ki aas bhi jaae
aayi bahaar khile fulawa,
more sapanen kaun sajaae

chaand ko badara garawa lagaae
aur bhi mora man lalachaae
yaar hasin gale lag ja, aa
yaar hasin gale lag ja mori umr gujarati jaae

AJAHUN NA AAYE BAALMA

dha	ge	n	ti	n	ke	dhi	n	dha	ge	n	ti	n	ke	dhi	n
1	2	3	4	5	6	7	8	1	2	3	4	5	6	7	8

prelude: sarangi: E^b – F C .A^b .B C

C----- E^b C .A^b .B C

aa ………………………………… -2

E^b F A^b B C'

aa …………… -2

G – A^b G F E^b C E^b ---- .A^b .B .B C---

aa …………………… aa……………aa………………… -2

1	2	3	4	5	6	7	8	1	2	3	4	5	6	7	8
	BB	-C'	C'	A^bB	C'	A^b	G	-	FA^b	B	A^b	G	F	E^b	-
	aj	-hu	n	aa-	-	ye	-	-	ba-	-	l	ma	-	-	-
-	E^b	-F	G	E^b	-	C	.B	C	-	-	-	C	A^b	GF	E^b
-	sa	-v	n	bi	-	ta	-	ja	-	-	y	ha	ye	re-	-
-	E^b	-F	G	E^b	-	C	.B	C	-	-	-	FG	A^bB	C'	-
-	sa	-v	n	bi	-	ta	-	ja	-	-	y	aa-	--	-	-
-	BB	-C'	C	A^bB	C'	A^b	G	-	FA^b	B	A^b	G	F	E^b	-
-	aj	-hu	n	aa-	-	ye	-	-	ba	-	l	ma	-	-	-
-	E^b	-F	G	E^b	-	C	.B	C	-	-	-	C	A^b	GF	E^b
-	sa	-v	n	bi	-	ta	-	ja	-	-	y	ha	ye	re	-
-	E^b	-F	G	E^b	-	C	.B	C	-	-	-	E^bFGA^bBC'			$E^{b'}$
-	sa	-v	n	bi	-	ta	-	ja	-	-	y	aa-	--	--	-
C'	BB	-C'	C	A^bB	C'	A^b	G	-	FA^b	B	A^b	G	F	E^b	-
-	aj	-hu	n	aa-	-	ye	-	-	ba	-	l	ma	-	-	-
-	E^b	-F	G	E^b	-	C	.B	C	-	-	-	E^b	-	A^bG	F
-	sa	-v	n	bi	-	ta	-	ja	-	-	y	ha	ye	re-	-
-	E^b	-F	G	E^b	-	C	.B	C	-	-	-				
-	sa	-v	n	bi	-	ta	-	ja	-	-	y				

interlude:

sarangi:- $E^{b'}$ C' D' B C', $E^{b'}$—D' F'—D' $E^{b'}$ – D' C' D' – B C'

violin:-

G'F'G' F'E^b'F' E^b'D'E^b'-
F'E^b' F'E^b'D'C' E^b'D'C'B
BC'BA^{b}GFE^{b}DC

| E^b | F | F | A^b | A^b | B | B | - | C' | C' | B | C' | - | C' | - |
| nin | d | bhi | a | khi | y | n | - | dwa | r | n | aa | - | ye | - |

| D' | B | A^b | G | F | E^b | F | E^b | - | E^b | F | F | A^b | A^b | B | B |
| - | - | - | - | - | - | - | - | - | nin | d | bhi | a | khi | y | n |

| - | C' | C' | B | C' | - | C' | - | - | B | B | B | C' | C' | C' | - |
| - | dwa | r | n | aa | - | ye | - | - | to | se | mi | l | n | ki | - |

| - | B | C'A^b | G | FE^b | F | - | E^b | - | E^b | F | F | A^b | A^b | B | B |
| - | aa | -s | bhi | ja | ye | - | - | - | nin | d | bhi | a | khi | y | n |

| - | C' | C' | B | C' | - | C' | - | - | B | B | B | C' | C' | C' | - |
| - | dwa | r | n | aa | - | ye | - | - | to | se | mi | l | n | ki | - |

| - | B | C'A^b | G | FE^b | F | - | E^b | - | E^b' | -D' | -C' | E^b' | - | -D' | -C' |
| - | aa | s | bhi | ja- | ye | - | - | - | aa | -ii | -b | ha | - | -r | -khi |

| A^b | - | - | BB | C' | - | - | - | - | E^b' | -D' | -C' | E^b' | - | -D' | -C' |
| le | - | - | ful | va | - | - | - | - | aa | -ii | -b | ha | - | -r | -khi |

| A^b | - | - | BB | C' | - | - | - | - | F' | -E^b' | -C' | A^b | - | -B | -A^b |
| le | - | - | ful | va | - | - | - | - | aa | -ii | -b | ha | - | -r | -khi |

| BC'D'E^b' | F' | E^b'D' | C' | - | C' | B | - | D'C' | -C' | B | C' | - | -A^b | -G |
| le- | -- | - | ful | va | - | mo | re | - | sp | -ne | - | kau | - | -n | -s |

| FE^b | G | F | E^b | E^{b}FA^{b}B | C' | - |
| ja | ye | - | - | aa- | -- | - |

| - | BB | -C' | C' | A^{b}B | C' | A^b | G | - | FA^b | B | A^b | G | F | E^b | - |
| - | aj | -hu | n | aa- | - | ye | - | - | ba | - | l | ma | - | - | - |

interlude: 2 same

E^{b}F   F A^{b}A^{b}B C'C' BC'C' D'C'BA^{b}GE^{b}FE^b
chand ko bdra grva lgae

BB B C'C' BC' A^{b}GFE^{b}GFE^b
aur bhi mora mn llchhae

E^b'D' C'E^b'D' C'A^b BB C'
yar   hsiin   gle   lg ja

A^{b}BC'D' E^b'D' C'E^b'D' C'A^b BB C'
aa..   yar   hsiin   gle   lg ja

F'E^b'   C'A^{b}B A^{b}BC'D'E^b'F' E^b'D' C'
yar   hsiin   gle   lg   ja

C'B   D'C'C'   BC'C'A^b FE^{b}GFE^b
mori umr   guzrti   jae

E^{b}FA^{b}BC' BBC' C'
aa ...   ajhu   n -

4. APNE PIYA KI MAIN TO BANI RE JOGANIYA

Film: Kan Kan me Bhagwan (1963)   Music: Shivram
Lyrics: Bharat Vyas   Singer: Suman K.
Taal: Kaharwa dugun   Chord: FA^{b}C'   S=C#
Transpose +1 and play from C Scale

piya charan ki babhoot ramaayi,
preet ki pahni mala
ab kaahe ka darna jag se,
man mein huaa ujala, aaa

apne piya ki main to bani re joganiya
hansi udaaye chaahe saari duniya,
main to bani re joganiya
apne piya ki main to bani re joganiya

saawariya ke rang mein chunariya
rangaungi -2
chandrma ka jhumka pahan piya aaungi
jhan jhan baaje mori ho o.. o..
jhan jhan baaje mori jhaanjhariya
main to bani re joganiya

tere liye maine to sharam laaj chhodi re -2
tere sang jodi to jagat sang todi re
tu hai mohan mera, ho, o.. o..
tu hai mohan main teri mohaniya,
main to bani re joganiya

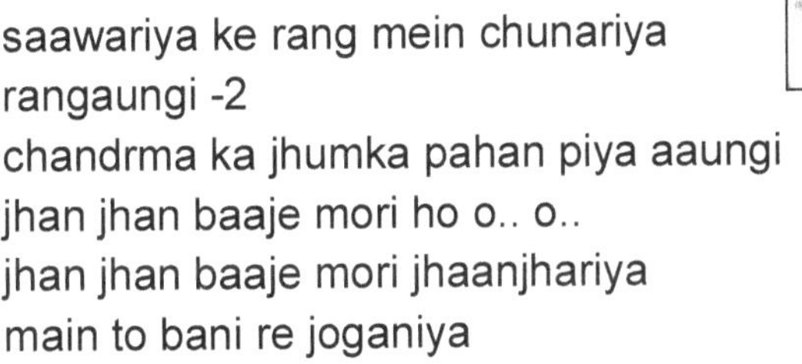

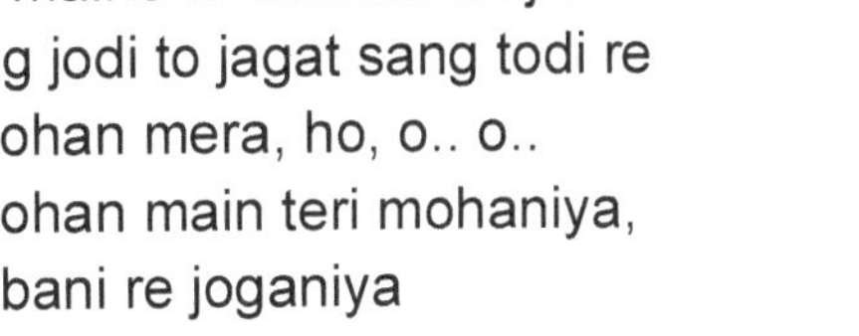

APNE PIYA KI MAIN TO BANI RE JOGANIYA

dhage	nti	nke	dhin	dhage	nti	nke	dhin	dhage	nti	nke	dhin	dhage	nti	nke	dhin
12	34	56	78	12	34	56	78	12	34	56	78	12	34	56	78
C'C'	C'C'C'	C'		C'F'F'		E^b'F'F'	C'F'E^b'	C'	B^{b}C'B^{b}A^b		B^{b}C'D^b'	C'			
piya	chrn	ki		bhbhut		rmaii,	pri-t	ki	p h ni-		ma---	la			
FA^b	D^b'D^b'	D^b'		B^{b}C'D^b'		B^{b}C'	A^b	A^b	A^b	A^{b}B^{b}C'		A^{b}A^{b}B^{b}F$^#$F			
ab	kahe	ka		drna		jg	se,	mn	me	huaa-		uja-la-,			
FA^{b}B^{b}D^b'---		C'B^{b}C'		B^{b}A^{b}B^b	E^{b}F										
aa -----		aa-------		aa------											
tune:															
	FB^b	B^b	B^b	A^b	A^b	A^b	F	F	A^b	A^b	A^b	F	F	F	-
-	B^b	B^b	B^b	B^b	C'	B^b	A^b	A^b	B^b	C'	A^b	B^b	-	A^b	F
F	A^b	A^b	A^b	F	F	F	-								
F	F	A^b	A^b	B^b	B^b	C'	F	F	F	A^b	A^b	B^b	B^b	C'	-
saan	vri	ya	ke	rn	g	mainchu		n	ri	ya rn		ga	un	gi	-
F	F	A^b	A^b	B^b	B^b	C'	F	F	F	A^b	A^b	B^b	B^b	C'	-
chn	dr	ma	ka	jhu	m	ka	p	h	n	pi ya		aa	un	gi	-
-	C'	C'C'	C'	C'	D^b'	C'	B^b	B^b	-	B^b	-	B^b	A^b	B^{b}D^b'	C'
-	jh	njh	n	ba	je	mo	ri	o	-	o	-	o	-	o	-
-	C'	C'C'	C'	C'	D^b'	C'	B^b	B^b	-	C'A^b		B^b	-	A^b	F
-	jh	njh	n	ba	je	mo	ri	jhan	-	jh ri		ya	-	main to	
F	A^b	A^b	A^b	F	F	F	-	-	FB^b	B^b	B^b	A^b	A^b	A^b	F
b	ni	re	jo	g	ni	ya	-	-	ap	ne pi		ya	ki	main to	
F	A^b	A^b	A^b	F	F	F	-	-	B^b	B^b	B^b	B^b	C'	B^b	A^b
b	ni	re	jo	g	ni	ya	-	-	hn	sii u		da	ye	chha	he
A^b	B^b	C'	A^b	B^b	-	A^b	F	F	A^b	A^b	A^b	F	F	F	-
sa	ri	du	ni	ya	-	main to		b	ni	re jo		g	ni	ya	-
-	FB^b	B^b	B^b	A^b	A^b	A^b	F	F	A^b	A^b	A^b	F	F	F	-
-	ap	ne	pi	ya	ki	main to		b	ni	re jo		g	ni	ya	-

interlude: play sthayi.

F	F	A^b	A^b	B^b	B^b	C'	F	F	F	A^b-A^b	B^b	B^{b}C'	C'	-
te	re	li	ye	main	ne	to	sh	r	m	la -j	chho	di-	re	-

F	F	A^b	A^b	B^b	B^b	C'	F	F	F	A^b-A^b	B^b	B^{b}C'	C'	-
te	re	sn	g	jo	di	to	j	g	t	sn g	to	di	re	-

-	C'	C'	C'	C'	D^b'	C'	B^b	B^b	-	B^b	-	B^b	A^b	B^{b}D^b'	C'
-	tu	hai	mo	h	n	me	ra	ho	-	o	-	o	-	o-	-

-	C'	C'	C'	C'	D^b'	C'	B^b	B^b	-	C' A^b	B^b	-	A^b	F
-	tu	hai	mo	hn	main	te	ri	mo	-	h ni	yan	-	main	to

F	A^b	A^b	F	F	F	F	-	-	FB^{b}B^b	B^b	A^b	A^b	A^b	F
b	ni	re	jo	g	ni	ya	-	-	ap ne pi	ya	ki	main	to	

F	A^b	A^b	A^b	F	F	F	-
b	ni	re	jo	g	ni	ya	-

5. ALLAH KARAM KARNA

Film: Dada (1979)   Music: Usha Khanna
Lyrics: Gauhar Kanpuri   Singer: Suman K.
Taal: Daadra   Chord: FA^{b}D' S=D

Transpose +2 and play from C Scale

hum sabko nek raah chalana mere allaah
bandon ko buraai se bachana mere allaah
allaah karam karna maula tu reham karna
allaah karam karna maula tu reham karna

ik vaakayaa sunaati hun main apni zubaani
apne badon se maine suni hai ye kahaani
rehtaa thaa kisi shehar mein ek aisa bhi insaan
jo naam ka muslim tha magar kaam ka shaitaan

zaalim ko zor e baazu pe apne gurur thaa
yaani ke bekhudi mein khuda se wo dur thaa
sab log use kehte thhe jallaad sitamgar
maasum ki fariyaad ka us pe na tha asar
jo waadaa us ne kar liyaa wo kar ke dikhaayaa
paison ke liye qatl kiye khun bahaya
ik din wo behtaa khun asar us pe kar gayaa
insaan zindaa ho gayaa shaitaan mar gayaa
allaah karam karna maula tu reham karna
allaah karam karna maula tu reham karna

imaan jise kehte hain farmaan e khuda hai
quraan ke har lafz mein us ki hi sadaa hai
allaah ne bakshi hai jo imaan ki daulat
ye sab se badi chiz hai insaan ki daulat
soye huye dilon ko jagata hai ye imaan
bhatke huyon ko raah dikhaataa hai ye imaan
imaan ki garmi se pighal jaate hain patthar
is nur se bante hain sanwarte hain muqaddar
jo sab se pyaar karta hai insaan wohi hai
muslim hai wohi saahib e imaan wohi hai

allaah karam karna maula tu reham karna
allaah karam karna maula tu reham karna

jis kaam ke karne pe na ho raazi koi dil
wo kaam bhi is duniya mein nafrat ke hai kaabil
jo kuchh bhi zubaan keh de wo iqraar nahin hai
laghzish hai labon ki wo gunehgaar nahin hai
jo dil se nahin karta buraai ka iraadaa
allaah se wo taubaa kare tod de waadaa
jaldi jo sambhal jaaye wo nadaan nahin hai
imaan jis mein ho wo beimaan nahin hai
duniya mein hameshaa to nahin rehtaa andheraa
insaan jahaan jaage wahin pe hai saveraa
allaah karam karna maula tu reham karna
allaah karam karna maula tu reham karna

jo sacche dil se karta hai imaan ki aarzu
allaah ki nazaron mein wo hotaa hai surkh ruh
imaan mein kya kya na sahaa pyaare nabi ne
kya aisi musibat bhi utthaayi hai kisi ne
karbal ke shahidon ne sabak hum ko padhaayaa
sajde mein de ke jaan ko imaan bachaayaa
iss raah mein jo sehte hain taqlif o musibat
ik roz un pe hoti hai allaah ki rehmat
insaan hai wo jo dusron ka dil na dukhaaye
pad jaaye agar jaan pe to jaan lutaaye
allaah karam karna maula tu reham karna
allaah karam karna maula tu reham karna.

ALLAH KARAM KARNA

dha	-	ti	ghe	dhin	-	dha	-	ti	ghe	dhin	-	dha	-	ti	ghe	dhin	-
1	2	3	4	5	6	1	2	3	4	5	6	1	2	3	4	5	6
																C'	-
																h	m
C'	-	C'	C'	-	C'	C'	-	C'	C'	C'	-	D'	-	C'	C'	B^b	-
s	b	ko	ne	-	k	ra	-	h	ch	la	-	na	-	me	re	a	l
B^b	-	A^b	-	A^b	-	A^b	-	A^b	A^b	A^b	-	G	-	G	G	G	A^b
la	-	-	-	bn	-	do	-	ko	bu	ra	-	ii	-	se	b	chha	-
B^b	-	A^b	G	F	-	F	G	E	-	E	-	E	-	E	F	G	-
na	-	me	re	a	l	la	-	-	-	a	l	la	-	h	k	r	m
F	-	F	G	E	-	E	-	E	F	G	-	F	-	F	-		
k	r	na	-	mau	-	la	-	tu	r	h	m	k	r	na	-		

interlude: 1 flute:
A^{b}B^{b}C'----- B^{b}C'D'C'D'---- B^b------
GB^{b}B^b---A^b---- GA^b--   A^b- F G-E F -
B^{b}A^{b}A^b- A^b- F G-E F -

dha	-	ti	ghe	dhin	-	dha	-	ti	ghe	dhin	-	dha	-	ti	ghe	dhin	-
																E	E
																i	k
E	-	E	E	-	E	E	-	E	D	C	-	C	F	F	F	F	-
va	-	k	ya	-	su	na	-	ti	hu	main	-	a	p	ni	zu	ba	-
F	G	E	-	E	E	E	-	E	E	-	E	E	-	E	D	C	-
ni	-	-	-	a	p	ne	-	b	do	-	se	main	-	ne	su	ni	-
F	-	F	F	F	-	F	-	-	-	A^b	A^b	A^b	-	A^b	A^b	A^b	-
hai	-	ye	k	ha	-	ni	-	-	-	r	h	ta	-	tha	ki	sii	-
A^b	A^b	A^b	A^b	A^b	A^b	B^b	-	A^b	A^b	A^b	-	A^b	-	-	-	G	-
sh	h	r	me	i	k	ae	-	sa	bhi	in	-	san	-	-	-	jo	-
G	-	G	G	G	G	G	-	G	F	F	F	C	F	F	F	F	-
na	-	m	ka	mu	k	li	mtha		m	g	r	ka	-	m	ka	shai	-
F	-	-	-														
tan	-	-	-														

interlude: flute: C’$B^b$$A^b$G- A^b-F G-E F-

					C’ -
					za -
C’ - C’	C’ - C’	C’ - C’	C’ C’ C’	B^b - A^b	B^b - C’
li m ko	zo - re	ba - ju	pe a p	ne - gu	ru - r
C’ - -	- C’ -	C’ - C’	C’ - C’	C’ - C’	C’ C’ -
tha - -	- ya -	ni - ki	be - khu	di - me	khu da -
B^b - A^b	B^b - C’	C’ - -	- G G	B^b - B^b	B^b B^b -
se - vo	du - r	tha - -	- s b	lo - g	u se -
B^b - B^b	B^b A^b -	C’ - B^b	A^b A^b -	A^b - -	- G -
k h te	the j l	la - d	si t m	gr - -	- ma -
G - G	G G G	G - G	G F C	F - F	F - F
su - m	ki f ri	ya - d	ka u s	pe - n	tha - a
F - -	-				
sr - -	-				

interlude: FF GG $A^b$$A^b$ $B^b$$B^b$ C’--

					C’ -
					jo -
C’ - C’	C’ - C’	C’ - C’	C’ C’ -	B^b - A^b	B^b C’ -
va - da	u s ne	k r li	ya vo -	k r ke	di kha -
C’ - -	- C’ -	C’ - C’	C’ C’ -	C’ - C’	C’ C’ -
ya - -	- pai -	so - ke	li ye -	q t l	ki ye -
B^b - A^b	B^b C’ -	C’ - -	- D’ D’	D’ D’ D’	D’ D’ D’
khu - n	b ha -	ya - -	- i k	di n vo	b h ta
C’ D’ D’	D’ D’ D’	D’ D’ C’	B^b - B^b	B^b A^b -	- G -
khu - n	a s r	u s pe	k r g	ya - -	- i n
G B^b B^b	B^b - B^b	A^b - A^b	G A^b -	B^b - A^b	G G F
sa - n	zin - da	ho - g	ya shai -	ta - n	m r g
F G E	- E -	E - E	F G -	F - F	G E -
ya - -	- a l	la - h	k r m	k r na	- mau -
E - E	F G -	F - F	-		
la - tu	r h m	k r na	-		

interlude: 1

Suman Kalyanpur Songs' Western Notes

															E		-
															ii		-
E	-	E	E	E	-	E	-	E	D	C	-	F	-	F	F	F	-
ma	-	n	ji	se	-	k	h	te	hain	f	r	ma	-	ne	khu	da	-
G	-	E	-	E	-	E	-	E	E	E	-	E	-	E	D	C	-
hai	-	-	-	qu	-	ra	-	n	ke	h	r	l	f	j	me	u	s
F	-	F	F	F	-	F	-	-	-	A^b	A^b	A^b	-	A^b	A^b	A^b	-
ki	-	hi	s	da	-	hai	-	-	-	a	l	la	-	h	ne	b	k
A^b	-	A^b	A^b	A^b	-	B^b	-	A^b	A^b	A^b	-	A^b	-	-	-	G	-
shi	-	hai	jo	ii	-	ma	-	n	ki	dau	-	l	t	-	-	ye	-
G	-	G	G	G	-	G	-	G	F	F	-	C	-	F	F	F	-
s	b	se	b	di	-	chi	-	z	hai	in	-	sa	-	n	ki	dau	-
F	-	-	-	C'	-	C'	-	C'	C'	-	C'	C'	-	C'	C'	C'	-
l	t	-	-	so	-	ye	-	hu	e	-	di	lo	-	ko	j	ga	-
B^b	-	A^b	B^b	C'	-	C'	-	-	-	C'	-	C'	-	C'	C'	-	C'
ta	-	hai	ye	ii	-	ma	-	n	-	bh	t	ke	-	hu	on	-	ko
C'	-	C'	C'	C'	-	B^b	-	A^b	B^b	C'	-	C'	-	-	-	G	-
ra	-	h	di	kha	-	ta	-	hai	ye	ii	-	ma	-	n	-	ii	-
B^b	-	B^b	B^b	B^b	-	B^b	-	B^b	B^b	B^b	-	C'	-	B^b	A^b	A^b	-
ma	-	n	ki	g	r	mi	-	se	pi	gh	l	ja	-	te	hain	p	t
A^b	-	-	-	G	-	G	-	G	G	G	-	G	-	G	F	C	-
thr	-	-	-	i	s	nu	-	r	se	b	n	te	-	hain	sn	v	r
F	-	F	F	F	-	F	-	-	-	C'	-	C'	C'	C'	C'	-	C'
te	-	hain	mu	q	d	d	r	-	-	jo	-	s	b	se	pya	-	r
C'	-	C'	C'	C'	-	B^b	-	A^b	B^b	C'	-	C'	-	-	-	G	-
k	r	ta	hai	i	n	sa	-	n	v	hi	-	hai	-	-	-	mu	s
B^b	-	B^b	B^b	B^b	-	B^b	-	A^b	G	G	-	B^b	-	A^b	G	G	-
li	m	hai	vo	hi	-	sa	-	hi	be	ii	-	ma	-	n	v	hi	-

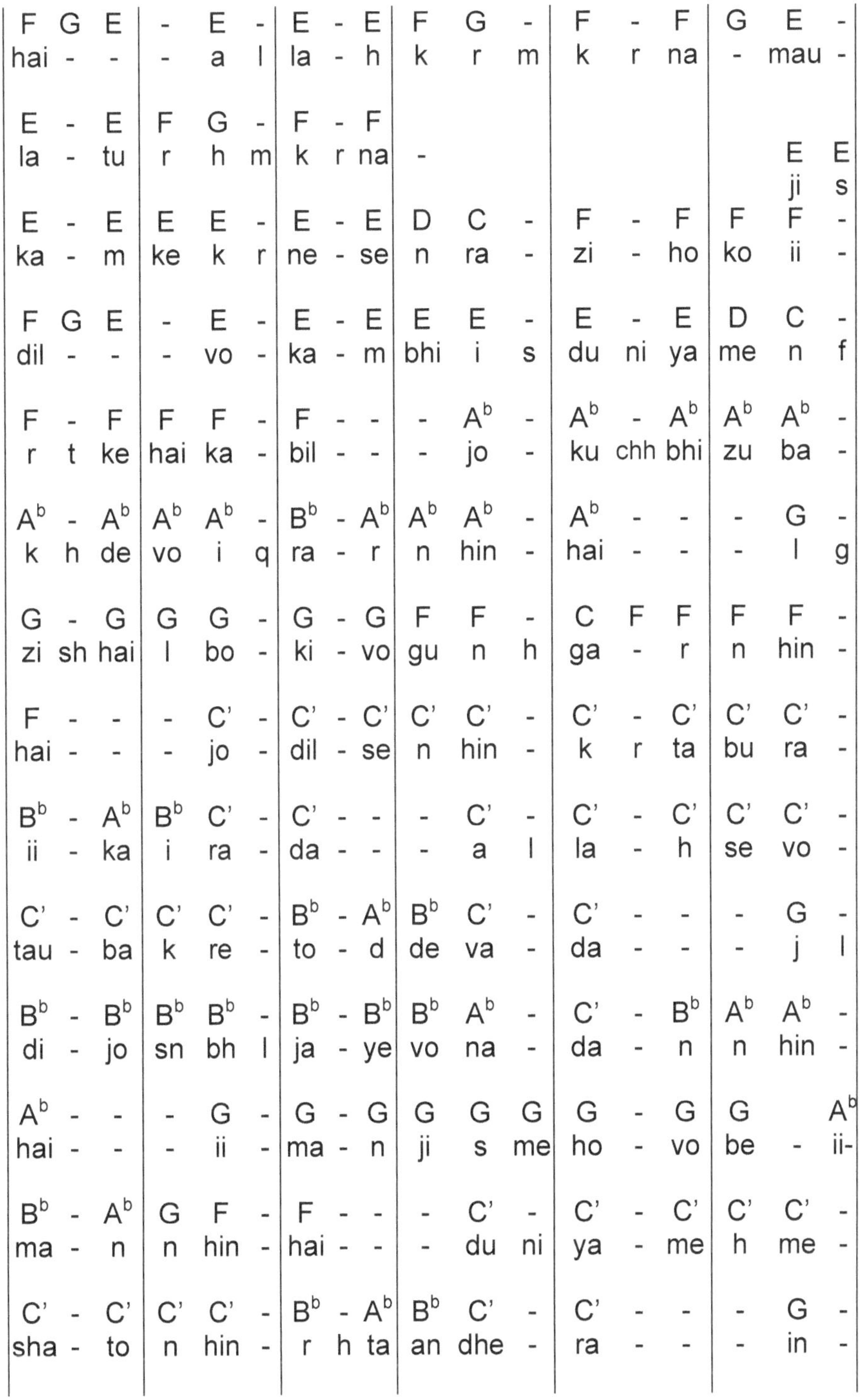

F	G	E	-	E	-	E	-	E	F	G	-	F	-	F	G	E	-
hai	-	-	-	a	l	la	-	h	k	r	m	k	r	na	-	mau	-

E	-	E	F	G	-	F	-	F							E	E	
la	-	tu	r	h	m	k	r	na	-						ji	s	

E	-	E	E	E	-	E	-	E	D	C	-	F	-	F	F	F	-
ka	-	m	ke	k	r	ne	-	se	n	ra	-	zi	-	ho	ko	ii	-

F	G	E	-	E	-	E	-	E	E	E	-	E	-	E	D	C	-
dil	-	-	-	vo	-	ka	-	m	bhi	i	s	du	ni	ya	me	n	f

F	-	F	F	F	-	F	-	-	-	Ab	-	Ab	-	Ab	Ab	Ab	-
r	t	ke	hai	ka	-	bil	-	-	-	jo	-	ku	chh	bhi	zu	ba	-

Ab	-	Ab	Ab	Ab	-	Bb	-	Ab	Ab	Ab	-	Ab	-	-	-	G	-
k	h	de	vo	i	q	ra	-	r	n	hin	-	hai	-	-	-	l	g

G	-	G	G	G	-	G	-	G	F	F	-	C	F	F	F	F	-
zi	sh	hai	l	bo	-	ki	-	vo	gu	n	h	ga	-	r	n	hin	-

F	-	-	-	C'	-	C'	-	C'	C'	C'	-	C'	-	C'	C'	C'	-
hai	-	-	-	jo	-	dil	-	se	n	hin	-	k	r	ta	bu	ra	-

Bb	-	Ab	Bb	C'	-	C'	-	-	-	C'	-	C'	-	C'	C'	C'	-
ii	-	ka	i	ra	-	da	-	-	-	a	l	la	-	h	se	vo	-

C'	-	C'	C'	C'	-	Bb	-	Ab	Bb	C'	-	C'	-	-	-	G	-
tau	-	ba	k	re	-	to	-	d	de	va	-	da	-	-	-	j	l

Bb	-	Bb	Bb	Bb	-	Bb	-	Bb	Bb	Ab	-	C'	-	Bb	Ab	Ab	-
di	-	jo	sn	bh	l	ja	-	ye	vo	na	-	da	-	n	n	hin	-

Ab	-	-	-	G	-	G	-	G	G	G	G	G	-	G	G		Ab
hai	-	-	-	ii	-	ma	-	n	ji	s	me	ho	-	vo	be	-	ii-

Bb	-	Ab	G	F	-	F	-	-	-	C'	-	C'	-	C'	C'	C'	-
ma	-	n	n	hin	-	hai	-	-	-	du	ni	ya	-	me	h	me	

C'	-	C'	C'	C'	-	Bb	-	Ab	Bb	C'	-	C'	-	-	-	G	-
sha	-	to	n	hin	-	r	h	ta	an	dhe	-	ra	-	-	-	in	-

B♭	-	B♭	B♭	B	-	A♭	-	A♭	G	G	-	B♭	-	A♭	G	F	-
sa	-	n	j	ha	-	ja	-	ge	v	hin	-	pr	-	hai	s	ve	-

F	G	E	-	E	-	E	-	E	F	G	-	F	-	F	G	E	-
ra	-	-	-	a	l	la	-	h	k	rm	-	kr	-	na	-	mau	-

E	-	E	F	G	-	F	-	F	-		further play like above.
la	-	tu	r	hm	-	kr	-	na	-		

6.   AA HAM AHAD E VAFA KAR LEN

Film: Do Bhai (1969)
Lyrics: Anand Bakshi
Taal: Kaharwa

Music: Laxmikant Pyarelal
Singer: Md. Rafi, Suman K.
Chord: EGB   S=C

aa ham ahad e wafa kar lein, ye rasm ada kar lein
saamne aaj dono jahaan ke
aa ham ahad e wafa kar lein, ye rasm ada kar lein

veerano me bhi phool vo khil jaate hain, khilna hai jinhein -2
deewaren saari tod ke mil jaate hain milna hai jinhein
saamne, saamne is zamin aasmaan ke
aa ham ahad e wafa kar lein, ye rasm ada kar lein

dekho duayein deta hai hamko bhari bahaar ka dil -2
kahta hai ban ke phool khile tere mere pyar ka dil
saamne, saamne is hasiin gulsitaan ke
aa ham ahad e wafa kar lein, ye rasm ada kar lein
o….o…. o…. o…..
o….o…. o…. o…..
aa… aa… aa…

tumne banaa diya hai mohobbat mein bas deewaana mujhe
lagta hai ek jhuth zamane ka har fasaana mujhe
saamne, saamne aaj dono jahaan ke
aa ham ahad e wafa kar lein, ye rasm ada kar lein

Vinod Kumar

AA HAM AHAD E VAFA KAR LEN

dha	ge	n	ti	n	ke	dhi	n	dha	ge	n	ti	n	ke	dhi	n
1	2	3	4	5	6	7	8	1	2	3	4	5	6	7	8
								B	-	-	-	B	C'	B	A
								aa	-	-	-	-	-	hm	-
G	G	B	G	E	A	A	G	G	-	-	-	-	-	G	-
a	h	de	v	fa	-	k	r	le	-	-	-	-	-	ye	-
D	E	G	E	D	E	G	A	B	-	-	-	B	C'	B	A
r	s	m	a	da	-	k	r	le	-	-	-	aa	-	h	m
G	G	B	G	E	-	A	G	G	-	E	-	-	-	G	-
a	h	de	v	fa	-	k	r	le	-	-	-	-	-	ye	-
D	E	G	E	D	E	G	A	B	-	-	-	-	-	B	D'
r	s	m	a	da	-	k	r	le	-	-	-	-	-	sa	m
D'	C'	-	-	-	-	B	D'	D'	C'	B	D'	D'	C'	A	C'
ne	-	-	-	-	-	aa	j	do	-	no	j	ha	-	ke	-
B	-	-	-	B	C'	B	A	G	G	B	G	E	A	A	G
aa	-	-	-	-	-	hm	-	a	h	de	v	fa	-	k	r
G	-	E	-	-	-	G	D	D	E	G	E	D	E	G	A
le	-	-	-	-	-	ye	-	r	s	m	a	da	-	k	r
B	-	-	-												
le	-	-	-												

interlude: D' D' D' D' D'D'D' D' C' B

dha	ge	n	ti	n	ke	dhi	n	dha	ge	n	ti	n	ke	dhi	n
1	2	3	4	5	6	7	8	1	2	3	4	5	6	7	8
C'	-	C'	-	C'	C'	-	C'	B	D'	C'	D'	B	B	B	B
vi	-	ra	-	no	me	-	bhi	fu	-	-	-	l	vo	khi	l
A	C'	B	-	A	A	A	A	G	B	A	-	G	G	G	-
ja	-	-	-	te	hain	khi	l	na	-	-	-	hai	ji	nhe	-
C'	-	C'		C'	C'	-	C'	C'	E'	D'	-	C'	C'	B	B
di	-	va	-	ren	sa	-	ri	to	-	-	-	d	ke	mi	l
A	C'	B	-	A	A	A	A	G	B	A	-	G	G	G	-
ja	-	-	-	te	hain	mi	l	na	-	-	-	hain	ji	nhe	-

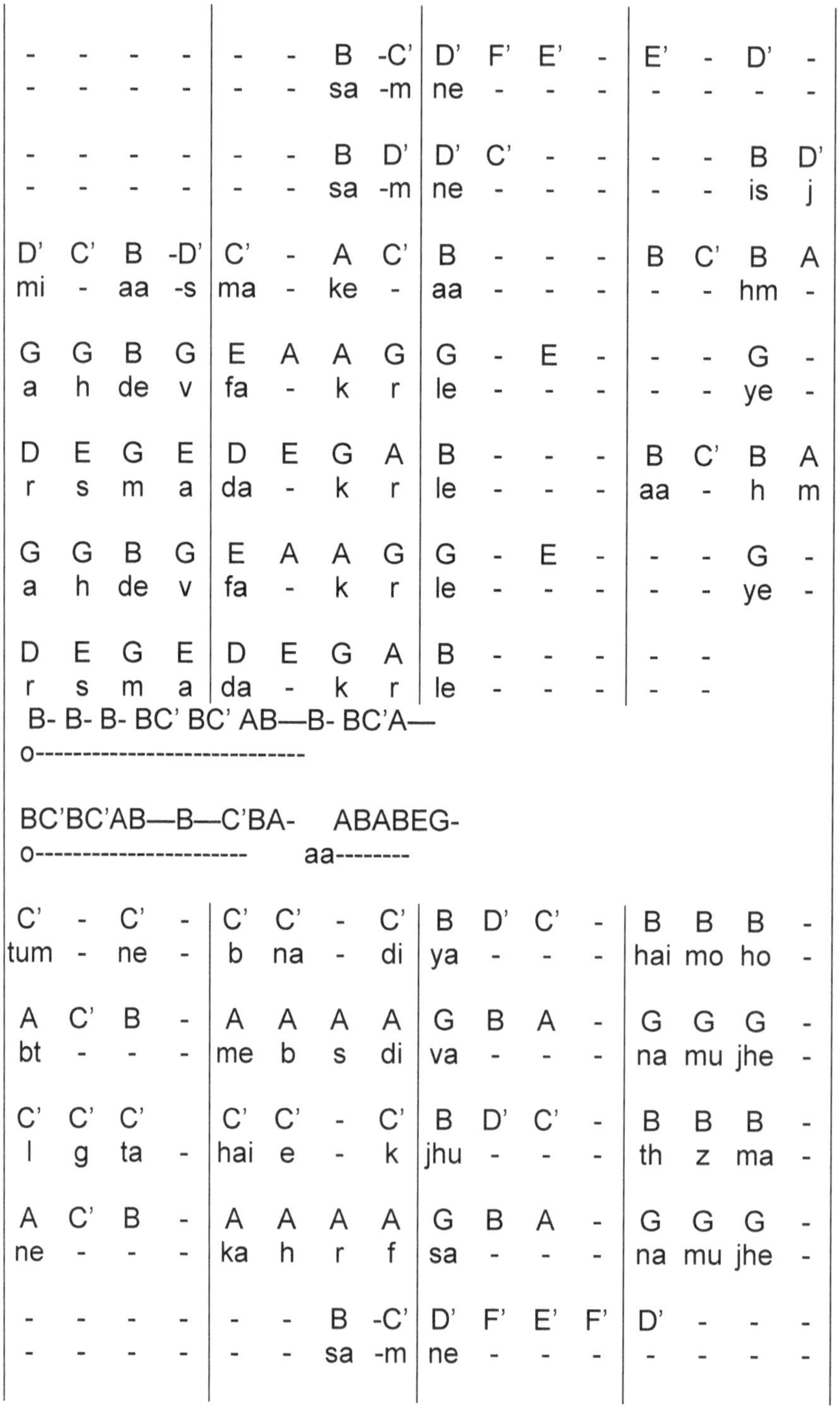

```
-    -    -    -  | -    -    B   -C' | D'  F'  E'  -  | E'  -   D'  -
-    -    -    -  | -    -    sa  -m  | ne  -   -   -  | -   -   -   -

-    -    -    -  | -    -    B   D'  | D'  C'  -   -  | -   -   B   D'
-    -    -    -  | -    -    sa  -m  | ne  -   -   -  | -   -   is  j

D'   C'   B   -D' | C'   -    A   C'  | B   -   -   -  | B   C'  B   A
mi   -    aa  -s  | ma   -    ke  -   | aa  -   -   -  | -   -   hm  -

G    G    B    G  | E    A    A   G   | G   -   E   -  | -   -   G   -
a    h    de   v  | fa   -    k   r   | le  -   -   -  | -   -   ye  -

D    E    G    E  | D    E    G   A   | B   -   -   -  | B   C'  B   A
r    s    m    a  | da   -    k   r   | le  -   -   -  | aa  -   h   m

G    G    B    G  | E    A    A   G   | G   -   E   -  | -   -   G   -
a    h    de   v  | fa   -    k   r   | le  -   -   -  | -   -   ye  -

D    E    G    E  | D    E    G   A   | B   -   -   -  | -   -
r    s    m    a  | da   -    k   r   | le  -   -   -  | -   -
 B- B- B- BC' BC' AB—B- BC'A—
o----------------------------------

BC'BC'AB—B—C'BA-     ABABEG-
o------------------------     aa--------

C'   -    C'   -  | C'   C'   -   C'  | B   D'  C'  -  | B   B   B   -
tum  -    ne   -  | b    na   -   di  | ya  -   -   -  | hai mo  ho  -

A    C'   B    -  | A    A    A   A   | G   B   A   -  | G   G   G   -
bt   -    -    -  | me   b    s   di  | va  -   -   -  | na  mu  jhe -

C'   C'   C'      | C'   C'   -   C'  | B   D'  C'  -  | B   B   B   -
l    g    ta   -  | hai  e    -   k   | jhu -   -   -  | th  z   ma  -

A    C'   B    -  | A    A    A   A   | G   B   A   -  | G   G   G   -
ne   -    -    -  | ka   h    r   f   | sa  -   -   -  | na  mu  jhe -

-    -    -    -  | -    -    B   -C' | D'  F'  E'  F' | D'  -   -   -
-    -    -    -  | -    -    sa  -m  | ne  -   -   -  | -   -   -   -
```

D'	C'	B	D'	D'	C'	A	C'	B	-	-	-	B	C'	B	A
-	-	-	-	-	-	B	D'	D'	C'	-	-	-	-	B	D'
-	-	-	-	-	-	sa	-m	ne	-	-	-	-	-	aa	j
D'	C'	B	D'	D'	C'	A	C'	B	-	-	-	B	C'	B	A
do	-	no	j	ha	-	ke	-	aa	-	-	-	-	-	hm	-
G	G	B	G	E	A	A	G	G	-	E	-	-	-	G	-
a	h	de	v	fa	-	k	r	le	-	-	-	-	-	ye	-
D	E	G	E	D	E	G	A	B	-	-	-				
r	s	m	a	da	-	k	r	le	-	-	-				

7. AAJKAL TERE MERE PYAR KE CHARCHE

Film: Brahmchari (1968)
Lyrics: Shailendra
Taal: Kaharwa

Music: Shanker Jaikishan
Singer: Md. Rafi, Suman K.
Chord: GB^{b}D'   S=C

aajkal tere mere pyar ke charche har zubaan par
sab ko maloom hai aur sabko khabar ho gayi

(humne to pyar mein aisa kaam kar liya
pyar ki raah mein apna naam kar liya) -2
pyar ki raah mein apna naam kar liya
aajkal tere mere pyar…….

(do badan ek dil ek jaan ho gaye
manzilen ek hui humsafar ban gaye) -2
manzilen ek hui humsafar ban gaye
aajkal tere mere pyar…

(kyon bhala hum daren dil ke malik hain hum
har janam mein tujhe apna mana sana)-2
har janam mein tujhe apna mana sanam
aajkal tere mere pyar…

AAJKAL TERE MERE PYAR KE CHARCHE

dhin	tete	dhin	dhin	dhin	tete	dhindhin		dhintete	dhin	dhin		dhin	tetedhindhin		
1	2	3	4	5	6	7	8	1	2	3	4	5	6	7	8

prelude:

guitar: $B^bC'B^bA^b$ $B^bC'B^bA^b$ B^b –

$B^bC'B^bA^b$ $B^bC'D'E^{b'}$ $E^{b'}D'C'B^b$ $C'D'E^{b'}F'$

$F'E^{b'}D'C'$ $F'F'$ $E^{b'}E^{b'}$ $D'D'$ C'-

$C'E^{b'}D'C'B^bAGF$

F –B^b F –FB^b- F –B^b F –FB^b- F –B^b F –FB^b- B^b---

synthe: B^b C' D'---- $D'E^{b'}G'F'E^{b'}F'$- $G'F'G'F'E^{b'}$—$E^{b'}F'E^{b'}D'$---

$C'D'C'B^b$-- G—A $B^bC'B^bAB^b$

accordian: $C'AB^bD'$--- $E^{b'}F'G'F'E^{b'}F'$---

$F'F'G'F'E^{b'}$--- $E^{b'}F'E^{b'}D'$—$C'D'C'B^b$

G –A $B^bC'B^bAB^b$--

guitar: F –B^b F –FB^b- F –B^b F –FB^b- F –B^b F –FB^b- B^b---

												-B^b	-B^b	C'	
												-aa	-j	kl	
D'	D'	D'	D',D'	D'	D'	C'	B^b	G	-G	G	(B^b	D')	-	A	B^b
tere	mere	pya	r,ke	ch	rche	hr	z	ba	-n	pr	(a	chha)	-	sb	ko
C'	C'	C'	C'	C'	D'	-G	A	B^b	-B^b	B^b	(D'	B^b)			
ma	lum	hai	aur	sb	ko	-kh	br	ho	-g	yi	(to	kya)			

interlude: saxophone:

$F'F'F'F'$ $E^{b'}$ –$E^{b'}F'$-- $E^{b'}F'$ $E^{b'}F'$

$D'D'D'D'$ C' –$C'D'$ -- $C'D'$ $C'D'$

$B^bB^bB^bB^b$ A^b –A^bB^b A^bB^b A^bB^b

$B^bB^bB^bB^b$ A^b –A^bB^b A^bB^b A^bB^b

synthe:

B^b $C'D'$ B^b $E^{b'}$ $D'E^{b'}$ D' B^b

$B^bB^bB^bB^b$ $B^bB^bB^bB^b$ B^b

												-F	-G		
												-hm	-ne		
F	-	-F	-G	F	-	-F	-G	B^b	-	-A	-C'	B^b	-	-C'	-D'
to	-	-pya	-r	me	-	-ae	-sa	ka	-	m,kr	-li	ya	-	-pya	-r

C'	-	-C'	-D'	C'	-	-D'	$E^{b'}$	F'	-	-A	-C'	B^b	-	-$E^{b'}$	-F'
ki	-	-ra	-h	me	-	-a	pna	na	-	m,kr	-li	ya	-	-pya	-r

$E^{b'}$	-	-D'	-$E^{b'}$	D'	-	-C'	B^b	D'	-	-C'	-B^b	B^b	-
ki	-	-ra	-h	me	-	-a	pna	na	-	m,kr	-li	ya	-

8. AAP SE HAMKO BICHHDE HUE

Film: Vishwas (1969)
Lyrics: Gulshan Bawra
Taal: Kaharwa dugun
Transpose +2 and play from C Scale

Music: Kalyanji Anandji
Singer: Manhar Udas, Suman K.
Chord: FA^{b}C'   S=D

apase hamako bichhade huye, ek jamaana bit gaya
apana mukaddar bigade huye, ek jamaana bit gaya

apase milake in ankhon ne kitane khwaab sajaaye the
jis gulashan men hamane milake git wafa ke gaaye the
us gulashan ko ujade huye, ek jamaana bit gaya

kismat hamako le ayi hai gulashan se wiraane men
ansu bhi naakaam rahe hain dil ki ag bujhaane men
is wiraane men jalate huye, ek jamaana bit gaya

27

AAP SE HAMKO BICHHDE HUE

dhage	nti	nke	dhin	dhage	nti	nke	dhin	dhage	nti	nke	dhin	dhage	nti	nke	dhin
12	34	56	78	12	34	56	78	12	34	56	78	12	34	56	78

prelude:
F' E' E^{b}' D' D^{b}' C' -2
C D^{b} E^{b} E A^{b} –
A^{b} A^{b} G G F F F   A^{b} A^{b} G G F - -
F C E F G B^{b} - C' B^{b} A^{b} F G –
A^{b} A^{b} G G F F F   A^{b} A^{b} G G F - -

	F	-F	-F	F	G	F	E	F	FA^{b}	-	G	A^{b}	-	(G	F)
	aa	-p	-se	hm	-	ko	-	bi	chhde	-	hu	e	-	-	-
-	A^{b}	-B^{b}	-B	B	B^{b}	A^{b}	G	A^{b}		G	F	E	F	-	-	-
-	e	-k	-z	ma	-	na	-	bi		-	t	g	ya	-	-	-
-	F	-F	-F	F	G	F	E	F	FA^{b}	-	G	A^{b}	-	(G	F)
-	ap	na	mu	q	-	dd	r	bi	gde	-	hu	e	-	-	-
-	A^{b}	-B^{b}	-B	B	B^{b}	A^{b}	G	A^{b}		G	F	E	F	-	-	-
-	e	-k	-z	ma	-	na	-	bi		-	t	g	ya	-	-	-

interlude: F B ------- B^{b} A^{b} B B^{b} ---
       A^{b} B – B^{b} – A^{b} B^{b} ^{Ab} B^{b} - A^{b} GA^{b} F -

	C'	-D^{b}'	-C'	B^{b}	B^{b}	B^{b}	-	B	BB^{b}	-A^{b}	G	F	-	F	-
	aa	-p	-se	mi	l	ke	-	-	in	-aan	-	khon	-	ne	-
-	C'C'	-D^{b}'	C'	B^{b}	-	B^{b}	B^{b}	B^{b}B	B^{b}	A^{b}	G	F	-	-	-
-	kit	-ne	-	kha	-	b	s	ja-	-	ye	-	the	-	-	-
-	C'C'	-D^{b}'	-C'	B^{b}	B^{b}	B^{b}	-	B	BB^{b}	-A^{b}	G	F	F	F	-
-	jis	-gu	-l	sh	n	me	-	-	hm	-ne	-	mi	l	ke	-
-	C'	-D^{b}'	-C'	B^{b}	-	B^{b}	-	B	BB^{b}	-A^{b}	G	F	-	-	-
-	gi	-t	-v	fa	-	ke	-	-	ga-	-ye	-	the	-	-	-
C	F	F	F	F	G	F	E	FF	-A^{b}	-	G	A^{b}	-	G	F
u	s	gu	l	sh	n	ko	-	uj	-de	-	hu	e	-	-	-
-	F	-F	-F	FG	-	F	E	FF	-A^{b}	-	G	A^{b}	-	-	-
-	us	-gu	-l	shn	-	ko	-	uj	-de	-	hu	e	-	-	-

- A^b -B^b -B | B B^b A^b G | A^b G F E | F - - -
- e- -k -z | ma - na - | bi - t g | ya - - -
interlude: F B ------ B^b A^b B B^b ---
          A^b B – B^b – A^b B^b ^{Ab} B^b - A^b GA^b F –

C'C'D$^{b'}$C' B^b B^{b}B BB^b A^{b}GF F
kismt   hm ko- le-   aa-yi hai

C'-D$^{b'}$C' B^b B^b B^{b}BB^{b}A^{b}G F
Gulshn   se   vira------ne-   me

C'D$^{b'}$C'   B^b B^b BB^{b}A^b GF F
aansu-   bhi   naka--m rhe hain

C'C' D$^{b'}$C' B^{b}B^b B^{b}B^{b}BB^{b}A^{b}G   F
dil   ki-   aag   bujha-----ne- me

FF   F FGGF E   FA^b GA^b (GF)
Is   vira—ne- me jlte huye -2

A^{b}B^b BBB^{b}A^{b}G A^{b}GF EF
ek   zma-na-   bi-t   gya

9. AAYA NA HAMKO PYAR JATANA

Film: Pahchaan (1970)　　　Music: Shanker Jaikishan
Lyrics: Indeevar　　　Singer: Mukesh, Suman K.
Taal: Kaharwa　　　Chord: EGB FAC' S=C#
Transpose +1 and play from C Scale

M: aya na hamako pyaar jataana pyaar kabhi se tujhe karate hain
S: bholaapan tera bha gaya hamako saadagi par teri marate hain

M: jisane hamaare dil ko samajha wo ek tera hi dil hai
　tera anchal, teri baahen, <u>apani yahin to mnjil hai -2</u>
　ham to tere ho hi chuke hain apana kahate darate hain
S: bholaapan tera bha gaya hamako saadagi par teri marate hain

S: surat achchhi, sirat achchhi tu to ek hai laakhon men
　dil karata hai dil se laga lun rakh lun chhupa ke ankhon men
　khud pe bharosa badh jaata hai jab tere saath gujrate hain

M: ek hi jiwan men to dil ki pyaas bujha nahin paayenge
S: tujhako fir paane ke liye ham fir duniya men ayenge
B: pyaar amar hai amar hi rahega, marane do insaan marate hain

S: bholaapan tera bha gaya hamako saadagi par teri marate hain
M: aya na hamako pyaar jataana pyaar kabhi se tujhe karate hain
S: bholaapan tera bha gaya hamako saadagi par teri marate hain

AAYA NA HAMKO PYAR JATANA

dha	ge	n	ti	n	ke	dhi	n	dha	ge	n	ti	n	ke	dhi	n
1	2	3	4	5	6	7	8	1	2	3	4	5	6	7	8

prelude:
C' B A - GA BA C'B D'C'- GC' AGFA
GC'--- C'BD'- C'B
C' E' D' C' B A G F   F G A B C'-

B	A	A	A	A	-	G	B	B	-	-	A	A	-	A	-
aa	-	ya	n	h	m	ko	-	pya	-	r	j	ta	-	na	-
C'	-	-	B	A	G	F	A	G	-	F	-	E	-	-	-
pya	-	-r	k	bhi	se	tu	jhe	k	r	te	-	hain	-	-	-
G	-	G	F$^\#$	G	-	G	B	B	-	A	A	A	-	A	-
bho	-	la	-	pn	-	te	ra	bha	-	g	ya	h	m	ko	-
C'	E'	E'	E'	D'	D'	C'	B	C'	-	B	-	A	-	^{F}G	E
sa	-	d	gi	p	r	te	re	m	r	te	-	hain	-	-	-

interlude:
A B G A B C' D' E'   E' G' F' D' E'-
E' E' E' F'- D' E'   C' C' C' D'- B C'
A' A' A' A'—G' A' G' F' E' F'—E' F' E' D' C'- A C' D' E'-

C'	B	B	B	B	-	B	-	C'	B	B	-	C'	B	B	-
ji	s	ne	h	ma	-	re	-	di	l	ko	-	s	m	jha	-
G	B	B	B	B	-	B	C'	D'	C'	B	A	A	-	-	-
vo	-	e	k	te	-	ra	-	hi	-	di	l	hai	-	-	-
A	C'	C'	-	C'	-	C'	B	D'	-	C'	-	C'	-	C'	-
te	-	ra	-	aan	-	ch	l	te	-	ri	-	ba	-	he	-
C'	E'	E'	D'	C'	-	A	B	C'	-	B	A	G	-	-	-
a	p	ni	y	hi	-	to	-	mn	-	zi	l	hai	-	-	-
G	C'	C'	B	A	-	F	A	G	-	F	E	E	-	-	-
a	p	ni	y	hi	-	to	-	mn	-	zi	l	hai	-	-	-
B	A	A	-	A	-	G	B	B	-	A	A	A	-	A	-
h	m	to	-	te	-	re	-	ho	-	hi	chu	ke	-	hain	-

| G | C' | C' | - | A | G | F | A | G | - | F | - | E | - | - | - |
| a | p | na | - | k | h | te | - | d | r | te | - | hain | - | - | - |

| G | - | G | F# | G | - | G | B | B | - | A | A | A | - | A | - |
| bho | - | la | - | pn | - | te | ra | bha | - | g | ya | h | m | ko | - |

| C' | E' | E' | E' | D' | D' | C' | B | C' | - | B | - | A | - | ^FG | E |
| sa | - | d | gi | p | r | te | re | m | r | te | - | hain | - | - | - |

interlude:
AGBG x 3 E-   BABG x 3 E-
EF FG GA- ABC'D'E'- EF FG GA-
D'---- BC' ABGB
C'------ AB—GA---

| C' | B | B | B | B | - | B | - | G | B | B | B | C' | D' | D' | - |
| su | - | r | t | a | ch | chhi | - | sii | - | r | t | a | ch | chhi | - |

| B | D' | D' | | C' | - | C' | C' | B | A | B | G | A | - | - | - |
| tu | - | to | - | e | - | k | hai | la | - | khon | - | me | - | - | - |

| E | E | E | - | D | - | C | D | E | A♭ | A♭ | A♭ | A♭ | A | A | - |
| di | l | k | r | ta | - | hai | - | di | l | se | l | ga | - | lu | - |

| A | C' | C' | C' | E' | - | E' | - | D' | - | C' | B | A | - | - | - |
| r | kh | lu | chhu | pa | - | ke | - | aan | - | khon | - | me | - | - | - |

| B | A | A | A | A | - | A | G | B | A | A | - | A | - | A | - |
| khu | d | pe | bh | ro | - | sa | - | b | dh | ja | - | ta | - | hai | - |

| A | C' | C' | B | A | G | F | A | G | - | F | - | E | - | - | - |
| j | b | te | re | sa | - | th | gu | z | r | te | - | hain | - | - | - |

| G | - | G | F# | G | - | G | B | B | - | A | A | A | - | A | - |
| bho | - | la | - | pn | - | te | ra | bha | - | g | ya | h | m | ko | - |

| C' | E' | E' | E' | D' | D' | C' | B | C' | - | B | - | A | - | ^FG | E |
| sa | - | d | gi | p | r | te | re | m | r | te | - | hain | - | - | - |

interlude:
A B G A B C' D' E'   E' G' F' D' E'-
E' E' E' F'- D'E'   C' C' C' D'- BC'
A' A' A' A'—G' A' G' F' E' F'—E' F' E' D' C'- AC' D' E'-

| C' | B | B | B | B | - | B | B | C' | B | B | - | C' | B | B | - |
| e | - | k | hi | ji | - | v | n | me | - | to | - | di | l | ki | - |

G	B	B	B	B	-	B	C'	D'	C'	B	A	A	-	-	-
pya	-	s	bu	jha	-	n	hin	pa	-	yen	-	ge	-	-	-
E	E	E	-	D	C	C	D	E	A^b	A^b	A^b	A^b	A	A	-
tu	jh	ko	-	fi	r	pa	-	ne	-	ke	li	e	-	hm	-
A	C'	C'	C'	E'	-	E'	-	D'	-	C'	B	A	-	-	-
fi	r	du	ni	ya	-	me	-	aa	-	yen	-	ge	-	-	-
B	A	A	A	A	A	A	G	B	A	A	A	A	-	A	-
pya	-	r	a	m	r	hai	a	m	r	hi	r	he	-	ga	-
G	C'	C'	B	A	-	F	A	G	-	F	-	E	-	-	-
m	r	ne	ko	in	-	san	-	m	r	te	-	hain	-	-	-
G	-	G	F$^\#$	G	-	G	B	B	-	A	A	A	-	A	-
bho	-	la	-	pn	-	te	ra	bha	-	g	ya	h	m	ko	-
C'	E'	E'	E'	D'	D'	C'	B	C'	-	B	-	A	-	^{F}G	E
sa	-	d	gi	p	r	te	re	m	r	te	-	hain	-	-	-
B	-	A	A	A	-	G	B	B	-	-	A	A	-	A	-
aa	-	ya	n	h	m	ko	-	pya	-	r	j	ta	-	na	-
C'	-	-	B	A	G	F	A	G	-	F	-	E	-	-	-
pya	-	-r	k	bhi	se	tu	jhe	k	r	te	-	hain	-	-	-
G	-	G	F$^\#$	G	-	G	B	B	-	A	A	A	-	A	-
bho	-	la	-	pn	-	te	ra	bha	-	g	ya	h	m	ko	-
C'	E'	E'	E'	D'	D'	C'	B	C'	-	B	-	A	-	^{F}G	E
sa	-	d	gi	p	r	te	re	m	r	te	-	hain	-	-	-

10. BAHNA NE BHAI KI KALAI SE

Film: Resham ki Dor (1974)
Lyrics: Shailendra
Taal: Kaharwa
Transpose +1 and play from C Scale

Music: Shanker Jaikishan
Singer: Suman K.
Chord: DFA FAC' S=C#

bahana ne bhaai ki kalaai se pyaar baandha hai
pyaar ke do taar se snsaar baandha hai
resham ki dori se-3 snsaar baandha hai

sundarata men jo kanhaiya hai mamata men yashoda maiyya hai
wo aur nahin duja koi wo te mera raaja bhaiyya hai
bahana ne bhaai ki kalaai se pyaar baandha hai

mera ful hai tu, talawaar hai tu meri laaj ka paharedaar hai tu
main akeli kahaan is duniya men mera saara snsaar hai tu
bahana ne bhaai ki kalaai se pyaar baandha hai

hamen dur bhale kismat kar de apane man se n juda karana
saawan ke paawan din bhaiyya bahana ko yaad kiya karana
bahana ne bhaai ki kalaai se pyaar baandha hai

BAHNA NE BHAI KI KALAI SE

dha	ge	n	ti	n	ke	dhi	n	dha	ge	n	ti	n	ke	dhi	n
1	2	3	4	5	6	7	8	1	2	3	4	5	6	7	8
prelude: E^b G A B^b B^b --- G B^b B^b—B^{b}AGFE^{b}D--															
	A	A	A	A	A	A	B^b	A	A	A	-	D	F	G	A
	bh	na	ne	bha	ii	ki	k	la	ii	se	-	-	-	-	-
-	A	A	A	A	A	A	B^b	A	A	A	-	G	-F	FG	A
-	bh	na	ne	bha	ii	ki	k	la	ii	se	-	pya	-r	ba-	dha
G	-	-	-	-	B^b	B^b	A	G	F	E^b	E^b	G	-F	E^b	E^b
hai	-	-	-	-	pya	r,ke	do	ta	-r	se	sn	sa	-r	ba	dha

| D | - | - | - | - | C' | C' | C' | B♭ | B♭ | A | G | - | B♭ | B♭ | A |
| hai | - | - | - | - | re | shm | ki | do | ri | se | - | - | re | shm | ki |

| F | A | G | F | - | B♭ | B♭ | A | G | F | E♭ | E♭ | G | -F | E♭ | E♭ |
| do | ri | se | - | - | re | shm | ki | do | ri | se | sn | sa | -r | ba | dha |

| D | - | - | - | - |
| hai | - | - | - | - |

interlude: 1
F' E♭' D'--- C'D'E♭'F'E♭' C'-- D'C' C'B♭ B♭A
AB♭E♭'D'C'B♭GFD—
DD FF EE F—AA FF E♭E♭ D
DD FF EE F—AA FF E♭- D-

| | | | | | | | | | | | | | C' | B |
| | | | | | | | | | | | | | sun | - |

| C' | C' | C' | B | C' | - | C' | C' | D' | C' | B♭ | A | A | - | B♭ | A |
| d | r | ta | - | me | - | jo | k | nhai | - | ya | - | hai | - | m | m |

| B♭ | - | B♭ | A | B♭ | - | B♭ | - | F | - | B♭ | A | A | - | C' | - |
| ta | - | me | y | sho | - | da | - | main | - | ya | - | hai | - | vo | - |

| C' | - | C' | C' | B♭ | - | G | A | C' | - | B♭ | - | B♭ | - | B♭ | B♭ |
| au | - | r | n | hin | - | du | - | ja | - | ko | - | ii | - | vo | to |

| B♭ | - | B♭ | - | F | - | A | - | - | F | -E♭ | D | D | - | - | - |
| me | - | ra | - | ra | - | ja | - | - | bhai | -ya | - | hai | - | - | - |

interlude: 2
GAB♭C'D'—D'E♭'D'--- D'E♭'D'C'- C'D'C'B♭-
B♭C'B♭A- GAGF- G- A-
FGFE♭ F- G- E♭FG G-F- E♭D
D'E♭'F'G'A'—F'A'G'E♭'D'—F'- E♭'D'C'---

| | | | | | | | | | | | | | C' | B |
| | | | | | | | | | | | | | me | ra |

| C' | - | C' | B | C' | - | C' | C' | D' | C' | B♭ | A | A | - | B♭ | A |
| fu | - | l | hai | tu | - | t | l | va | - | r | hai | tu | - | me | ri |

| B♭ | - | B♭ | A | B♭ | B♭ | B♭ | - | F | - | B♭ | A | A | - | C' | B |
| la | - | j | ka | p | h | re | - | da | - | r | hai | tu | - | main | a |

C'	-	C'	D'	B^b	-	G	A	C'	C'	B^b	-	B^b	-	B^b	-
ke	-	li	k	ha	-	i	s	du	ni	ya	-	me	-	me	-
B^b	-	B^b	-	F	-	A	-	-	F	-E^b	-D	D	-	-	-
ra	-	sa	-	ra	-	sn	-	-	sa	-r	-hai	tu	-	-	-

interlude: 1 play

C'B	C'C'	BC'	C'C'D'C'	B^{b}B^b	A
hme	dur	bhle	kismt	kr	de

B^{b}AB^b	B^{b}A	B^b	B^b	GDF	B^{b}AA
apne	mn	se	n	juda	krna

C'BC'	C'	B^b-GA	C'	B^{b}B^b
savn	ke	pa-vn	din	bhaiya

B^{b}B^b	B^b	FA	A F	E^b-D
bhna	ko	yad	kiya	krna

11. BAAD MUDDAT KE YE GHADI AAYI

Film: Jahan Aara (1964)
Lyrics: Rajendra Krishna
Taal: Kaharwa
Transpose +3 and play from C Scale

Music: Madan Mohan
Singer: Md. Rafi, Suman K.
Chord: CEG   S=D#

Rafi: baad muddat ke yah ghadi aayi ap aye to jindagi aayi
         ishq mar-mar ke kaamayaab hua aaj ek zrra afataab hua

Suman: shukriya ai hujur ane ka wakt jaaga garibakhaane ka
         ek jmaane ke baad did hui id se pahale meri id hui

Rafi: id ka chaand aj dekha hai id ka kyon na aitabaar aaye
         hath uthakar dua yah karta hun id fir aisi bar-bar aaye
         din jmaane ka, raat apani hai is ghadi kaayanaat apani hai
         ishq par husn ki inayat hai mere pahalu men meri jnnat hai

Suman: faasale waqt ne mita hi die dil tadpate huye mila hi diye
         kaash is waqt maut aa jaaye zindagani pe aake chha jaaye

Both: baad muddat ke yah ghadi aayi ap aye to jindagi aayi
         ishq mar-mar ke kaamayaab hua aj ek jrra afataab hua

BAAD MUDDAT KE YE GHADI AAYI

dha	ge	n	ti	n	ke	dhi	n	dha	ge	n	ti	n	ke	dhi	n
1	2	3	4	5	6	7	8	1	2	3	4	5	6	7	8
prelude:		E F A F E		E F A F D		E F G E C									
		E F D D G		--- B A C'---		G E G F		E F E D --							
			E	D	E	F	G								
			ba	-	d	mu	-								
F	-	E	-	D	.B	-	C	E	D	E	-	EF	G	F	-
d	-	-	t	ke	ye	-	gh	di	-	-	-	aa-	-	yi	-
E	D	-	E	D	E	F	G	F	E	-	-	D	.B	-	C
-	-	-	aa	-	p	aa	-	ye	-	-	-	to	zin	-	d
D	E	-	D	F	G	F	-	E	-	-	G	-	G	A	B
gi	-	-	-	aa	-	yi	-	-	-	-	i	sh	q	m	r
C'	-	-	-	C'	Bb	-	G	F	D	E	-	F	G	F	-
mr	-	-	-	ke	ka	-	m	ya	-	-	-	b	hu	aa	-
E	D	-	E	D	E	F	G	F	-	E	-	D	.B	-	C
-	-	-	aa	-	j	i	k	z	-	r	-	ra	aa	-	f
E	D	E	-	F	G	F	-	E	-	-	E	D	E	Bb	A
ta	-	-	-	b	hu	aa	-	-	-	-	aa	-	j	i	k
F	-	E	-	D	.B	-	C	E	D	E	-	F	G	F	-
z	-	r	-	ra	aa	-	f	ta	-	-	-	b	hu	aa	-
E	-	-	E	D	E	F	G	F	-	E	-	D	.B	-	C
-	-	-	shu	k	ri	ya	-	hai	-	-	-	hu	zu	-	r
E	D	E	-	F	G	F	-	E	D	-	G	G	G	A	B
aa	-	-	-	ne	-	ka	-	-	-	-	shu	k	ri	ya	-
C'	-	-	-	C'	Bb	-	G	FE	D	-	E	F	G	F	-
hai	-	-	-	hu	zu	-	r	aa-	-	-	-	ne	-	ka	-
E	D	-	E	D	E	F	G	F	-	E	-	D	.B	-	C
-	-	-	v	-	qt	ja	-	ga	-	-	-	g	ri	-	b

E	D	E	-	F	G	F	-	E	-	-	A	A	A	A	-
kha	-	-	-	ne	-	ka	-	-	-	-	i	k	z	ma	-
C'	Bb	C'	-	A	A	E	G	C'	-	G	-	E	G	F	-
ne	-	-	-	ke	ba	-	d	ii	-	-	-	d	hu	ii	-
E	-	-	E	D	E	F	G	F	F	E	-	D	.B	-	C
-	-	-	ii	-	d	se	-	p	h	-	-	le	me	-	ri
E	D	E	-	F	G	F	-	E	-	-	E	D	E	F	Bb
ii	-	-	-	d	hu	ii	-	-	-	-	ii	-	d	se	-
F	F	E	-	D	.B	-	C	E	D	E	-	F	G	F	-
p	h	-	-	le	me	-	ri	ii	-	-	-	d	hu	ii	-
E	-	-	E	-	G	A	Bb	A	-	-	-	A	G	-	F
-	-	-	ii	-	d	ka	-	chan	-	-	-	d	aa	-	j
FE	D	-	-	G	-	G	-	-	-	-	G	E	G	C'	-
de-	-	-	-	kha	-	hai	-	-	-	-	ii	-	d	ka	-
Bb	-	Bb	G	-	G	E	G	G	Bb	-	- A	B	-	C'	-
kyu	-	na	-	-	ae	-	t	ba	-	-	r	aa	-	ye	-
-	-	-	B	-	B	B	-	C'	C'	-	-	C'	Bb	-	G
-	-	-	ha	-th	u	tha	-	k	r	-	-	du	aa	-	ye
FE	D	E	-	F	G	F	-	E	-	-	E	D	E	F	G
k-	r	-	-	ta	-	hu	-	-	-	-	ii	-	d	fi	r
F	-	E	-	D	.B	-	C	E	D	E	-	EF	G	F	-
ae	-	sii	-	-	ba	-	r	ba	-	-	r	aa-	-	ye	-
E	-	-	E	D	E	Bb	A	F	-	E	-	D	.B	-	C
-	-	-	ii	-	d	fi	r	ae	-	sii	-	-	ba	-	r
E	D	E	-	EF	G	F	-	E	-						
ba	-	-	r	aa-	-	ye	-	-	-						

E		GBC'BbA		G		FF		EED	EFG		G
din		zma—ne-		ka		rat		ap-	ni--		hai

EE GABC'   B♭AGCD   GGF♯ G
is ghdi---   qa-ynat   apni hai

AA   AA B♭AC'A   E   GABC'-G EG F E
ishq pr hu---sn   ki ina------ yt hai—

 EDE FGF E   D.BC   EDEFG F E
me-re phlu me me--ri j--nnt hai—

EDE   B♭AF E   D.BC   EDEFG F E
me-re   phlu me me--ri j--nnt hai—

E GBC' GG   D   EG   F♯   F♯G
fasle- v-qt ne mita hi   diye

E   GBC'G GC   DG   F♯ F♯G
dil tdpte hue   mila hi diye

AA   AA B♭AC' AEG   C' EGF E
kash is v--qt mau-t aa ja-e—

EDE FGFE D   .BC   EDE   FGF E -
zin-dgani- pe aake chha-- ja-e—

EDEB♭AFE   D   .BC   EDE   FGF E -
zindga--ni pe aake chha-- ja-e--

12. BUJHA DIYE HAIN KHUD APNE HATHO

Film: Shagun (1964)
Lyrics: Sahir Ludhiyanvi
Taal: Kaharwa
Transpose +1 and play from C Scale

Music: khaiyyam
Singer: Suman K.
Chord: EGB FAC' S=C#

bujha diye hain khud apane haathon mohabbaton ke diye jala ke
meri wafa ne ujaad di hai ummid ki bastiyaan basa ke

tujhe bhula denge apane dil se ye faisala to kiya hai lekin
na dil ko maalum hai na hamako jienge kaise tujhe bhula ke

kabhi milenge jo raaste men to munh firaakar palat padenge
kahin sunenge jo naam tera to chup rahenge najr jhuka ke

na sochane par bhi sochati hun ke zindagaani men kya rahega
teri tamanna ko dafn kar ke tere khyaalon se dur jaake

BUJHA DIYE HAIN KHUD APNE HATHO

dha	-	tin	tin	ta	-	dhin	dhin	dha	-	tin	tin	ta	-	dhin	dhin
1	2	3	4	5	6	7	8	1	2	3	4	5	6	7	8
prelude: F'----- E'C'E'-----															
E	A	-	F	G	-	E	-	F	F	A	A	GA	B♭	G	-
bu	jha	-	di	ye	-	hain	-	khud	a	p	ne	ha-	-	tho	-
-	B	B	B	A	B	G	-	F♯	F♯	-	E	F♯	G	G	-
-	mo	h	bb	to	-	ke	-	di	ye	-	j	la	-	ke	-
flute: E- FAG- E C E--															
E	A	-	F	G	-	E	-	F	A	-	G	GA	B♭	G	-
me	ri-	-	v	fa	-	ne	-	u	ja	-	d	di-	-	hai	-
B	B	-	B	A	B	G	-	F♯	F♯	-	E	F♯	G	G	-
um	mi	-	d	ki	-	b	s	ti	ya	-	b	sa	-	ke	-
interlude: E--- F GAC'----C'---B---															
A B C' B G--- E--- G F♯AG--															
G	AB	C'	C'	C'	-	B	-	A	A	A	A♭	AB	C'	C'	
tu	jhe-	-	bhu	la	-	de	-	ge	a	p	ne	dil-	-	se	-
D'	D'	-	C'	B	-	D'	-	B	A	-	G	G	-	G	
ye	fai	-	s	la	-	to	-	ki	ya	-	hai	le	-	kin	-
music: E – FGB—AGFEG--															
E	A	-	F	G	-	E	-	F	A	-	A	GA	B♭	G	-
n	dil	-	ko	ma	-	lu	-	m	hai	-	n	hm	-	ko	-
B	B	-	B	A	B	G	-	F♯	F♯	-	E	F♯	G	G	-
ji	yen	-	ge	kai	-	se	-	tu	jhe	-	bhu	la	-	ke	-
interlude: E--- F GAC'----C'---B---															
A B C' B G--- E--- G F♯AG--															
G	AB	C'	C'	C'	-	B	-	A	A	-	A	AB	C'	C'	
k	bhi-	-	mi	le	-	ge	-	jo	ra	-	s	te-	-	me	-
D'	D'	-	C'	B	-	D'	-	B	A	-	G	G	-	G	
to	muh	-	fi	ra	-	kr	-	p	l	t	p	den	-	ge	-
E	A	-	F	G	-	E	-	F	A	-	G	GA	B♭	G	-
k	hin	-	su	ne	-	ge	-	jo	na	-	m	te-	-	ra	-
-	B	B	B	A	B	G	-	F♯	F♯	-	E	F♯	G	G	-
-	to	chup	r	hen	-	ge	-	n	zr	-	jhu	ka	-	ke	-

interlude: G—F# GAC--- F# GAE—A♭---

A♭	A♭	-	A♭	A♭	-	A♭	-	A	A	-	A	AB	C'	A	
n	so	-	ch	ne	-	pr	-	bhi	so	-	ch	ti-	-	hu	-

A	A	-	G	B	-	A	-	G	AG	B	A	F#	A	G	-
ke	zin	-	d	ga	-	ni	-	me	kya	-	r	he	-	ga	-

E	A	-	F	G	-	E	-	F	A	A	A	GA	B♭	G	-
te	ri	-	t	mn	-	na	-	ko	d	f	n	kr	-	ke	-

B	B	-	B	A	B	G	-	F#	F#	-	E	F#	G	G	-
te	re	-	kh	ya	-	lo	-	se	du	-	r	ja-	-	ke	-

flute: E- FAG- E C E--

E	A	-	F	G	-	E	-	F	F	A	A	GA	B♭	G	-
bu	jha	-	di	ye	-	hain	-	khud	a	p	ne	ha-	-	tho	-

-	B	B	B	A	B	G	-	F#	F#	-	E	F#	G	G	-
-	mo	h	bb	to	-	ke	-	di	ye	-	j	la	-	ke	-

E	A	-	F	G	-	E	-	F	A	-	G	GA	B♭	G	-
me	ri-	-	v	fa	-	ne	-	u	ja	-	d	di-	-	hai	-

B	B	-	B	A	B	G	-	F#	F#	-	E	F#	G	G	-
um	mi	-	d	ki	-	b	s	ti	ya	-	b	sa	-	ke	-

13.   CHALE JA 3 JAHAAN PYAR MILE

Film: Jahaan Pyar Mile (1969)
Lyrics: Hasrat Jaipuri
Taal: Kaharwa dugun
Transpose +2 and play from C Scale

Music: Shanker Jaikishan
Singer: Md. Rafi, Suman K.
Chord: FA^{b}C'   S=D

chale ja chale ja chale ja, jaha pyar mile, jaha pyar mile -3

itane bade jahan me koyi toh miit hoga
is gam ki bansuri me koyi toh giit hoga
chale ja chale ja chale ja…

chalana hi zindagi hai rukana hain maut teri
ae zindagi ke rahi kis baat ki hai deri
chale ja chale ja chale ja…

aawaz de rahi hai manzil tuje suhani
badhata hi chal musafir har saans ek kahaani
chale ja chale ja chale ja…

CHALE JA 3 JAHAAN PYAR MILE

dhage nti nke dhin	dhage nti nkedhin	dhage nti nkedhin	dhage nti nkedhin
12 34 56 78	12 34 56 78	12 34 56 78	12 34 56 78
prelude: D$^{b'}$ C'---- F' ---- D$^{b'}$--- C'—F'-----			
C D^b F G	A^b C' B^b A^b	A^{b}B^b - - -	- - C' A^b
ch le ja ch	le ja ch le	ja- - - -	- - j ha
G F - F	F - C' A^b	G F - F	F - - -
pya - -r mi	le - j ha	pya - -r mi	le - - -

interlude:
C'C'C' F'—F' C' D$^{b'}$ C'
C'C'C' E$^{b'}$—E$^{b'}$ C' D$^{b'}$ B^b
B^{b}B^{b}B^b E$^{b'}$—E$^{b'}$ D$^{b'}$- C'-
A^{b}A^{b}A^b D$^{b'}$—D$^{b'}$ C'- B^b-
GGG C'—C' A^{b}GF--

			C'	C'
			i	t

C'D' E♭'D'E♭'	-	D♭'	C'	-	B♭	C'	- C'	-	-	- C'	-
ne	- - -	b	de	-	j	ha	- me	-	-	- ko	-

C'D' E♭'D'E♭'	-	D♭'	C'	-	B♭	C'	- C'	-	-	- A	A
ii	- - -	to	mi	-	t	ho	- ga	-	-	- i	s

A	- - -	G	A	F	F	AB♭ D♭'D♭'	-	-	- D♭'	-
gm	- - -	ki	ba	- su	ri-	- me	-	-	- ko	-

C'	- A	-	F	A	-	B♭	C'	- C'	-	-	- -	-
ii	- - -	to	gi	-	t	ho	- ga	-	-	- -	-

interlude: C'D♭'E♭' A♭'G'A♭'G' F'E♭'F'E♭' D♭'C'D♭'C' B♭-
GA♭B♭ F'E♭'F'E♭' D♭'C'D♭'C' B♭A♭ GA♭ C'-

			C'	C'
			ch	l

C'D' E♭'D'E♭'	-	D♭'	C'	-	B♭	C'	- C'	-	-	- C'	C'
na	- - -	hi	zin	-	d	gi	- hai	-	-	- ru	k

C'D' E♭'D'E♭'	-	D♭'	C'	-	B♭	C'	- C'	-	-	- A	-
na	- - -	hai	mau	-	t	te	- ri	-	-	- hai	-

A	- - -	G	A	F	F	AB♭ D♭'D♭'	-	-	- D♭'	C'
zin	- - -	d	gi	- ki	ra-	- he	-	-	- ki	s

C'	- A	-	F	A	-	B♭	C'	- C'	-	-	- -	-
ba	- - -	t	ki	- hai	de	- ri	-	-	- -	-

14.   CHURA LE NA TUMKO YE MAUSAM

Film: Dil hi to hai (1963)   Music: Roshan
Lyrics: Sahir Ludhiyanvi   Singer: Mukesh, Suman K.
Taal: Kaharwa   Chord: D^bEA $DF^\#A$ S=C

M: chura le na tum ko ye mausam suhaana
       khuli waadiyon men akeli na jaana
S: lubhaata hai mujhako ye mausam suhaana
       main jaaungi tum mere pichhe na aana

M: lipat jaaega koi bebaak jhonka
       jawaani ki rau men na anchal udaana
S: mere waaste tum pareshaa n hona
       mujhe khub ata hai daaman bachaana -2
       main jaaungi tum mere pichhe na aana

M: ghata bhi kabhi chum leti hai chehara
       samajh soch kar rukh se zulfen hataana
S: ghata mere nazadik aa ke to dekhe
       in ankhon ne sikha hai bijali giraana -2
       main jaaungi tum mere pichhe na aana

M: tum ek phool ho tumko dhundhunga kaise
       kahin milke phoolon mein gum ho na jaana
S: jo phoolon me rangat mile bhi to kya hai,
       juda meri khushbu juda muskurana -2
       main jaaungi tum mere pichhe na aana

Vinod Kumar

CHURA LE NA TUMKO YE MAUSAM

dha	ge	n	ti	n	ke	dhi	n	dha	ge	n	ti	n	ke	dhi	n
1	2	3	4	5	6	7	8	1	2	3	4	5	6	7	8

```
prelude:
B E'- B E'- F#'G'F#'G' F#' E' F#'–
B F#'- B F#'- G'A'G'A' G' F#' E'-
A'-B'A' G'-A'G' F#'-G'F#' E'-
E EG  BA BA E EG B-
Chord : (EGB)
```

dha	ge	n	ti	n	ke	dhi	n	dha	ge	n	ti	n	ke	dhi	n
														E	-
														chu	-
F#	-	-	D	-	E	-	F#	A	-	-	-	A	-	A	-
ra	-	-	-	-	le	-	n	tum	-	-	-	ko	-	ye	-
-	-	A	-	B	B	-	A	A	-	-	-	G	-	F#	-
-	-	mau	-	-	sm	-	su	ha	-	-	-	na	-	-	-
E	-	E	E	-	E	-	E	E	F#	-	-	E	-	D	-
-	-	khu	li	-	va	-	di	yon	-	-	-	me	-	-	-
D	-	F#	F#	-	G	-	F#	E	-	-	-	E	-	E	-
-	-	a	ke	-	li	-	n	ja	-	-	-	na	-	lu	-
F#	-	-	D	-	E	-	F#	A	-	A	-	A	-	A	-
bha	-	-	-	-	ta	-	hai	mu	-	jh	-	ko	-	ye	-
-	-	A	-	B	B	-	A	A	-	-	-	G	-	F#	-
-	-	mau	-	-	sm	-	su	ha	-	-	-	na	-	-	-
E	-	E	E	-	E	-	E	E	F#	-	-	E	-	D	-
-	-	main	ja	-	un	-	gi	tum	-	-	-	me	-	re	-
-	-	F#	-	-	G	-	F#	E	F#	E	-	E	-	-	-
-	-	pi	-	-	chhe	-	n	aa	-	-	-	na	-	-	-

antra:

dha	ge	n	ti	n	ke	dhi	n	dha	ge	n	ti	n	ke	dhi	n
		Db'	Db'	Db'	B	-	Db'	Db'	-	A	-	A	-	A	-
		li	p	t	ja	-	ye	ga	-	-	-	ko	-	ii	-
-	-	Db'	-	-	B	-	Db'	Db'	-	A	-	A	-	-	-
-	-	be	-	-	ba	-	q	jhau	-	-	-	ka	-	-	-

-	-	A	A	-	E	-	F#	B	-	-	-	B	-	B	-
-	-	j	va	-	ni	-	ki	rau	-	-	-	me	-	na	-
-	-	Db'	-	-	B	-	B	A	-	-	-	A	-	Db'	B
-	-	aan	-	-	chl	-	u	da	-	-	-	na	-	o	
B	Db'	Db'	Db'	-	B	-	Db'	Db'	-	A	-	A	-	-	-
o	-	me	re	-	va	-	s	te	-	-	-	tum	-	-	-
-	-	Db'	Db'	-	B	-	Db'	Db'	-	A	-	A	-	-	-
-	-	p	re	-	sha	-	n	ho	-	-	-	na	-	-	-
-	-	A	A	-	E	-	F#	B	-	-	-	B	-	B	-
-	-	mu	jhe	-	khu	-	b	aa	-	-	-	ta	-	hai	-
A	-	Db'	-	-	B	-	B	A	-	-	-	A	-	E	-
-	-	da	-	-	mn	-	b	chha	-	-	-	na	-	mu	-
F#	-	-	D	-	E	-	F#	A	-	-	-	A	-	A	-
jhe	-	-	-	-	khu	-	b	aa	-	-	-	ta	-	hai	-
-	-	A	-	B	B	-	A	A	-	-	-	G	-	F#	-
-	-	da	-	-	mn	-	b	chha	-	-	-	na	-	-	-
E	-	E	E	-	E	-	E	E	F#	-	-	E	-	D	-
-	-	main	ja	-	un	-	gi	tum	-	-	-	me	-	re	-
-	-	F#	-	-	G	-	F#	E	F#	E	-	E	-	E	-
-	-	pi	-	-	chhe	-	n	aa	-	-	-	na	-	chu	-
F#	-	-	D	-	E	-	F#	A	-	-	-	A	-	A	-
ra	-	-	-	-	le	-	n	tum	-	-	-	ko	-	ye	-
-	-	A	-	B	B	-	A	A	-	-	-	G	-	F#	-
-	-	mau	-	-	sm	-	su	ha	-	-	-	na	-	-	-
E	-	E	E	-	E	-	E	E	F#	-	-	E	-	D	-
-	-	khu	li	-	va	-	di	yon	-	-	-	me	-	-	-
D	-	F#	F#	-	G	-	F#	E	-	-	-	E	-		
-	-	a	ke	-	li	-	n	ja	-	-	-	na	-		

15. CHHODO CHHODO MORI BAIYAAN

Film: Miyan Bivi Razi (1960) Music: Sachindev Burman
Lyrics: Shailendra Singer: Suman K.
Taal: Daadra Chord: $DF^{\#}A$ S=C#
Transpose +1 and play from C Scale

chodo chodo mori bainya sanwre
laj ke mare mai to pani pani hui jaun

nar naweli mai ganv ki gwalan janu na ye preet ki paheli
mohe dar lage -2 jhuth muth mai kahi badnam na ho jaun
chodo chodo mori bainya sanwre
o mitwa o mitwa

neer bharan ke roz bahane karun chori chori aau tose milne
tujhse nit jane kya -2 kya kahne ko aau bin kahe chali jau
chodo chodo mori bainya sanwre

aaj nahi to kal bhed khulega tab aate jate dunia degi tane
more man bhaye -2 kahe tohe dil diya mai badi pachtaun
chodo chodo mori bainya sanwre

CHHODO CHHODO MORI BAIYAAN

| dha | dhi | na | dha | tun | na | dha | dhi | na | dha | tun | na |
1	2	3	4	5	6	1	2	3	4	5	6
									A	B♭	-
									chho	do	-
G	-	A	G	F#	-	G	-	-	A	-	-
chho	-	do	mo	ri	-	bai	-	-	ya	-	-
-	-	C'D'	-	-	B♭	A	-	-	-	-	-
-	-	saan-	-	-	v	re	-	-	-	-	-
A	-	A	C'	C'	-	D'	-	D'	E♭'	D'	-
la	-j	ke	ma	re	-	main	-	to	pa	ni	-
B	-	B	C'	D'	-	B♭	-	A	A	B♭	-
pa	-	ni	hu	ii	-	ja	-	un	chho	do	-
-	-	G	A	G	F#	G	-	-	A	-	-
-	-	chho	do	mo	ri	bai	-	-	ya	-	-
-	-	C'D'	-	-	B♭	A	-	-	-	-	-
-	-	saan	-	-	v	re	-	-	-	-	-

interlude: AAD'D♭'D' AAC'BC' AAC'-B♭-A-
AAAB♭- C'- D'E♭'D'--- C'- B♭A---

| dha | dhi | na | dha | tun | na | dha | dhi | na | dha | tun | na |
1	2	3	4	5	6	1	2	3	4	5	6
A	-	B♭	-	A	-	G	-	G	F#	E	-
na	-	r	-	n	-	ve	-	li	main	-	-
-	-	E	-	F#	-	G	-	-	A	-	-
-	-	gan	v	ki	-	gva	-	-	ln	-	-
A	-	D'	D♭'	D'	-	C'	-	B	C'	-	D'
ja	-	nu	n	hin	-	pri	-	t	ki	-	p
B♭	-	-	A	-	-	-	-	-	A	A	-
he	-	-	li	-	-	-	-	-	mo	he	-
A	-	-	C'	-	-	D'	-	-	-	-	-
d	dr	-	la	-	-	ge	-,	-	-,	-,	-

$^{C'}$D'	-	-	B^b	-	-	A	-	-	A	A	-
-	-	-	-	-	-	-	-	-	mo	he	-
A	-	-	C'	-	-	D'	-	-	-	-	-
d	r	-	la	-	-	ge	-	-	-	-	-
A	-	A	C'	-	C'	D'	-	D'	$E^{b'}$	D'	D'
jhu	-	th	mu	-	th	main	-	k	hin	b	d
B	-	B	C'	D'	-	B^b	-	A	A	B^b	-
na	-	m	na	ho	-	ja	-	un	chho	do	-
B^b	-	G	A	G	$F^\#$	G	-	-	A	-	-
o	-	chho	do	mo	ri	bai	-	-	ya	-	-
-	-	$^{C'}$D'	-	-	B^b	A	-	-	-	-	-
-	-	saan	-	-	v	re	-	-	-	-	-

A--- BE'D'---- B---- AGD---
o— mitva---- o----mitva—

interlude:2 D ^{G}A—BE'D'--- BGB--- AGD---

AB^b AGG F$^\#$E E F$^\#$GG AA
nir bhrn ke- roz bhane kru

AD' D$^{b'}$D' BB C'D' B^b A
chori chori aaun tose milne

AA AA C'C' $^{C'}$D'--- $^{C'}$$B^b$---A
tose nit jane kya----------

AA AA C'C' D' AAC' C' D'D'
tose nit jane kya khne ko aaun

E$^{b'}$D' BB C'D' B^bA
bina khe chli jaun

AB^b B^b GA GF$^\#$ GA $^{C'}$D' B^b A
chhodo o chhodo mori baiyan saan v re...

play rest song as above.

16. DAGABAZI PIYA TERE DIL ME HAI

Film: Aulad (1968)

Music: Chitragupta

Lyrics: Majrooh Sultanpuri

Singer: Suman K.

Taal: Kaharwa dugun

Chord: $E^bF^\#B^b$ CE^bG

Transpose +1 and play from C Scale

S=C#

dil dhadkta hai paanv rukte hai dekhte log ye kis nazar se mujhe

dagabazi piya tere dil me hai -2
tera dil mere gaalo ke til me hai -2 til me hai til me hai
dagabazi piya tere dil me hai -2

tere naino ka uthna haye re mera anchal sarkata jaye re -2
mera uljhe hai man, kanpe hai tan, payal badi, mushkil me hai
dagabazi piya tere dil me hai -2

yahan lali uchhalti shishe me pariyan hain machalti shishe me -2
sab ko chodkar, teri nazar, mujhpe hi kyun, mehfil me hai
dagabazi piya tere dil me hai -2

pehle tum kalaiyaan, thamoge, fir gauri ye baaiyan, thamoge
sab janu balam teri kasam kya kya nahi, tere dil me hai
dagabazi piya tere dil me hai -2

DAGABAZI PIYA TERE DIL ME HAI

dhage	nti	nke dhin	dhage	nti	nke dhin	dhage	nti	nke dhin	dhage	nti	nke dhin
12	34	56 78	12	34	56 78	12	34	56 78	12	34	56 78

prelude:

$GB^bD^{b'}C'B^bGB^b$—GB^b—$D^bC'A^bB^b$—

G-FE^bF G-FE^bF C'-B^bA^bC' C'-B^bA^bC'

$F'F'$ $F'F'$ $F'F'$ $F'D^bC'$

$D^{b'}D^{b'}$ $D^bD^{b'}$ $D^bD^{b'}$ $E^bD^{b'}B^b$

$D^{b'}C'D^{b'}B^bC'A^b$ $C'B^bC'A^bB^bF^\#A^b$- $F^\#B$—

B^b --- C'$B^b A^b$G A^b—C'B^bG--
aa----aa---   aa---------

G GGFG G GG GFB^b B^b C'A^bG F F CD^b E^bG F $E^b E^b$
dil dhdkta hai pav rukte   hain, dekhte log, ye kis   nzr se mujhe

| | | | $F^\#$ F |
| | | | d ga |

| E^b -C - D^b | E^b - E^b E^b | - G - A^b | $F^\#$ G A^b |
| ba -ji - pi | ya - te re | - dil - me | hai - te ra |

| B^b - B^b B^b | B^bC' D^b' C' B^b | - G - A^b | $F^\#$ - G A^b |
| dil - me re | ga- - lo ke | - til - me | hai - te ra |

| B^b - B^b B^b | B^bC' D^b' D^b' D^b' | C' E^b' - D^b' | C' D^b' - C' |
| dil - me re | ga- - lo ke | - til - me | hai til - me |

| B^b B^b - A^b | $F^\#$ - $F^\#$ F | E^bF -C - D^b | E^b - E^b E^b |
| hai til - me | hai - d ga | ba- -ji - pi | ya - te re |

| - G - A^b | $F^\#$ - $F^\#$ F | E^bF -C - D^b | E^bF G F C |
| - dil - me | hai - d ga | ba- -ji - pi | ya- - te re |

| - F - E^b | E^b - |
| - dil - me | hai - |

interlude:
GA^{b}B^b—D'—C'— GA^{b}B^b – C'—B^b— E^b'- C'- D^b'- B-
GA^{b}B^b – C'—B^b-
CD^{b}E^{b}FGA^b B^bC'F'E^b' B^bC'F'E^b' E^b'E^b'E^b'E^b'
A^{b}B^{b}D^b'C' B^{b}D^b'C' C'C'C'C'
F'E'D^b' C'B^{b}A^b F$^\#$FD^b C   CD^{b}E^{b}FGA^{b}B^b—

| | | | B^b B^b |
| | | | te re |

| B^b -$F^\#$ - $F^\#$ | F $F^\#$ E^b - | - $F^\#$ - $F^\#$ | F - F $F^\#$ |
| nai -no - ka | u th na - | - ha - ye | re - me ra |

| B^b -B^b - B^b | C' C' G A^b | D^b' - C' - | B^b $^\#$ A^b B^b |
| aan -ch -l s | r k ta - | ja - ye - | re - me ra |

| D' | -D' | - | E^{b,} | C' | - | A^b | B^b | D' | -D' | - | E^{b,} | C' | - | A^b | B^b |
| ul | -jhe | - | hai | mn | - | - | - | kan | -pe | - | hai | tn | - | - | - |

| D^{b,} | -D^{b,} | - | C' | E^{b,} | - | - | C' | C' | B^b | - | A^b | F[#] | - |
| pa | -y | -l | b | di | - | - | mu | sh | kil | - | me | hai | - |

interlude:

GA^bB^b—D'—C'-- GA^bB^b—C'—B^b—
E^{b,}—C'—D^{b,}—B^b-- GA^bB^b—C'—B^b—
CD^bE^bFGA^b B^bC'F'E^{b,} B^bC'F'E^{b,} E^{b,} E^{b,} E^{b,} E^{b,}
A^bB^bD^{b,}C' B^bD^{b,}C' C' C' C' C'
F'E^{b,}D^{b,} C'B^bA^b F[#]FD^bC CD^bE^bFGA^bB^b—

| | | | | | | | B^b | B^b |
| | | | | | | | y | ha |

| B^b | -F[#] | - | F[#] | F | F[#] | E^b | - | - | F[#] | - | F[#] | F | - | F | F[#] |
| la | -li | - | u | chh | l | ti | - | - | shi | - | she | me | - | p | ri |

| B^b | -B^b | - | B^b | C' | - | G | A^b | D^{b,} | - | C' | - | B^b | # | A^b | B^b |
| ya | -hain | - | m | chl | - | ti | - | shi | - | she | - | me | - | s | b |

| D' | -D' | - | E^{b,} | C' | - | A^b | B^b | D' | -D' | - | E^{b,} | C' | - | A^b | B^b |
| ko | -chho | - | d | kr | - | - | - | te | -ri | - | n | zr | - | - | - |

| D^{b,} | -D^{b,} | - | C' | E^{b,} | - | - | C' | C' | B^b | - | A^b | F[#] | - |
| mujh | -pe | - | hi | kyu | - | - | m | h | fi | -l | me | hai | - |

B^bB^bB^b F[#] F[#]FF[#]E^b F[#]F[#]F   FF[#] B^bB^b B^b C'GA^b D^{b,}C'B^b
phle   tum klai-ya, thamoge, fir gori ye baiya- thamoge

A^bB^b D'D' E^{b,} C' A^bB^b D'D' E^{b,} C'A^bB^b
sb   janu   blm -- teri   ksm --

D^{b,}   D^{b,} C'E^{b,} C'C' B^b A^b F[#]
kya kya   nhin, tere dil me hai

F[#]F FC D^b E^b E^bE^b G A^b F[#]
dgabazi piya tere dil me hai

F[#]F FC D^b E^bFG FC   F   E^b E^b
dgabazi piya---   tere   dil me hai

F[#] B^b D^{b,} C'D^{b,} — C'D^{b,}-- C'D^{b,}B^b- F[#]AB^b--

17. DIN HO YA RAAT HAM RAHEIN

Film: Miss Bombay (1957) Music: Hansraj Bahal
Lyrics: Prem Dhawan Singer: Md. Rafi, Suman K.
Taal: Kaharwa dugun Chord: CEG   S=E
Transpose +4 and play from C Scale

din ho yaa raat ham rahen tere saath yah hamaari marzi
tumhaari marazi…. ji hamaari marzi…
tumhaari to hamaari bhi yahi hai marzi
din ho yaa raat …

too dor main patang udoon tere sang sang
ho ho ho ho ho ho aa ha ha ha ha
too hai phool to main rang rahoon tere sang sang
ho ho ho hu hu hu ho ho, ho ho ho
rang daalo is rang mein hamaara ang ang -2
ye tumhaari marazi… ji hamaari marzi…
tumhaari to hamaari bhi yahi hai marzi din ho yaa raat …

le ke aaoon main baraat thamun mehandi wale haath
ho ho ho ho ho ho aa ha ha ha ha
main to mukh se na boloon chali chaloon tere saath
ho ho ho hu hu hu ho ho, ho ho ho
nit nit kare chanda se chakori mulaaqaat -2
ye tumhaari marazi… ji hamaari marzi…
tumhaari to hamaari bhi yahi hai marzi din ho yaa raat …

ik bangalaa ho pyaara saari duniya se nyara
ho ho ho ho ho ho aa ha ha ha ha
jisaki chaandi ki diwaaren aur sone ka dwara
ho ho ho hu hu hu ho ho, ho ho ho
jiske angana mein aake bhool jaaoon jag sara -2
ye tumhaari marazi… ji hamaari marzi…
tumhaari to hamaari bhi yahi hai marzi din ho yaa raat …

DIN HO YA RAAT HAM RAHEIN

dhage nti	nke	dhin	dhage nti	nke	dhin	dhage nti	nke	dhin	dhage nti	nke	dhin
12 34	56	78	12	34 56	78	12	34 56	78	12	34 56	78

```
C'C'C'C'C' Bᵇ A G F E D C
ho--------------------------

C    C    D      G   G  G  G      C    C   D      G   G  G  G
ho ho ho         ho ho ho ho      ho ho ho        ho ho ho ho

C     C    C   .Bᵇ  │.Bᵇ  CC .Bᵇ .G │ C    C    C  .Bᵇ │.Bᵇ  CC .Bᵇ .G
di    n    ho  ya    ra   -t  h   m   r    he  te  re   sa   -th ye  h

.Bᵇ  .Bᵇ   C   D    │ C    -   -   G │ G    G  C' C' │Bᵇ C'  -   C'  G
ma    ri   m   r      zi   -   - tum  ha    ri  m  r   zi    -   ji  h

G   GC'  Bᵇ   A    │ G    -   -   G │ G    C'  Bᵇ  A │ G    G   F   F
ma  ri-  m    r      zi   -   - tum  ha    ri  to  h   ma   ri  bhi y

E    E    D    C  │ DE  FE  D   -
hi   hai  m    r    zi-  -   -   -
```

interlude:
```
G Bᵇ BᵇC'C' C' BᵇC' -2
G Bᵇ C'D'D'-  D' D'------- D'--- D'---- D'C'-----
```

```
                                                               G   Bᵇ
                                                               tu   -

C'  -C'  C'   Bᵇ │ Bᵇ  C'  G   Bᵇ │ C'  C'  C'  Bᵇ │ Bᵇ  C'  G   Bᵇ
do  -r  main  p    tn   g   u   du   te  re  sn   g   sn   g   ho  ho

C'  -    G    Bᵇ │ C'  -   G   Bᵇ │ D'  -   C'  -  │ C'  -   G   Bᵇ
ho  -    ho   ho    ho   -  ha  ha   ha   -  ha   -   ha   -   tu  hai

C'  -C'  C'   Bᵇ │ Bᵇ  C'  G   Bᵇ │ C'  C'  C'  Bᵇ │ Bᵇ  C'  G   Bᵇ
fu  -l   to  main   rn   g   r   hu  te  re  sn   g   sn   g   ho  ho

C'  -    G    Bᵇ │ C'  -   G   Bᵇ │ D'  -   C'  -  │ C'  -   G   A
ho  -    ho   ho    ho   -  ha  ha   ha   -  ha   -   ha   -   rn  g

Bᵇ  Bᵇ   A    G  │ A    A   G   D │ C    Bᵇ  C   D │ C    C   G   G
da  ro   i    s    rn   g   me  h   ma   ra  an  g   an   g   ye tum
```

| G G C' C' | B♭ C' C' G | G GC'B♭ A | G - - G |
| ha ri m r | zi - ji h | ma ri- m r | zi - - tum |

| G C' B♭ A | G G F F | E E D C | DE FE D - |
| ha ri to h | ma ri bhi y | hi hai m r | zi - - - |

interlude:
G B♭ B♭C'C' C' B♭C' -2
G B♭ C'D'D'- D' D'------- D'--- D'---- D'C'-----

GB♭ C'C' C' B♭C'C' GB♭ C' C' C'B♭ C'C'
leke aaun main barat, thamu mehndi vale ha th

G B♭ C' – G B♭ C' - G B♭ D' – C'- C'-
hohoho- hohoho- ha ha ha – ha- ha-

G B♭ C'C' C' B♭ C'C' GB♭ C'C' C'B♭ C'C'
main to mukh se na bolu, chli chlu tere Cth

G B♭ C' – G B♭ C' - G B♭ D' – C'- C'-
hohoho- hohoho- ha ha ha – ha- ha-

GA B♭B♭ AG AA G DC.B♭ CDCC
nit- nit kre chnda se chkori mulakat -2

G GGG C'C'C' C' GGC' B♭AG
ye tumhari mrji-- ji hmari mrji--

GGC' B♭ AGG F FE E DC DE FE D -
tumhari to hmari bhi yhi hai mr ji--------

18.   DIL EK MANDIR HAI

Film: Dil Ek Mandir (1963)
Lyrics: Hasrat Jaipuri
Taal: Daadra
Transpose +2 and play from C Scale

Music: Shanker Jaikishan
Singer: Md. Rafi, Suman K.
Chord: FA^{b}C'   S=D

jaanewaale kabhi nahin ate, jaanewaalon ki yaad ati hai

dil ek mndir hai, dil ek mndir hai -2
pyaar ki jis men hoti hai puja, ye pritam ka ghar hai
dil ek mndir hai, dil ek mndir hai -2

har dhadkan hai arati wndan, ankh jo michi ho ge darshan -2
maut mita de chaahe hasti, yaad to amar hai -2

ham yaadon ke ful chadhaayein, aur ansu ke dip jalaayein -2
saanson ka har taar pukaare ye prem nagar hai -2

DIL EK MANDIR HAI

dha	tin	tin	ta	dhin	dhin	dha	tin	tin	ta	dhin	dhin
1	2	3	4	5	6	1	2	3	4	5	6

C F A^b D^b' C'   A^b F C'
aa----------   aa-----

C'D^b' C'D^b'--------   C'C'D^b'E'   D^b'D^b'   C'C'--
jane vale--------   kbhi-----   nhin   aate---,

B^{b}B^b B^{b}B^b B^b B^{b}A^{b}A^b G—F   F
jane vale ki ya-d   aa--ti hai

CD^b	D^{b}F	-F	G	A^b	A^b	G	-	-	-	A^b	F
dil	e-	-k	mn	di	r	hai	-	-	-	-	-

FG	GC'	-C'	C'	E'	D^b'	C'	-	-	-	-	-
dil	e-	-k	mn	di	r	hai	-	-	-	-	-

B^bA^b	-	A^b,A^b	GA^b	G	F	A^b	A^b	A^b	GA^b	G	-F
pya	-	r,ki	jis	me	-	ho	ti	hai	pu-	ja	-ye
G	A^b	-G	F	F	$-D^b$	C	-	-	-	-	-
pri	t	-m	ka	gh	-r	hai	-	-	-	-	-
CD^b	D^bF	-F	G	A^b	A^b	G	-	-	-	A^b	F
dil	e-	-k	mn	di	r	hai	-	-	-	-	-
FG	GC'	-C'	C'	E'	$D^{b'}$	C'	-	-	-	-	-
dil	e-	-k	mn	di	r	hai	-	-	-	-	-

interlude:
$A^bB^bC'D^{b'}F'$---
E'F' E'F' E'F' E'F' G'F'E'C' G'—
F'G' F'G' F'G' F'G' $A^{b'}$G'F'$D^{b'}$ G'—
C' F' E'---- $D^{b'}$ C' --- B^b A^b
F $D^{b'}$C' B^bA^b GF--

F	F	F	F	F	E	F	G	F	D^b	C	-
hr	dh	d	kn	hai	-	aa	r	ti	vn	dn	-
G	G	G	G	G	F	A^b	A^b	A^b	GA^b	G	F
aan	kh	jo	mi	chi	-	ho	g	ye	dr	shn	-
A^b	A^b	A^b	A^b	A^b	F	A^b	C'	-	C'	C'	-
mau	t	mi	ta	de	-	chha	he	-	h	sti	-
$D^{b'}$	$D^{b'}$	$D^{b'}$	$D^{b'}$	$D^{b'}$	$D^{b'}$	C'	-	-	-	-	-
ya	d	to	a	m	r	hai	-	-	-	-	-

interlude:
FGA^b-G- FGA^b-G- D^bE^bF-E- D^bE^bF-E^b-
.B^bCD^b-C- .B^bCD^b-C-   .F.G.A^b-.G- F—

F	F	-	F	F	E	G	G	F	D^b	C	-
hm	ya	-	do	ke	-	fu	l	ch	dha	yen	-
G	G	-	G	G	F	A^b	A^b	A^b	GA^b	G	F
aur	aan	-	su	ke	-	di	p	j	la-	yen	-
A^b	A^b	-	A^b	F	A^b	C'	C'	C'	C'	C'	C'
san	so	-	ka	h	r	ta	r	pu	ka	re	ye
$D^{b'}$	-	$D^{b'}$	$D^{b'}$	$D^{b'}$	$D^{b'}$	C'	-	-	-	-	-
pre	-	m	n	g	r	hai	-	-	-	-	-

19.   DIL KI KITAB KORI HAI

Film: Yaar Mera (1971)
Lyrics: Hasrat Jaipuri
Taal: Kaharwa dugun

Music: Shanker Jaikishan
Singer: Suman K., Md. Rafi
Chord: GBD' S=C

ho dil ki kitab kori hai, kori hi rahne do -2
haaye jo ab tak chhori hai chhori hi rahne do
dil ko churana chori hai chori hi rahne do
agar ye zora zori hai zori hi rahne do

chnda ko lage grahan suraj ko lage grahan -2
chnda ko lage suraj ko lage, lagne do lage grahan
haye pyar ki chandani gori hai, gori hi rahne do
ho dil ki kitab kori hai, kori hi rahne do

jab phul koi khil jaye lahraake bhawra aaye -2
aane do agar aata hai idhar, phir apne aap ud jaye
harjayi ye aadat tori hai, tori hi rahne do
ho dil ki kitab kori hai, kori hi rahne do

chal doge muskuraake, nazro se tum girake -2
jab pyar kiya iqrar kiya, manenge ham nibhake
haay teri meri ye jodi hai jodi hi rahne do
ho dil ki kitab kori hai, kori hi rahne do

Vinod Kumar

DIL KI KITAB KORI HAI

dhage	nti	nke	dhin	dhage	nti	nke	dhin	dhage	nti	nke	dhin	dhage nti nke dhin
12	34	56	78	12	34	56	78	12	34	56	78	12 3456 78
												B o
B	B	AB	-G	G	AB	B	A	E	GC'	-	C'	B A G -
dil	ki	kita	-b	ko	ri-	hai	-	ko	ri-	-	hi	rh nedo -
B	-B	AB	AG	G	AB	B	A	E	GC'	-	C'	B A G -
ha	y,jo	ab	tk	chho	ri-	hai	-	chho	ri-	-	hi	rh nedo -
B	BB	AB	AG	G	AB	B	A	E	GC'	-	C'	B A G -
dil ko,chu	ra-	na		cho	ri-	hai	-	cho	ri-	-	hi	rh nedo -
B	B	AB	AG	G	AB	B	A	E	GC'	-	C'	B A G -
gr	ye	zo-	ra	zo	ri-	hai	-	zo	ri-	-	hi	rh nedo -

interlude:
E'—D' B D' D' B D' E'—D' B D' D' B D' E'—D' B D'
D' B D' D' D' E' E' F' G' E'
A'- A' - G' E' E' D' A'- A' - G' E' E' D'
AA BB C'C' D'D' E'—G--

												D' chn
D'	D'	D'D'	-E'	E'	-	-	C'	C'	C'	AA	-D'	D' - - E'
da	ko	lge	-gr	hn	-	-	su	rj	ko	lge	-gr	hn - - chn
E'	E'D'	C'	E'	E'	E'D'	C'	C'C'	C'	C'	AA	-D'	D' - - B
da	ko,l	ge	su	rj	ko,l	ge	lg	ne	do	lge	-gr	hn - - hay
B	BB	A	BG	G	AB	B	A	E	GA	-	C'	B A G -
pya	r,ki	chan	dni	go	ri-	hai	-	go	ri-	-	hi	rh nedo -
												D'D' jb
D'	D'D'	D'D'D'E'		E'	E'	-	C'C'	C'	C'	A	AD'	D' D' - E'
fu	l,ko	ii	khil	ja	ye	-	lh	ra	ke	bhnv	ra-	aa ye - aa
E'	E'D'	C'	E'	E'	E'D'C'	C'		AA	BA	-D'	D'	D' D' - B
ne	do,a	gr	aa	ta	hai,idhr	fir		ap	ne,aa	-p	ud	ja ye - hr

B	B	A GG	G AB B A	E GA - C'	B A G -
ja	ii	aa dt	to ri- hai -	to ri- - hi	rh nedo -

20. DIL NE FIR YAAD KIYA

Film: Dil Ne Fir Yaad Kiya (1966)
Lyrics: G L Rawal
Taal: Kaharwa
Transpose +1 and play from C Scale

Music: Sonik Omi
Singer: Suman K., Md. Rafi, Mukesh
Chord: CFA   S=C#

dil ne fir yaad kiya bark si lahar aai hai
fir koi chot mohobbat ki ubhar aai hai

wo bhi kya din the hamen dil men bithhaaya tha kabhi
aur hns hns ke gale tum ne lagaaya tha kabhi
khel hi khel men kyon jaan pe ban aayi hai

kya bataaye tumhen ham shamma ki kismat kya hai
gam men jalane ke siwa aur mohobbat kya hai
ye wo gulashan hai ke jisame na bahaar aai hai

ham wo parawaane hai jo shamma ka dam bharte hai
husn ki aag men khaamosh jala karte hai
ah bhi nikale to ye pyaar ki ruswaayi hai

DIL NE FIR YAAD KIYA

dha	ge	n	ti	n	ke	dhi	n	dha	ge	n	ti	n	ke	dhi	n
1	2	3	4	5	6	7	8	1	2	3	4	5	6	7	8

prelude:
A--- G F , A --- G F, F F C, C' B^b A GF GF
flute: B^{b}C' B^{b}C' B^{b}C' – B^b A G F E^b D^b C

 C   D FG AB^b AGF GG G FE^{b}F E^{b}D^{b}E^{b}D^b C
dil ne fir yad kiya brk sii lhra   ii...   hai

F   F AB^b C'C' C'B^b C'B^b A GFG AG   F- G-FE^{b}D^{b}C
dil ne fir   yad kiya brk   sii lhra ii...   hai

C   DFG AB^b AGFGG   G GFE^b F E^{b}D^{b}E^{b}D^b C
fir koii- chot mohbbt   ki ubhr   aa ii...   hai

C   D FG AB^b AGF
dil ne fir yad kiya

music: flute
C' --- E^b'D' F' – C'
E^b'D'B^b – D'D'E^b'D'F' – C'
D' --- C'B^{b}AGF – A –B^b C' D' – A
synthe:
F E^b D --- C F E^b D --- C .B^b C D F C ---

C' D' C' B^b B^b AG   A   A   FAB^{b}D'- B^b B^b D'C'
vo bhi kya din the hme dil   me bitha-ya-   tha kbhi

C' D' ^{C}D' B^b B^b AG   A A FAB^{b}D'- B^b B^b D'C'
vo bhi kya   din the hme dil me bitha-ya-   tha kbhi

C'D' C'B^b D'D' D' D'C' E^b'---- D^b'   E^b'D^b'C' C'   B^{b}C' AGF
aur hns hns   ke gle tum---ne   lga- ya tha- kbhi-

FF   AB^b C'D^b' C' B^b C'B^{b}A GF G AG F- GFE^{b}D^{b}C
khel hi- khel me kyu jan pe bn aa ii hai -------

C   DFG AB^b AGFGG G GFE^b F E^{b}D^{b}E^{b}D^b C
fir koii- chot mohbbt ki ubhr   aa ii...   hai

C   D FG AB^b AGF
dil   ne fir   yad kiya

interlude:
F GF FB^b A --- A F
G AG G D' C' ---D' C'
E^b' F' – E^b' F' – E^b' F' –
flute: F G A G – D' C' A G C'--

C'   D'C'-B^b B^{b}C'   AG   AA   F AB^{b}D'D'B^b D' C'
kya bta-en   tumhe hm shmma ki kismt-   kya hai -2

C'   D'C'D'B^b B^{b}C' AG   AA   F AB^{b}D'D'B^b D' C'
kya bta-en   tumhe hm shmma ki kismt-   kya hai -2

C'   D' C'B^{b}D' C' D'C'B^b E^b'--D^b' E^b'D^b'C'C'C' ^{Bb}C'   A-- GF
gm me jlne   ke siva-   au-r   moh-bbt   kya   hai--

F F AB^{b}C' C'   C' B^{b}B^{b}C' B^b AGF GFAG F- GFE^{b}D^{b}C
ye vo gulshn hai ke jisme n bhar aani   hai

C   DFG AB^b AGFGG   G GFE^b F E^{b}D^{b}E^{b}D^b C
fir   koii- chot mohbbt   ki ubhr   aa ii…   hai

C D FG AB^b AGF
dil ne fir yad   kiya

G   A^b GFFF   GF E^{b}C   CE^b F G   G A^b GF
hm vo prvane hai- jo- shmma ka dm bhrte   hain - - 2

B^b A^b GFFF   GF E^{b}C   CE^b F G G A^b F
hm vo prvane hai- jo- shmma ka dm bhrte hain -2

AB^b C'B^b B^{b}B^b B^b C'D'C'D'--D' C'B^{b}D' C'----A GF
husn ki- aag   me kha-mo---sh jla-   kr---te hain-

FF   AB^b C'C'C' C' B^b C'B^b A GFGFAG F- GFE^{b}D^{b}C
aah   bhi nikle to ye pyar ki rusva-ii-   hai -------

21. GARJAT BARSAT SAAWAN AAYO

Film: Barsaat ki Raat (1960)　　Music: Raushan
Lyrics: Sahir Ludhiyanvi　　Singer: Kamal Barot, Sudha
Taal: Teen Taal　　Malhotra, Suman K.
Transpose +1 and play from C Scale　　Chord: EGC' DFA   S=C#

garajat barasat saawan ayo re -2
laayo n sng me hamre bichhade balamawa,
sakhi ka karun haay, garajat barasat saawan ayo re
garajat barasat saawan
ayo re, saawan ayo, saawan ayo re, garajat barasat saawan

rimajhim rimajhim meha barase, rimajhim rimajhim
meha – barase – barase -, meha
rimajhim rimajhim meha barase
tadape jiyarawa miin samaan
pad gayi fiki laal chunariya, piya nahin aaye
garajat barasat saawan ayo re garajat barasat saawan

pal-pal chhin-chhin pawan jhakore -3
laage tan par tir samaan, tir samaan, aa……
sakhi laage tan par tir samaan
nainan jal son bhigi chadariya, agan lagaae
garajat barasat saawan ayo re
laayo n sng me hamre bichhade balamawa
sakhi ka karun haay, garajat barasat saawan ayo –
laayo na – sang me – hamre – bhichhade – balamva,
sakhi ka karun haay re haay

GARJAT BARSAT SAAWAN AAYO

dha	dhin	dhin	dha	dha	dhin	dhin	dha	dha	tin	tin	ta	ta	dhin	dhin	dha
1	2	3	4	5	6	7	8	9	10	11	12	13	14	15	16
								D	D	G	G	G	G	F	G
								g	r	j	t	b	r	s	t
C'	-	A	G	E	G	F	-	D	D	G	G	G	G	F	G
sa	-	v	n	aa	yo	re	-	g	r	j	t	b	r	s	t
C'	-	A	G	E	G	F	-	F	B^b	A	G	E	G	F	-
sa	-	v	n	aa	yo	re	-	la	-	yo	re	sn	g	me	-
E	D	E	-	E	G	F	D	.B	D	C	-	-	-	F	E
h	m	re	-	bi	chh	de	b	l	m	va	-	-	-	s	khi
F	B^b	A	G	F	-	-	D	D	D	G	G	G	G	F	G
ka	-	k	ru	ha	-	-	y	g	r	j	t	b	r	s	t
C'	-	A	G	E	G	F	-	D	D	G	G	G	G	F	G
sa	-	v	n	aa	yo	re	-	g	r	j	t	b	r	s	t
C'	-	C'	C'	-	C'	C'	C'	E'	D'	E'	F'	D'	-	C'	-
sa	-	v	n	-	aa	yo	re	sa	-	v	n	aa	-	yo	-
-	C'	A	G	E	G	F	-	D	D	G	G	G	G	F	G
-	sa	v	n	aa	yo	re	-	g	r	j	t	b	r	s	t
C'	-	C'	C'	-	-	-	-								
sa	-	v	n	-	-	-	-								
G	G	G	G	G	G	C'	A	C'	-	C'	-	B	D'	C'	-
ri	m	jhi	m	ri	m	jhi	m	me	-	ha	-	b	r	se	-
G	G	G	G	G	G	C'	A	C'	-	C'	-	-	-	G	G
ri	m	jhi	m	ri	m	jhi	m	me	-	ha	-	-	-	b	r
C'	-	-	-	-	-	G	G	GA	B^b	-	-	B^b	-	F	G
se	-	-	-	-	-	b	r	se-	-	-	-	me	-	ha	-
G	G	G	G	G	G	C'	A	C'	-	C'	-	B	D'	C'	-
ri	m	jhi	m	ri	m	jhi	m	me	-	ha	-	b	r	se	-

A	A	A	A	C'	C'	C'	-	C'	-	C'	C'	A	-	G	G
t	r	pe	ji	y	r	va	-	mi	-	n	s	ma	-	-	n
D	D	G	G	G	-	F	G	C'	-	A	G	E	G	F	-
p	d	g	yi	fi	-	ki	-	la	-	l	chu	n	ri	ya	-
F	B^b	-A	G	F	-	-	D	D	D	G	G	G	G	F	G
pi	ya	-n	hin	aa	-	-	y	g	r	j	t	b	r	s	t
C'	-	C'	C'	-	-	-	-								
sa	-	v	n	-	-	-	-								
G	G	G	G	G	G	C'	A	C'	C'	C'	C'	B	D'	C'	-
p	l	p	l	chhi	n	chhi	n	p	v	n	jh	ko	-	re	-
A	A	F	G	B^b	A	F	G	C'	C'	C'	C'	B	D'	C'	-
p	l	p	l	chhi	n	chhi	n	p	v	n	jh	ko	-	re	-
G	G	G	G	G	G	C'	A	C'	C'	C'	C'	B	D'	C'	-
p	l	p	l	chhi	n	chhi	n	p	v	n	jh	ko	-	re	-
C'	E'	E'	F'	D'	D'	C'	C'	B	D'	C'	C'	A	-	G	G
la	-	ge	-	t	n	p	r	ti	-	r	s	ma	-	-	n
G	-	C'	A	C'	-	-	C'	C'A	GG	FF	GG	AA	C'-	C'	C'
ti	-	r	s	ma	-	-	n	aa-	--	--	--	--	-	s	khi
C'	E'	E'	F'	D'	D'	C'	C'	B	D'	C'	C'	A	-	G	G
la	-	ge	-	t	n	p	r	ti	-	r	s	ma	-	-	n
D	-	G	G	G	G	F	G	C'	-	A	G	E	G	F	-
nai	-	n	n	j	l	so	-	bhi	-	gi	ch	d	ri	ya	-
F	B^b	-A	G	F	-	-	D	D	D	G	G	G	G	F	G
a	g	-n	l	ga	-	-	y	g	r	j	t	b	r	s	t
C'	-	A	G	E	G	F	-	D	D	G	G	G	G	F	G
sa	-	v	n	aa	yo	re	-	g	r	j	t	b	r	s	t
C'	-	A	G	E	G	F	-	F	B^b	A	G	E	G	F	-
sa	-	v	n	aa	yo	re	-	la	-	yo	re	sn	g	me	-

E	D	E	-	E	G	F	D	.B	D	C	-	-	-	F	E
h	m	re	-	bi	chh	de	b	l	m	va	-	-	-	s	khi
F	B♭	A	G	F	-	-	D	D	D	G	G	G	G	F	G
ka	-	k	ru	ha	-	-	y	g	r	j	t	b	r	s	t
C'	-	A	G	E	G	F	-	D	D	G	G	G	G	F	G
sa	-	v	n	aa	yo	re	-	g	r	j	t	b	r	s	t
C'	-	C'	C'	-	C'	C'	C'	E'	D'	E'	F'	D'	-	C'	-
sa	-	v	n	-	aa	yo	re	sa	-	v	n	aa	-	yo	-
-	C'	A	G	E	G	F	-	D	D	G	G	G	G	F	G
-	sa	v	n	aa	yo	re	-	g	r	j	t	b	r	s	t
E'	-	-	D'	C'	B	D'	C'	x	AC'	D'	C'	A	-	G	-
sa	-	-	v	n	aa	-	yo	x	la-	-	yo	na	-	-	-
x	C'	B	C'	x	B♭	A	B♭	x	A	G	A	x	G	F	A
x	sn	g	me	x	h	m	re	x	bi	chh	de	x	b	l	m
FA	GF	ED	C-	F	G	F	G	A	B♭	-	B♭	-	A	F	G
va-	--	--	--	s	khi	ka	-	k	ru	-	ha	-	y	re	-
C'	-	-	-												
ha	-	-	y												

22.   HAMNE MANA HAMPE SAJAN

Film: Dada (1979)
Lyrics: Mahendra Dehlavi
Taal: Kaharwa
Transpose +1 and play from C Scale

Music: Usha Khanna
Singer: Suman K.
Chord: EGC' S=C#

humne mana hum pe sajan jobanva bharpur hai -2
ye to mahima ram ki ie me hamra ka kasur hai -2

saal solva laga humko ye to hum bhi janat hai
hamari bagiya mehake phulwa ye to hum bhi manat hai
chingari se aag bhaye ham sach ye baat zarur hai -2
ye to mahima ram ki ie me hamra ka kasur hai -2

daar ke kazra khaa ke gilaori hum jis aur nikal jaye
than jaaye hai diwano me chakku chhuriyaa chal jaye
sara shehar hai aashiq hamra hamka bahut garur hai -2
ye to mahima ram ki ie me hamra ka kasur hai -2

pehle gaona karvaiyenge fir sun meethi batiyaan
sabka thenga dikhlaai ke rang deihai tohri satiyaan
ab hu paas na aao hamre ab hu dilli dur hai -2
ye to mahima ram ki ie me hamra ka kasur hai -2
humne mana hum pe sajan jobanva bharpur hai -2
ye to mahima ram ki ie me hamra ka kasur hai -2

HAMNE MANA HAMPE SAJAN

dha	ge	n	ti	n	ke	dhi	n	dha	ge	n	ti	n	ke	dhi	n
1	2	3	4	5	6	7	8	1	2	3	4	5	6	7	8

prelude:
GAC'D'E' GAE'D'C' GAC'D' E'- D'C' D'- C'- C'- BA B- A-
B- AG A- G- ABC' BAG EDC

	C'	-	C'	C'	-	C'$^{D'}$	-	B	-	B	C'	A	-	A	G
	hm	-	ne	ma	-	na	-	hm	-	pe	-	sa	-	j	n
G	-	A	A	G	-	F	F	G	-	-	G	B	A	C'	-
jo	-	b	n	va	-	bh	r	pu	-	-	r	hai	-	-	-
-	C'	-	C'	C'	-	C'$^{D'}$	-	B	-	B	C'	A	-	A	G
-	hm	-	ne	ma	-	na	-	hm	-	pe	-	sa	-	j	n
G	-	A	A	G	-	F	F	G	-	-	F	E	D	C	-
jo	-	b	n	va	-	bh	r	pu	-	-	r	hai	-	-	-
-	E	-	E	E	D	D	E	E	C	-	C	C	-	G	G
-	ye	-	to	m	hi	ma	-	ra	-	-	m	ki	-	i	ma
G	A	A	C'	-	C'	-	B	A	-	-	G	G	-	-	-
h	m	ra	-	-	ka	-	k	su	-	-	r	hai	-	-	-
-	E	-	E	E	D	D	E	E	C	-	C	C	-	G	G
-	ye	-	to	m	hi	ma	-	ra	-	-	m	ki	-	i	ma
G	A	A	C'	-	C'	-	B	A	-	-	G	G	-	-	-
h	m	ra	-	-	ka	-	k	su	-	-	r	hai	-	-	-

interlude: G – A D' C' – B A   G – A D' C' – B B
A – B E' E$^{b'}$ – D' C' ^{A}C' D'E$^{b'}$D'E$^{b'}$ C'---

C'	-	C'	D'	-	D'	E'	-	E'	-	E'	-	E'	-	E'	-
sa	-	l	so	-	l	va	-	la	-	ga	-	h	m	ko	-
C'	-	C'	-	D'	-	E'	-	C'	-	C'	C'	C'	-	-	-
ye	-	to	-	h	m	bhi	-	ja	-	n	t	hain	-	-	-
C'	C'	D'	-	D'	D'	D'	-	D'	D'	D'	-	D'	D'	D'	-
h	m	ri	-	b	gi	ya	-	m	h	ke	-	fu	l	va	-

B	-	B	-	A	-	B	-	G	-	G	G	G	GE'D'A'	C'-
ye	-	to	-	h	m	bhi	-	ma	-	n	t	hain	-	- -

C'	-	C'	-	C'	-	C'	-	B	-	B	C'	B	-	A	-
chin	-	ga	-	ri	-	se	-	aa	-	g	bh	ye	-	h	m

G	G	A	-	G	-	F	F	G	-	-	G	B	A	C'	-
s	ch	ye	-	ba	-	t	z	ru	-	-	r	hai	-	-	-

C'	-	C'	-	C'	-	C'	-	B	-	B	C'	B	-	A	-
chin	-	ga	-	ri	-	se	-	aa	-	g	bh	ye	-	h	m

G	G	A	-	G	-	F	F	G	-	-	F	E	D	C	-
s	ch	ye	-	ba	-	t	z	ru	-	-	r	hai	-	-	-

-	E	-	E	E	D	D	E	E	C	-	C	C	-	G	G
-	ye	-	to	m	hi	ma	-	ra	-	-	m	ki	-	i	ma

G	A	A	C'	-	C'	-	B	A	-	-	G	G	-	-	-
h	m	ra	-	-	ka	-	k	su	-	-	r	hai	-	-	-

-	E	-	E	E	D	D	E	E	C	-	C	C	-	G	G
-	ye	-	to	m	hi	ma	-	ra	-	-	m	ki	-	i	ma

G	A	A	C'	-	C'	-	B	A	-	-	G	G	-
h	m	ra	-	-	ka	-	k	su	-	-	r	hai	-

interlude:

G – A D' C' – B A   G – A D' C' – B B
A – B E' E^b' – D' C'   ^A C' D'E^b'D'E^b' C'---

C'	-	C'	C'	D'	D'	E'	-	E'	-	E'	E'	E'	-	E'	-
da	-	r	ke	k	j	ra	-	kha	-	ke	gi	lau	-	ri	-

C'	-	C'	C'	D'	-	E'	E'	C'	-	C'	C'	C'	-	-	-
h	m	ji	s	o	-	r	ni	kl	-	ja	-	yen	-	-	-

C'	-	D'	-	D'	-	D'	-	D'	-	D'	-	D'	-	D'	-
thn	-	ja	-	ye	-	hai	-	di	-	va	-	no	-	me	-

B	-	B	-	A	B	B	-	G	-	G	-	G	GE'D'A'	C'-
ch	k	ku	-	chhu	ri	ya	-	chl	-	ja	-	yen	-	- -

C'	-	C'	C'	C'	C'	C'	-	B	-	B	C'	B	A	A	-
sa	-	ra	sh	h	r	hai	-	aa	-	shi	k	h	m	ra	-
G	G	A	-	G	G	F	F	G	-	-	G	B	A	C'	-
h	m	ka	-	b	hu	t	g	ru	-	-	r	hai	-	-	-
C'	-	C'	C'	C'	C'	C'	-	B	-	B	C'	B	A	A	-
sa	-	ra	sh	h	r	hai	-	aa	-	shi	k	h	m	ra	-
G	G	A	-	G	G	F	F	G	-	-	F	E	D	C	-
h	m	ka	-	b	hu	t	g	ru	-	-	r	hai	-	-	-
-	E	-	E	E	D	D	E	E	C	-	C	C	-	G	G
-	ye	-	to	m	hi	ma	-	ra	-	-	m	ki	-	i	ma
G	A	A	C'	-	C'	-	B	A	-	-	G	G	-	-	-
h	m	ra	-	-	ka	-	k	su	-	-	r	hai	-	-	-

23. HAAN, MAINE BHI PYAR KIYA

Film: Boond Jo Ban Gayi Moti (1967)
Lyrics: Bharat Vyas
Taal: Kaharwa

Music: Satish Bhatia
Singer: Mukesh, Suman K.
Chord: DFA   S=D

Transpose +2 and play from C Scale

M: haan, maine bhi pyaar kiya, pyaar se kab inkaar kiya
       bhigi bhigi raate, mithhi mithhi baaten
       aur maine dil ko nisaar kiya, haan,

S: maine bhi pyaar kiya

M: pyaar se kab inkaar kiya

S: pyaar se kab inkaar kiya
       bhigi bhigi raate, mithhi mithhi baaten
       aur maine dil ko nisaar kiya,

M: haan, maine bhi pyaar kiya

M: pyaar kiya kaliyon ke mahakate angon se
       pyaar kiya maine gul ke gulaabi gaalon se

S: aa ha ha aa ha ha aa
       pyaar kiya nargis ki nashili ankhon se
       pyaar kiya badali ki rngili zulfon se
       khuli chaandani men aa haa haa
       khuli chaandani men maine abhisaar kiya

B: haan, maine bhi pyaar kiya

M: thaam liya siine pe uchhalti laharon ko
       jhum uthha baahon men pakad tufaanon ko

S: aa ha ha aa ha ha aa

M: chum liya bijali se machalate hothhon ko
       lut liya maine mast ubharti bahaaron ko
       raat ki dulhan ka

S: aa ha ha

M: raat ki dulhan ka maine singaar kiya

B: haan, maine bhi pyaar kiya

HAAN, MAINE BHI PYAR KIYA

dha	ge	n	ti	n	ke	dhi	n	dha	ge	n	ti	n	ke	dhi	n
1	2	3	4	5	6	7	8	1	2	3	4	5	6	7	8

prelude:

flute: A--- B♭C'D'- A— B♭A AG GF

Cynthe: DD FD DD GD DD GD DA DF AA C'A AD'C'B♭ A-

piyano: D' C' A G, F E D C .A

```
                        F   -  |  -   -  F   -  | E   -  C   -
                        ha  -  |  -   -  main -  | ne  -  bhi  -

D   -  D   D  | D   -   -   -  | F   -  F   F  | E   E  C   C
pya -  r   ki | ya  -   -   -  | pya -  r   se | k   b  i   n

D   -  D   D  | D   -   -   -  | G   G  G   G  | A   -  G   -
ka  -  r   ki | ya  -   -   -  | bhi gi bhi gi | ra  -  te  -

G   G  G   G  | A   -   G   -  | G   G  G   A  | G   G  F   E
mi  thi mi thi| ba  -   te  -  | au  r  main ne| di  l  ko  ni

F   -  F   F  | F   -   F   -  | -   -  F   -  | E   -  C   -
sa  -  r   ki | ya  -   ha  -  | -   -  main -  | ne  -  bhi  -

D   -  D   D  | D   -   -   -
pya -  r   ki | ya  -   -   -
```

interlude:

flute: A--- B♭C'D'- A—C'B♭ B♭A AG

synthe: DD FD DD GD DD GD DA DG AA C'A AD'C'B♭ A-

piyano: D' C' A G, F E D C .A

```
A   -  A   A  | A   -   A   B♭ | D'  -  A   A  | A   A  G   F
pya -  r   ki | ya  -   k   li | yon -  ke  m  | h   k  te  -

G   -  G   -  | G   -   -   -  | G   -  G   G  | G   -  A   B♭
an  -  go  -  | se  -   -   -  | pya -  r   ki | ya  -  main ne

C'  -  A   A  | G   -   F   E  | F   -  F   -  | F   -  -   -
gul -  ke  gu | la  -   bi  -  | ga  -  lo  -  | se  -  -   -


F D' C'  F D' C'  A  C'  B♭  | G  B♭ A   A  A  D'
ha ha ha ha ha ha  aa aa aa   aa aa aa  aa aa aa
```

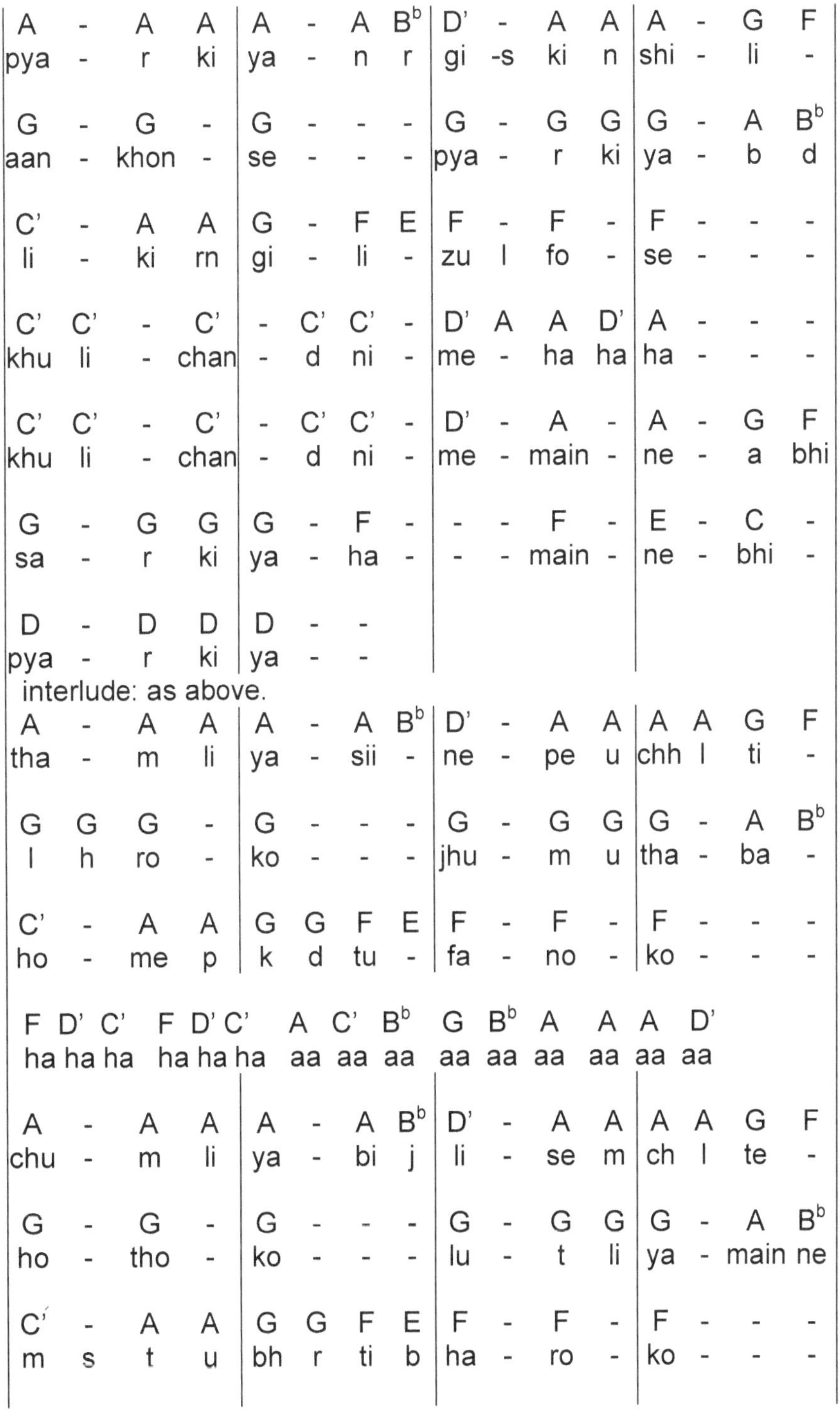

```
A   -   A   A | A   -   A   B♭| D'  -   A   A | A   -   G   F
pya -   r   ki| ya  -   n   r | gi  -s  ki  n | shi -   li  -

G   -   G   - | G   -   -   - | G   -   G   G | G   -   A   B♭
aan -   khon - | se  -   -   - | pya -   r   ki| ya  -   b   d

C'  -   A   A | G   -   F   E | F   -   F   - | F   -   -   -
li  -   ki  rn| gi  -   li  - | zu  l   fo  - | se  -   -   -

C'  C'  -   C'| -   C'  C'  - | D'  A   A   D'| A   -   -   -
khu li  -   chan| -  d   ni  - | me  -   ha  ha| ha  -   -   -

C'  C'  -   C'| -   C'  C'  - | D'  -   A   - | A   -   G   F
khu li  -   chan| -  d   ni  - | me  -   main - | ne  -   a   bhi

G   -   G   G | G   -   F   - | -   -   F   - | E   -   C   -
sa  -   r   ki| ya  -   ha  - | -   -   main - | ne  -   bhi -

D   -   D   D | D   -   -
pya -   r   ki| ya  -   -
interlude: as above.

A   -   A   A | A   -   A   B♭| D'  -   A   A | A   A   G   F
tha -   m   li| ya  -   sii - | ne  -   pe  u | chh l   ti  -

G   G   G   - | G   -   -   - | G   -   G   G | G   -   A   B♭
l   h   ro  - | ko  -   -   - | jhu -   m   u | tha -   ba  -

C'  -   A   A | G   G   F   E | F   -   F   - | F   -   -   -
ho  -   me  p | k   d   tu  - | fa  -   no  - | ko  -   -   -

F D' C'  F D' C'|  A   C'  B♭| G   B♭  A | A   A   D'
ha ha ha ha ha ha|  aa  aa  aa| aa  aa  aa| aa  aa  aa

A   -   A   A | A   -   A   B♭| D'  -   A   A | A   A   G   F
chu -   m   li| ya  -   bi  j | li  -   se  m | ch  l   te  -

G   -   G   - | G   -   -   - | G   -   G   G | G   -   A   B♭
ho  -   tho - | ko  -   -   - | lu  -   t   li| ya  -   main ne

C'  -   A   A | G   G   F   E | F   -   F   - | F   -   -   -
m   s   t   u | bh  r   ti  b | ha  -   ro  - | ko  -   -   -
```

C'	-	C'	C'	C'	C'	C'	C'	D'	A	A	D'	A	-	-	-
ra	-	t	ki	du	l	h	n	ka	-	aa	ha	ha	-	-	-
C'	-	C'	C'	C'	C'	C'	C'	D'	-	A	-	A	-	G	F
ra	-	t	ki	du	l	h	n	ka	-	main	-	ne	-	sin	-
G	-	G	G	G	-	F	-	-	-	F	-	E	-	C	-
ga	-	r	ki	ya	-	ha	-	-	-	main	-	ne	-	bhi	-
D	-	D	D	D	-	-									
pya	-	r	ki	ya	-	-									

24. HAAL E DIL UNKO SUNANA THA

Film: Fariyad (1964)
Lyrics: Kedar Sharma
Taal: Daadra
Transpose +1 and play from C Scale

Music: Snehal Bhaatkar
Singer: Suman K.
Chord: DFA   S=C#

haal-e-dil unako sunaana tha -2
sunaaya na gaya, sunaaya na gaya
jo zubaan par mujhe laana tha
wo laaya na gaya, wo laaya na gaya

pyaar se sine pe sar rakhake to dil kadamon pe -2
apako apana banaana tha -2
banaaya na gaya, banaaya na gaya

khelati ankh-michauli rahi nazaren apani -2
jinako palakon men chhupaana tha -2
chhupaaya na gaya, chhupaaya na gaya

ek hi waar men haathon se jigar thaam liya -2
haay jis dil ko bachaana tha -2
bachaaya na gaya, bachaaya na gaya

HAAL E DIL UNKO SUNANA THA

dha	dhi	na	dha	tun	na	dha	dhi	na	dha	tun	na
1	2	3	4	5	6	1	2	3	4	5	6
prelude: C' F'- C' D'- C' F'- D' G'— C' D'-											
D'C'AGFD- DFGAD'- C'BA-											
								D'	D'	C'	A
								ha	le	dil	-
C'	D'	-	A	F	-	G	-	A	-	C'	-
un	ko	-	su	na	-	na	-	tha	-	-	-
D'	-	D'	D'	C'	A	C'	D'	-	A	F	-
-	-	ha	le	dil	-	un	ko	-	su	na	-
G	-	A	-	-	-	-	-	-	C'	G	A
na	-	tha	-	-	-	-	-	-	su	na	-
D'	-	-	-	A	G	A	-	-	C'	G	E'
ya	-	-	-	na	g	ya	-	-	su	na	-
E'	-	D'	-	A	G	A	-	-	GA	C'A	G
ya	-	-	-	na	g	ya	-	-	-	-	-
F	-	A	A	G	F	G	-	F	E	EF	G
-	-	jo	zu	ba	-	pr	-	mu	jhe	la-	-
E	-	D	-	-	-				C'	G	A
na	-	tha	-	-	-				vo	la	-
D'	-	-	-	A	G	A	-	-	C'	G	E'
ya	-	-	-	na	g	ya	-	-	vo	la	-
E'	-	D'	-	A	G	A	-	D'	D'	C'	A
ya	-	-	-	na	g	ya	-	ha	le	dil	-
C'	D'	-									
un	ko	-									
prelude: C' F'- C' D'- C' F'- D' G'— C' D'-											
D'C'AGFD- DFGAD'- C'BA-											
								C'	C'	C'	-
								pya	r	se	-

BC'	D'	B	A	A	-	G	-	A	G	F	-
sii-	-	ne	pe	sr	-	r	kh	ke	to	dil	-
F	G	A	C'	B	-	A	-	A	-A	G	F
q	d	mo	-	pr	-	-	-	aa	-p	ko	-
F	G	F	E	EF	G	E	-	D	-	-	-
a	p	na	b	na-	-	na	-	tha	-	-	-
-	-	-	C'	G	A	D'	-	-	-	C'	G
-	-	-	b	na	-	ya	-	-	-	na	g
A	-	-	C'	G	E'	E'	-	D'	-	C'	G
ya	-	-	b	na	-	ya	-	-	-	na	g
A	-	D'	D'	C'	A	C'	D'	-			
ya	-	ha	le	dil	-	un	ko	-			

prelude: C' F'- C' D'- C' F'- D' G'— C' D'-
D'C'AGFD- DFGAD'- C'BA-

GAD^b' D^b'D'D' D'D'C' AB GFFG AC'BA
khelti aankh-michauli rhi nzren- apni –

A A GF G F E EFG E D
jinko plko me chhupa-- na tha

C'GAD' C' GA D' GE'E'D' C' GA
chhupa-ya na gya, chhupa-ya- na gya

D'D' C'A C' D'
hale dil- unko

AC' GA D'D' D' D'C'C'D'E' D' C'C' BC' D' C'D' B A
ek hi- var me ha-tho--- se jigr tham liya------

A GF G F EEFG E D
hay jis dil ko bchha-- na tha

C'GAD' C' GA D' GE'E'D' C' GA
bchha-ya na gya, bchha-ya- na gya

```
D'D'   C'A   C' D'
hale   dil-  unko
```

25. HAI NA BOLO BOLO

Film: Andaz (1971)

Lyrics: Hasrat Jaipuri

Taal: Kaharwa

Transpose +2 and play from C Scale

Music: Shanker Jaikishan

Singer: Suman K., Md. Rafi, Sushma Shreshtha, Pratibha

Chord: EGB   S=D

hai na bolo bolo -2 paapa bolo bolo mammi bolo bolo

paapa ko mammi se, mammi ko paapa se, pyaar hai pyaar hai

paapa mammi milate hain, chupake chupake hansate hain -2

jaane kyaa kya kahate hain, baaten karate rahate hain

hai na bolo bolo….

mammi teri achchhi hai kitani bholi bhaali hai

paapa bhi to achchhe hain kitane pyaare pyaare hain

hai na bolo bolo-2 munni bolo bolo dipu bolo bolo

paapa ko mammi se mammi ko paapa se pyaar hai pyaar hai

hai na bolo bolo….

papa se main bolungi mammi ko ghar le aayein

mammi se main bolunga saath mujhe bhi le jaayein

mammi bolo bolo, papa bolo bolo,

paapa ko mammi se mammi ko paapa se pyaar hai pyaar hai

hai na bolo bolo -2

paapa ko dipu se mammi ko munni se pyaar hai pyaar hai.

HAI NA BOLO BOLO

dha	ge	n	ti	n	ke	dhi	n	dha	ge	n	ti	n	ke	dhi	n
1	2	3	4	5	6	7	8	1	2	3	4	5	6	7	8
prelude: C E C E C E C E															
E	-	E	-	-	E	E	E	E	-	-	-	F	-	F	-
hai	-	na	-	-	bo	lo	bo	lo	-	-	-	hai	-	na	-
-	F	F	F	F	-	-	-	E	-	E	-	-	E	E	E
-	bo	lo	bo	lo	-	-	-	pa	-	pa	-	-	bo	lo	bo
E	-	-	-	F	-	F	-	-	F	F	F	F	-	-	-
lo	-	-	-	m	-	mmi	-	-	bo	lo	bo	lo	-	-	-
G	G	G	-	G	G	G	-	A	A	A	-	A	A	A	-
pa	pa	ko	-	m	mmi	se	-	m	mmi	ko	-	pa	pa	se	-
B	-	-	-	A	-	-	-	B	-	-	-	A	-	-	-
pya	-	-	r	hai	-	-	-	pya	-	-	r	hai	-	-	-
interlude: B E' D' B B F' E' D'															
G' F#' G' F#' A' G' F' E' F' E' G' F' B' A' G' F' E'---															
A	A	B	B	A	A	A	-	A	A	B	B	A	A	A	-
pa	pa	m	mmi	mil	te	hain	-	chup	ke	chup	ke	hns	te	hain	-
E	E	F	G	F	F	F	-	B	A	G	F	E	E	E	-
ja	ne	kya	kya	kh	te	hain	-	ba	te	kr	te	rh	te	hain	-
A	A	B	B	A	A	A	-	A	A	B	B	A	A	A	-
m	mmi	te	ri	a	chchhi	hai	-	kit	ni	bho	li	bha	li	hai	-
E	E	F	G	F	F	F	-	B	A	G	F	E	E	E	-
pa	pa	bhi	to	a	chchhe	hain	-	kit	ne	pya	re	pya	re	hain	-
A	A	B	B	A	A	A	-	A	A	B	B	A	A	A	-
pa	pa	se	main	bo	lu	gi	-	m	mmi	ko	ghr	le	aa	yen	-
E	E	F	G	F	F	F	-	B	A	G	F	E	E	E	-
m	mmi	se	main	bo	lu	ga	-	sa	-th	mujhe	bhi	le	ja	yen	-
E	-	E	-	-	E	E	E	E	-	-	-	F	-	F	-
hai	-	na	-	-	bo	lo	bo	lo	-	-	-	hai	-	na	-

-	F	F	F	F	-	-	-	E	-	E	-	-	E	E	E
-	bo	lo	bo	lo	-	-	-	pa	-	pa	-	-	bo	lo	bo
E	-	-	-												
lo	-	-	-												

26. ITNA HAI TUMSE PYAR MUJHE

Film: Suraj (1966)   Music: Shanker Jaikishan
Lyrics: Hasrat Jaipuri   Singer: Md. Rafi, Suman K.
Taal: Daadra   Chord: CEG   S=D#
Transpose +3 and play from C Scale

R: itna hai tumse pyaar mujhe mere raazdaar
        jitne ke aasmaan par taare hai beshumaar

S: itna hai tumse pyaar mujhe mere raazdaar
        jitne ke iss zameen par zarre hai beshumaar

B: itna hai tumse pyaar mujhe mere raazdaar

R: tere siwaa kissi ko na laaya nigaah mein
        laakhon haseen aaye jawaani ki raah mein
        sadiyon se kar raha tha tumhaara hi intezaar

B: itna hai tumse pyaar mujhe mere raazdaar
        jitne ke aasmaan par taare hai beshumaar
        itna hai tumse pyaar mujhe mere raazdaar

S: maine bhi tere waaste kitne janam liye
        tab dil ke raasto pe jale pyaar ke diye
        ek din zaroor paaugi itna tha aitbaar

B: itna hai tumse pyaar mujhe mere raazdaar
        jitne ke iss zameen par zarre hai beshumaar
        itna hai tumse pyaar mujhe mere raazdaar

M: Bekhud banaa diya mujhe tere salaam ne
        Jannat agar mile to na loon tere saamne
        Yeh pyaar woh nasha hai ke jisska nahin utaar

Itna hai tumse pyaar mujhe mere raazdaar

B: Itna hai tumse pyaar mujhe mere raazdaar

R: Jitne ke aasmaan par taare hai beshumaar

S: Itna hai tumse pyaar mujhe mere raazdaar

Jitne ke iss zameen par zarre hai beshumaar

B: Itna hai tumse pyaar mujhe mere raazdaar.

ITNA HAI TUMSE PYAR MUJHE

dha	dhi	na	dha	tu	na	dha	dhi	na	dha	tu	na
1	2	3	4	5	6	1	2	3	4	5	6
prelude: C'D'D'C', BC'C'B, ABBA, GAAG, FGGF, EFFE, DEED, C-											
										C i	C t
F na	- -	D hai	E tum	C -	C se	F pya	- -	D r	E mu	C jhe	- -
G me	- -	G re	G ra	A -	F# z	G da	- -	-G -r	- -	E ji	G t
AB ne -	C' -	C' ke	C' aa	- -	C' s	BC' ma -	D' -	C' n	B pr	G -	G ta
B re	- -	B hain	A be	- -	F# shu	AG ma-	FE --	GF --	ED -r	- -	CC it
F na	- -	D hai	E tum	C -	C se	F pya	- -	D r	E mu	C jhe	- -
G me	- -	G re	G ra-	A -	F# z	G da	- -	-G -r	- -	E ji	G t
AB ne -	C' -	C' ke	C' i	C' s	C' j	BC' mi-	D' -	C' n	B pr	G -	G z
B rre	- -	B hain	A be	- -	F# shu	AG ma-	FE --	GF --	ED -r	- -	CC it

F	-	D	E	C	C	F	-	D	E	C	-
na	-	hai	tum	-	se	pya	-	r	mu	jhe	-
G	-	G	G	A	F#	G	-	-			
me	-	re	ra	-	z	da	-	-r			

interlude:
C' EGC' C' EGC' C'E'D'E'C'D' BC'ABG
B EGB B EGB BD' C'D' BC' AB G-
santur: EG C'BG- EG BAG- EG AGFE G- G- x2

										B	A
										te	-
B	G	G	G	-	F#	A	G	G	G	G	-
re	-	si	va	-	ki	sii	-	ko	n	la	-
G	C	D	EF	G	F	E	D	E	-	B	A
ya	-	ni	ga -	-	h	me	-	-	-	la	-
B	G	G	G	-	F#	A	G	G	G	G	-
khon	-	h	sii	-	n	aa	-	ye	j	va	-
C	-	D	EF	G	F	EC	E	-	-	E	G
ni	-	ki	ra -	-	h	me -	-	-	-	s	di
AB	C'	C'	C'	C'	C'	BC'	D'	C'	B	G	A
yon-	-	se	k	r	r	ha -	-	tha	tu	mha	-
B	-	C'	A	-	F#	AG	FE	GF	ED	-	CC
ra	-	hi	in	-	t	za-	--	--	-r	-	it
F	-	D	E	C	C	F	-	D	E	C	-
na	-	hai	tum	-	se	pya	-	r	mu	jhe	-
G	-	G	G	A	F#	G	-	-			
me	-	re	ra	-	z	da	-	-r			

interlude:
GEG-B-, GEG-B-, GEG-B- A- G- x2
EFGABC'D'E' G' G', AAAA B- C'C'C'C' C'-
EG F#G F#G, EG F#G F#G, EG F#G F#G B-

										B	A
										main	-

B	G	G	G	-	F#	A	G	G	G	G	G
ne	-	bhi	te	-	re	va	-	s	te	ki	t
G	C	D	EF	G	F	E	-	-	-	B	A
ne	-	j	nm	-	li	ye	-	-	-	t	b
B	G	G	G	-	F#	A	G	G	G	G	-
dil	-	ke	ra	-	s	to	-	pe	j	le	-
C	-	D	EF	G	F	E	-	-	-	E	G
pya	-	r	ke	-	di	ye	-	-	-	i	k
AB	C'	C'	C'	-	C'	BC'	D'	C'	B	G	EG
din	-	z	ru	-	r	pa	-	un	gi	-	it
B	-	B	A	-	F#	AG	FE	GF	ED	-	CC
na	-	tha	ae	-	t	ba-	--	--	-r	-	it
F	-	D	E	C	C	F	-	D	E	C	-
na	-	hai	tum	-	se	pya	-	r	mu	jhe	-
G	-	G	G	A	F#	G	-	-			
me	-	re	ra	-	z	da	-	-r			

interlude: C' EGC' C' EGC' C'E'D'E'C'D' BC'ABG
B EGB B EGB BD' C'D' BC' AB G-
santur: EG C'BG- EG BAG- EG AGFE G- G- x2

BABG   GG   F#AG   GG   GC   DEFGF   ECE
be-khud   bna   diya-   mujhe   tere   sla--m   ne—

BABG GG   F#AG   G G   G C-D   EGFECE
jnnt   agr   mile-   to n   lu te-re   sa-mne—

EG   ABC'C'   C'   C'C'D'   B   B   GA   B   BA F#AGFEGFED
ye   pya--r   vo   nsha-   hai   ke   jiska   nhin uta----------r

27.   JUHI KI KALI MERI LADLI

Film: Dil Ek Mandir (1963)   Music: Shanker Jaikishan
Lyrics: Shailendra   Singer: Suman K.
Taal: Daadra   Chord: DFA   S=C#
Transpose +1 and play from C Scale

juhi ki kali meri laadali naazo ki pali meri laadali
o aas kiran jug jug tu jiye
nanhi si pari meri laadali o meri laadali

dharti pe utar aaya chanda tera chehra bana
champe kaa salaunaa guladastaa tan tera bana -2
o meri laadali
komal titali meri laadali hire ki kani meri laadali
o aas kiran jug jug tu jie
nanhi si pari meri laadali o meri laadali

sharmaae divaali taaro ki tere naino se
koyal ne churaai hai pacham tere baino se -2
o meri laadali
gudiyaa si dhali meri laadali mohe laage bhali meri laadali
o aas kiran jug jug tu jie
nanhi si pari meri laadali o meri laadali

har bol tera sikhalaae hame dukh se ladanaa
muskaan teri kahati hai sada dhiraj dharna -2
o meri laadali
gangaa ki lahar meri laadali chanchal saagar meri laadali
o aas kiran jug jug tu jie
nanhi si pari meri laadali o meri laadali
juhi ki kali meri laadali……

JUHI KI KALI MERI LADLI

dhin	-	ti	na	dhin	na	dhin	-	ti	na	dhin	na
1	2	3	4	5	6	1	2	4	5	6	8
prelude: F- G- F D C D F -											
											A
											ju
A	A	G	G	F	E♭	D	-	D	D	-	A
hi	ki	k	li	me	ri	la	-	d	li	-	na
A	A	G	G	F	E♭	D	-	D	D	-	B♭
jo	se	p	li	me	ri	la	-	d	li	-	o
B♭	-	B♭	B♭	B♭	A	A	C'	B♭	B♭	-	D'
aa	-s	ki	rn	ju	g	jug	tu	ji	ye	-	nn
D'	D'	C'	B♭	A	G	F	-	F	F	-	E
hin	sii	p	ri	me	ri	la	-	d	li	-	-
F	-	D	E♭	F	-	D	-	D	D	-	-
-	-	o	me	ri	-	la	-	d	li	-	-

interlude:
C' A B♭ C' F' D' C' A –
C' A B♭ C' E♭' C' B♭ G –
GAB♭ --- F FGA--- E♭ E♭FG--- E♭ – D –

dhin	-	ti	na	dhin	na	dhin	-	ti	na	dhin	na
1	2	3	4	5	6	1	2	4	5	6	8
										D'	D'
										dh	r
D'	D'	D'	C'	C'	-	B♭	B♭	-	A	F	G
ti	pe	u	tr	aa	-	ya	chn	-	da	te	ra
A	A	A	A	-	-	-	-	-	-	D'	-
cheh	ra	b	na	-	-	-	-	-	-	chn	-
D'	D'	D'	C'	C'	-	B♭	B♭	-	A	F	G
pe	ka	s	lau	na	-	gul	d	-	sta	t	n
A	A	A	A	-	-	-	-	-	-	F'	-
te	ra	b	na	-	-	-	-	-	-	chn	-

F$'$	D$'$	C$'$	B^b	F	-	G	F	-	F	B^b	A
pe	ka	s	lau	na	-	gul	d	-	sta	t	n
G	F	F	F	-	E	F	-	D	E^b	F	-
te	ra	b	na	-	-	-	-	o	me	ri	-
D	-	D	D	-	-	-	-	-	-	-	A
la	-	d	li	-	-	-	-	-	-	-	ko
A	A	G	G	F	E^b	D	-	D	D	-	A
ml	ti	t	li	me	ri	la	-	d	li	-	hi
A	A	G	G	F	E^b	D	-	D	D	-	B^b
re	ki	k	ni	me	ri	la	-	d	li	-	o
B^b	-	B^b	B^b	B^b	A	A	C$'$	B^b	B^b	-	D$'$
aa	-s	ki	rn	ju	g	jug	tu	ji	ye	-	nn
D$'$	D$'$	C$'$	B^b	A	G	F	-	F	F	-	E
hin	sii	p	ri	me	ri	la	-	d	li	-	-
F	-	D	E^b	F	-	D	-	D	D	-	-
-	-	o	me	ri	-	la	-	d	li	-	-

28. KABHI HOTON SE MUJHE BHI LAGA

Film: Geet (1970)
Lyrics: Prem Dhawan
Taal: Kaharwa dugun
Transpose +1 and play from C Scale

Music: Kalyanji Anandji
Singer: Suman K.
Chord: EGB   S=C#

kya hai iss bansuriya mein
jo mujhme nahi sanvariya
kabhi hontho se mujhe bhi laga le
bansuri banai ke ho bansuri banai ke

mai toh gaaun, mai toh gaaun tere giit mere miit
sare jag ko bhulai ke
kabhi hontho se mujhe bhi laga le
bansuri banai ke ho bansuri banai ke -2

tore sang neha laga tore rang rachi -2
ban ban dware dware phiru madmati
tujhmein hi, tujhmein hi sama gayi
main tere pas aayi ke
kabhi hontho se mujhe bhi laga le
bansuri banai ke ho bansuri banai ke -2

sara jag jan gaya radha bhai shyam ki -2
chhede teraa nam leke sakhiyan sare ganv ki
ho chhaliya tune
chhaliya tune sudh naa lini baanvari banai ke
kabhi hontho se mujhe bhi laga le
bansuri banai ke ho bansuri banai ke -2

Vinod Kumar

KABHI HOTON SE MUJHE BHI LAGA

dhage 12	nti 34	nke 56	dhin 78	dhage 12	nti 34	nke 56	dhin 78	dhage 12	nti 34	nke 56	dhin 78	dhage 12	nti 34	nke 56	dhin 78

prelude:
G F#E F#G , A GF# GA
B C' B A -4
Db' D' Db' B -4
D' E' D' Db' -4
F#' G' F#' E' -4
D' B G F#E
flute: E' --- E' F#' E' G' F#' E' D' C' B
    B---- D' C' B B , D' C' B, B G-- D E

B B BB BD'Db'B B B B BBC'A GF#GE EF#AG-- F# E
kya hai.... is ba- suri ya me, jo mujhme...nhin.... C'vriya

                                                            E Eb
                                                            k bhi

dhage 12	nti 34	nke 56	dhin 78	dhage 12	nti 34	nke 56	dhin 78	dhage 12	nti 34	nke 56	dhin 78	dhage 12	nti 34	nke 56	dhin 78
E	G	A	B	A	-C'	B	F#	G	-	-	F#	G	-	E	-
ho	to	se	mu	jhe	bhi	-	l	ga	-	-	-	le	-	-	-
-	E	GA	-B	A	-G	-	F#	A	G	F#	E	E	-	F#	E
-	ba	suri	-b	naii	-ke	-	ho	ba	su	ri	b	na	ii	ke	-
-	E	GA	-B	A	-G	-	F#	A	G	F#	E	E	E	Ab	A
-	ba	suri	-b	naii	-ke	-	ho	ba	su	ri	b	naii	ke	main	to
B	-	A	Ab	-	-	-	-	-	-	-	-	-	-	Ab	A
ga	-	un	-	-	-	-	-	-	-	-	-	-	-	main	to
B	B	Ab	A	B	-	Ab	A	B	-	B	A	B	D'Db'	-	B
ga	un	te	re	gi	-t	me	re	mi	-t	sa	re	j	gko	-	bhu
A	-	GA	-	F#G	-	E	Eb	E	G	A	B	A	-C'	B	F#
la	ii	ke	-	-	-	k	bhi	ho	to	se	mu	jhe	bhi	-	l
G	-	-	F#	G	-	E	-	-	E	GA	-B	A	-G	-	F#
ga	-	-	-	le	-	-	-	-	ba	suri	-b	naii	-ke	-	ho
A	G	F#	E	E	-	F#	E	-	E	GA	-B	A	-G	-	F#
ba	su	ri	b	na	ii	ke	-	-	ba	suri	-b	naii	-ke	-	ho

A   G   F#   E | E   E   E   - | |
ba   su   ri   b | na ii ke - | |
interlude:
EGG F#AA GB
ADᵇ'Dᵇ' BD'D' Dᵇ'E'
E' G' F#' E' D' Dᵇ' B A
B D' Dᵇ' B A G F# E
flute:
E F# Eᵇ – E B- B-
B D' Dᵇ' B B- Dᵇ'BA
Aᵇ Aᵇ Aᵇ   Aᵇ A Aᵇ A
B A G F# E – Aᵇ-
Aᵇ Aᵇ Aᵇ   Aᵇ A Aᵇ A,   B A G F# E -

B   -   -   - | -   -   Dᵇ' D' | E' D' B   G | B   -   -   -
ho   -   -   - | -   -   -   - | -   -   -   - | -   -   -   -

-    B   C'A -A | G   F#   A   A | -   B   Dᵇ'D'-E'| D' -   Dᵇ'
-    to   resn -g | ne ha   la   ga| -   to rern -g | ra -   chi -

-    Dᵇ' D'B -A | G   F#   A   A | -   B   Dᵇ'D'-E'| D' -   Dᵇ'
-    to   resn -g | ne ha   la   ga| -   to rern -g | ra -   chi -

-    Dᵇ' D'B -A | G   F#   A   A | -   B   Dᵇ'D'-E'| D' -   Dᵇ' -
-    b   nb   -n | dwa re dwa   re| -   fi rum -d | ma -   ti -

A   Dᵇ'Dᵇ' D' E'E'| D' -   Dᵇ'   B | Aᵇ AᵇAᵇ -   Aᵇ| -   -   -   -
-    -   -   - | -   -   o   - | tu jhme -   hi| -   -   -   -

AᵇAᵇ Aᵇ Aᵇ Aᵇ | Aᵇ -Aᵇ Aᵇ   A | B   D' Dᵇ' -B| A   -   G   -
tujh me   hi s | ma -g   yi main| te re pa   -s| aa ii ke -

F#   -   E   Eᵇ | E   G   A   B | A   -C' B   F#| G   -   -   F#
-    -   k   bhi| ho to   se   mu| jhe -bhi -   l| ga -   -   -

G   -   E   - | -   E   GA   -B | A   -G   -   F#| A   G   F# E
le   -   -   - | -   ba suri -b | naii -ke -   ho| ba su ri b

E   -   F#   E | -   E   GA   -B | A   -G   -   F#| A   G   F# E
na   ii   ke   - | -   ba suri -b | naii -ke -   ho| ba su ri b

```
E    E    E    -  |                    |                    |
na   ii   ke   -  |                    |                    |
```
interlude:
E GG F# AA GB
A C'C' A D'D' C'E'
E'G'F#'E'D'Db'BA BD'Db'BAGF#E
flute:
E F# Eb – E B- B-
B D' Db' B B- Db'BA
Ab Ab Ab Ab A Ab A
B A G F# E – Ab-
Ab Ab Ab Ab A Ab A
B A G F# E –

```
          BBBB BDb'D'E' E'D'BG B---
          o.....................................
          BC'  AA  GF#  AA  BDb'  D'E'  D'Db'   Db'
          sara jg   jan  gya radha bhyi  shyam  ki

          Db'D'  BA  GF#  AA  BDb' D'E'  D'Db' Db'
          sara   jg   jan   gya radha bhyi shyam ki

          Db'D'    BA  GF# AA  B  Db'  D'E'  D'Db' Db'
          chhede tera   nam leke sakhiya sare  ganv  ki

          Db'BA  AbAb   AbAb
          ho     chhliya tune

          AbAb    AbAb  Ab   Ab  AbA BD'Db'  BA   G- F#-
          chhliya tune sudh na linhi bavri    bnaii ke

          EE   EG  A BA      C'B    F#G-F#   G E
          kbhi hoto se mujhe bhi-    lga--     le

          EGA  BA  G F# AGF#  EE  F#E
          basuri bnaii ke ho basuri bnaii  ke

          EGA  BA   G F# AGF#  EE  E
          basuri bnaii ke ho basuri bnaii ke
```

29. KE JAAN CHALI JAYE

Film: Anjana (1969)
Lyrics: Anand Bakshi
Taal: Kaharwa

Music: Laxmikant Pyarelal
Singer: Md. Rafi, Suman K.
Chord: CEG DGB^b S=C

qaraar khoyaa mohabbat mein is zamaane ne
yeh baat sach hi kahi hai kisi deewaane ne

ke jaan chali jaaye jiyaa nahin jaaye
jiyaa jaaye to phir jiyaa nahin jaaye
yeh ilzaam sar pe liyaa nahin jaaye
liyaa jaaye to phir jiyaa nahin jaaye
ke jaan chali jaaye ho ooooo

zamaane mein nahin deewaana ham saa -2
deewaana nahin yeh zamaana ham saa
yeh kya jaane, yeh kya samjhe, yeh baatein pyaar ki -2
ooo.. ke pyaar har kisi se kiyaa nahin jaaye
kiyaa jaaye to phir jiyaa nahin jaaye   ke jaan chali jaaye ho ooo

na aaye kabhi neend, na aaya hai qaraar -2
hamaari taubaa ham nahin karenge pyaar
bas laao dil hamaara ham ko de do o sanam-2
o o… yeh dil le ke waapas diyaa nahin jaaye
diyaa jaaye to phir jiyaa nahin jaaye ke jaan chali jaaye ho ooo

churaa ke nazren na dekho tum yeh phool -2
suno yeh be-rukhi hamen nahin qubool
yaa ham jaayen yaa keh du yeh bahaar chali jaaye -2
o o… bahaar chali jaaye piyaa nahin jaaye
piyaa jaaye to phir jiyaa nahin jaaye
ke jaan chali jaaye jiyaa nahin jaaye
jiyaa jaaye to phir jiyaa nahin jaaye ke jaan chali jaaye ho……..

Vinod Kumar

KE JAAN CHALI JAYE JIYA NAHIN JAAY

dhin	-	-	ta	-	-	ta	-	dhindhin	-	ta		-	-	ta	-
1	2	3	4	5	6	7	8	1	2	3	4	5	6	7	8
prelude:															
C'C'C'		D'D'		D'D'E'D'E'		C'	B♭B♭		B♭B♭D'A♭			G			
qrar		khoya		mohbbt		me	is		zmane			ne			
G	GG	A♭G	F	CDG	G	GG		GA♭GA♭		G	F				
yh	bat	sch	hi	khi-	hai	kisii		diva--ne		ne					
														C'	-
														ke	-
B	C'	-	-	-	A♭	G	-	G	A♭	-	G	F	-	F	-
ja	-	-	-	n	ch	li	-	ja	-	-	ye	-	-	ji	-
D	F	-	-	-	G	A♭	-	B♭	-	-	-	-	-	-	-
ya	-	-	-	-	n	hin	-	ja	-	-	-	-	y	-	-
-	-	E'	D'	-	E'	-	F'	E'	-	-	C'	-	-	C'	-
-	-	ji	ya	-	ja	-	ye	to	-	-	fi	-	r	ji	-
B	-	-	D'	-	C'	A♭	-	A♭	-	-	-	-	C'	C'	-
ya	-	-	-	-	n	hin	-	ja	-	-	-	-	y	ye	-
B	C'	-	A♭	-	-	G	-	G	A♭	-	G	F	-	F	-
il	-	-	ja	-	-	m	-	sr	-	-	pe	-	-	li	-
D	F	-	-	-	G	A♭	-	B♭	-	-	-	-	-	-	-
ya	-	-	-	-	n	hin	-	ja	-	-	-	-	y	-	-
-	-	E'	D'	-	E'	-	F'	E'	-	-	C'	-	-	C'	-
-	-	li	ya	-	ja	-	ye	to	-	-	fi	-	r	ji	-
B	-	-	D'	-	C'	A♭	-	A♭	-	-	-	-	C'	C'	-
ya	-	-	-	-	n	hin	-	ja	-	-	-	-	y	ke	-
B	C'	-	-	-	A♭	G	-	G	A♭	-	G	F	-	-	-
ja	-	-	-	n	ch	li	-	ja	-	-	ye	-	-	-	-
-	-	D	-	B♭	-	A♭	-	G	-	-	-	-	-	-	-
-	-	ho	-	o		o	-	o	-	-	-	-	-	-	-

interlude:
G G A♭ B♭ D' C' B♭ A♭ – 2 E' D' C' B♭ A♭ G
FGGF FA♭A♭G GB♭B♭A♭ A♭GGG – 2 E' D' C' B♭ A♭ G
FGGF GA♭A♭G GB♭B♭A♭ A♭GGG -2
E'D' E'D' E'D' G'---- E'D' E'D' E'D' C'----

														C'	-
														z	-
C'	-	D'	-	C'	-	D'	-	E'	-	-	-	-	-	E'	-
ma	-	ne	-	me	-	n	-	hin	-	-	-	-	-	di	-
D'	-	E'	-	-	-	D'	C'	C'	-	-	-	-	-	C'	-
va	-	na	-	-	-	h	m	sa	-	-	-	-	-	di	-
C'	-	D'	-	A♭	C'	D'	-	E'	-	-	-	-	-	E'	-
va	-	na	-	-	n	hin	-	ye	-	-	-	-	-	z	
D'	-	E'	-	-	-	D'	C'	C'	-	-	-	-	-	E'	-
ma	-	na	-	-	-	h	m	sa	-	-	-	-	-	ye	-
C'	-	E'	-	C'	-	D'	-	B♭	-	C'	-	A♭	-	B♭	-
kya	-	ja	-	ne	-	ye	-	kya	-	sm	-	jhe	-	ye	-
F	-	F	-	A♭	-	-	G	G	-	-	-	-	-	-	-
ba	-	te	-	pya	-	-	r	ki	-	-	-	-	-	-	-
C'	-	-	-	-	-	-	-	-	-	-	-	-	-	C'	-
o	-	-	-	-	-	-	-	-	-	-	-	-	-	ke	-
B	-	C'	-	A♭	A♭	-	A♭	G	A♭	-	G	F	-	F	-
pya	-	-	-	r	h	r	ki	sii	-	-	se	-	-	ki	-
D	F	-	-	-	G	A♭	-	B♭	-	-	-	▪	▪		▪
ya	-	-	-	-	n	hin	-	ja	-	-	-	-	y		
-	-	E'	D'	-	E'	-	F'	E'	-	-	C'	-	-	C'	-
-	-	ki	ya	-	ja	-	ye	to	-	-	fi	-	r	ji	-
B	-	-	D'	-	C'	A♭	-	A♭	-	-	-	-	C'		
ya	-	-	-	-	n	hin	-	ja	-	-	-	-	y		

interlude:
G GG G A^bGFG G C' C' C'C'
C'D'D'C' B^bC'C'B^b $A^b$$B^b$$B^b$$A^b$ $A^b$$B^b$$B^b$G
G GG G A^bGFG G C' C' C'C'
C'D'D'C' B^bC'C'B^b G----
G G F G A^bC' A^b— C' A^b C' G ----
G G F G A^bC' A^b— C' A^b C' G ----
G'F' G'- A^b'- G'F'E'D' E'- F'- E'D'C'B^b C'- D'- C'$B^b$$A^b$$B^b$ G—

														C'	-
														na	-
C'	-	D'	-	C'	-	D'	-	E'	-	-	-	-	-	E'	-
aa	-	ye	-	k	-	bhi	-	nin	-	-	-	-	d	na	-
D'	-	E'	-	-	D'	-	C'	C'	-	-	-	-	-	C'	-
aa	-	ya	-	-	hai	-	q	ra	-	-	-	-	r	h	-
C'	-	D'	-	C'	-	D'	-	E'	-	-	-	-	-	E'	-
ma	-	ri	-	tau	-	ba	-	hm	-	-	-	-	-	n	-
D'	-	E'	-	D'	-	C'	-	C'	-	-	-	-	-	E'	-
hin	-	k	-	ren	-	ge	-	pya	-	-	-	-	r	b	s
C'	-	E'	-	C'	-	D'	-	B^b	-	C'	-	A^b	-	B^b	-
la	-	o	-	di	l	h	-	ma	-	ra	-	h	m	ko	-
F	-	F	-	A^b	-	G	-	G	-	-	-	-	-	-	-
de	-	do	-	o	-	s	-	nm	-	-	-	-	-	-	-
C'	-	-	-	-	-	-	-	-	-	-	-	-	-	C'	-
o	-	-	-	-	-	-	-	-	-	-	-	-	-	ye	-
B	-	C'	-	A^b	-	A^b	-	G	A^b	-	G	-	F	F	-
dil	-	-	-	le	-	ke	-	va	-	-	p	-	s	di	-
D	F	-	-	-	G	A^b	-	B^b	-	-	-	-	-	-	-
ya	-	-	-	-	n	hin	-	ja	-	-	-	-	y	-	-
-	-	E'	D'	-	E'	F'	-	E'	-	-	C'	-	-	C'	-
-	-	di	ya	-	ja	y	-	to	-	-	fi	-	r	ji	-

B   -   - D' | - C' A^b - |A^b - - - | - C'
ya   -   - - | - n hin - |ja - - - | - y

interlude:
G C' C' --- F- G- GA^b- A^b
GFGF A^{b}GA^{b}G C'B^b D'C' B^{b}A^b A^{b}G
GFGF A^{b}GA^{b}G C'B^b B^{b}A^b A^{b}G
D'C'--- E'D'--- F'E'----

C'C'   D' C'D'E' E' D'E' D' C' C'
chura ke nzren n dekho tum yh ful -2

C'C'   D' C'D'E' E'D' E'D' C'C'
suno yh be-rukhi hme nhin qubul

E' C' E'C'D' B^b C' A^b B^{b}FA^b A^{b}G G
ya hm jaen ya kh do ye bahar chli jae -2

C'-------
o ------

C'BC' A^{b}G GA^{b}GF FDF GA^b B^b
bahar chli ja-e- piya- nhin jae

E'D'   E'F' E' C' C'BD' C'A^b A^{b}C'
piya jae to fir jiya- nhin jae

C' BC' A^{b}G GA^{b}GF FDF GA^b B^b
ke jan chli ja-e- jiya- nhin jae

E'D' E'F' E' C' C'BD' C'A^b A^{b}C'
jiya jae to fir jiya- nhin jae

C' BC' A^{b}G GA^{b}GF D B^b A^b G -
ke jan chli   ja-e-   o-------

30. KAUNE RANG MUNGWA

Film: Heera Moti (1959)   Music: Raushan Nagrath
Lyrics: Prem Dhawan   Singer: Suman K., Sudha Malhotra
Taal: Kaharwa dugun   Chord: FA^{b}C' S=C

kaune rang mungwa kawan rang motiyaa kaune rang mungwa
kaune rang mungwa kawan rang motiyaa
ho kaune rang ho kaune rang
nanadi tore birna ho o o o jee

sabaz rang mungwa safed rang motiyaa sabaz rang mungwa
sabaz rang mungwa safed rang motiyaa
saanwar rang ho saanwar rang bhave ri more birna
ho o o o jee

toot gayile mungwa bikhar gaile motiyaa toot gayile mungwa
toot gayile mungwa bikhar gaile motiyaa
bisar gaile haay bisar gaile bhave ri more birna
ho o o o jee

been laibo mungwa bator laibo motiyaa been laibo mungwa
been laibo mungwa bator laibo motiyaa
manaaye laibo, manaaye laibo nanadi tore birna
ho o o o jee

kit sohe mungwa kit sohe motiyaa kit sohe mungwa
kit sohe mungwa kit sohe motiyaa
ho kit sohe, ho kit sohe nanadi tore birna
ho o o o jee

mundri sohe mungwa bakiya sohe motiyaa mundri sohe mungwa
mundri sohe mungwa bakiya sohe motiyaa
titiriya sohe, ho titiriya sohe bhave ri more birna
ho o o o jee ho ho ho ho ho ho ho ho ho ho ho ho ho ho ho ho

KAUNE RANG MUNGWA

dhage	nti	nkedhin		dhage	nti	nkedhin		dhage	nti	nkedhin		dhage	nti	nkedhin	
12	34	56	78	12	34	56	78	12	34	56	78	12	34	56	78
prelude:															
F – A♭ G	F – E♭ D	FF A♭ G	F – E♭ D												
F – A♭ G	F – E♭ D	FF A♭ G	F F F -												
F	F	F	F	B♭	B♭	B♭	B♭	B♭	C'	B♭	B♭	A	G	A	-
kau	ne	rn	g	mun	g	va	k	v	n	rn	g	mo	ti	ya	-
F	F	F	F	B♭	B♭	B♭	-	F	-F	FDA♭G		F	GF	-	-
kau	ne	rn	g	mun	g	va	-	-	flute			-	-	-	-
F	F	F	F	B♭	B♭	B♭	B♭	B♭	C'	B♭	B♭	A	G	A	A
kau	ne	rn	g	mun	g	va	k	v	n	rn	g	mo	ti	ya	ho
G	A♭	G	F	GG	-A♭	G	A♭	G	A♭	F	G	A♭	-	G	-
kau	ne	rn	g	flute:			ho	kau	ne	rn	g	n	-	n	-
F	-	G	G	F	F	F	-	A♭	-	G	-	A♭	-	G	-
di	-	to	re	bi	r	na	-	ho	-	o	-	o	-	o	-
F	-	-	GA♭	F	-G	F	F	F	F	F	F	B♭	B♭	B♭	B♭
ji	-	-	-	-	-	-	s	b	j	rn	g	mun	g	va	s
B♭	C'	B♭	B♭	A	G	A	F	F	F	F	F	B♭	B♭	B♭	-
fe	d	rn	g	mo	ti	ya	s	b	j	rn	g	mun	g	va	-
F	-F	FDA♭G		F	GF	-	F	F	F	F	F	B♭	B♭	B♭	B♭
-	-	-	-	-	-	-	s	b	j	rn	g	mun	g	va	s
B♭	C'	B♭	B♭	A	G	A	A♭	C	A♭	F	F	G	-A♭	F	A♭
fe	d	rn	g	mo	ti	ya san		v	r	rn	g	flute:	ho	san	
G	A♭	F	G	A♭	-	G	-	F	-	A♭	G	F	F	F	-
v	r	rn	g	bha	-	v	-	ti	-	mo	re	bi	r	na	-
F	-	D	G	F	-	F	-								
ho	-	ho	o	ho	-	ji	-								

play rest of the song as above.

taan at the end
C'--------- D'E^b'D'E^b'C'---
ho---------------------

A^b – FG A^b- A^{b}A^b GG FF   FG A^{b}A^b GG FF
ho-------------------   ho-----------

GA^{b}GA^{b}F- GA^{b}GA^{b}F-
ho------- ho-------

31. MAN MOHAN MAN MEIN HO TUMHI

Film: Kaise Kahun (1964)
Lyrics: Shakeel Badayuni
Taal: Teen Taal
Transpose +1 and play from C Scale

Music: Sachindev Burman
Singer: Md. Rafi,Suman K.,
Shiv Dayal Batish
Chord: FA^{b}C' GB^{b}D' S=C#

aa tanu um aa aa aa aa aa aa aa aa aa aa
manmohan man me ho tumhi -2
more ang ang tumhi samaye
jano, ya jano na, ho tumhi
manmohan man me
manmohan man me, man me
ho tumhi, ho tumhi, ho tumhi
manmohan man me ho tumhi
more ang ang tumhi samaye
jano, ya jano na, ho tumhi manmohan man me

dekh dekh tori chhab sanwariya -2
bani hain radha tumri banwariya
rom rom tumhare gun gaaye
mano, ya mano na, ho tumhi manmohan man me
dekh dekh tori chhab sanwariya
hu bani hain radha tumhari banwariya
dekh dekh tori chhab sanwariya
bani hain radha tumri banwariya
rom rom tumhare gun gaaye
mano, ya mano na, ho tumhi manmohan man me -2

MAN MOHAN MAN MEIN HO TUMHI

dha	dhin	dhin	dha	dha	dhin	dhin	dha	dha	tin	tin	ta	ta	dhin	dhin	dha
1	2	3	4	5	6	7	8	9	10	11	12	13	14	15	16

prelude:

C'-------C'B^{b}A^{b}B^{b}FG----   G FGB^b E^b F
aa-------tanum--- -------- aa----------

F- C D --- C ---   F ----------
aa--------------- aa----------

F---- G----- FGB^b A^b B^b G – E^{b}FG--- E^b ---
aa---------- aa-------------------------

F—C--- D --- C   B^b G G F—G --
aa----------- aa---------

												F	G	
												m	n		
C'	-	C'	C'	B^b	D'	C'	-	-	A^b	-	B^b	G	-	G	G
mo	-	h	n	m	n	me	-	-	ho	-	tu	mhi	-	mo	re
F	G	G	F	E^b	E^b	E^b	E^b	F	-	-	C	D	-	C	-
an	-	g	an	-	g	tu	m	hi	-	-	s	ma	-	ye	-
C	C	C'	D'-	-	B^b	C'	-	-	A^b	-	A^b	B^b	G	F	G
ja	no	ya	ja	-	no	na	-	-	ho	-	tu	mhi	-	m	n
C'	-	C'	C'	B^b	D'	C'	-	-	-	A^b	B^b	C'	-	-	-
mo	-	h	n	m	n	me	-	-	-	-	-	-	-	-	-
F	G	A^b	-	B^b	C'	-	D'	B^b	C'	-	D'	C'	D'	C'	D'
m	n	mo	-	h	n	-	m	n	me	-	m	-	n	-	me
F'	E^{b,}	F'	D'	C'	B^b	A^b	B^b	G	F	E^b	F	D	-	F	G
ho	-	-	tu	mhi	ho	-	tu	mhi	ho	-	tu	mhi	-	m	n
C'	-	C'	C'	B^b	D'	C'	-	-	A^b	-	B^b	G	-	G	G
mo	-	h	n	m	n	me	-	-	ho	-	tu	mhi	-	mo	re
F	G	G	F	E^b	E^b	E^b	E^b	F	-	-	C	D	-	C	-
an	-	g	an	-	g	tu	m	hi	-	-	s	ma	-	ye	-

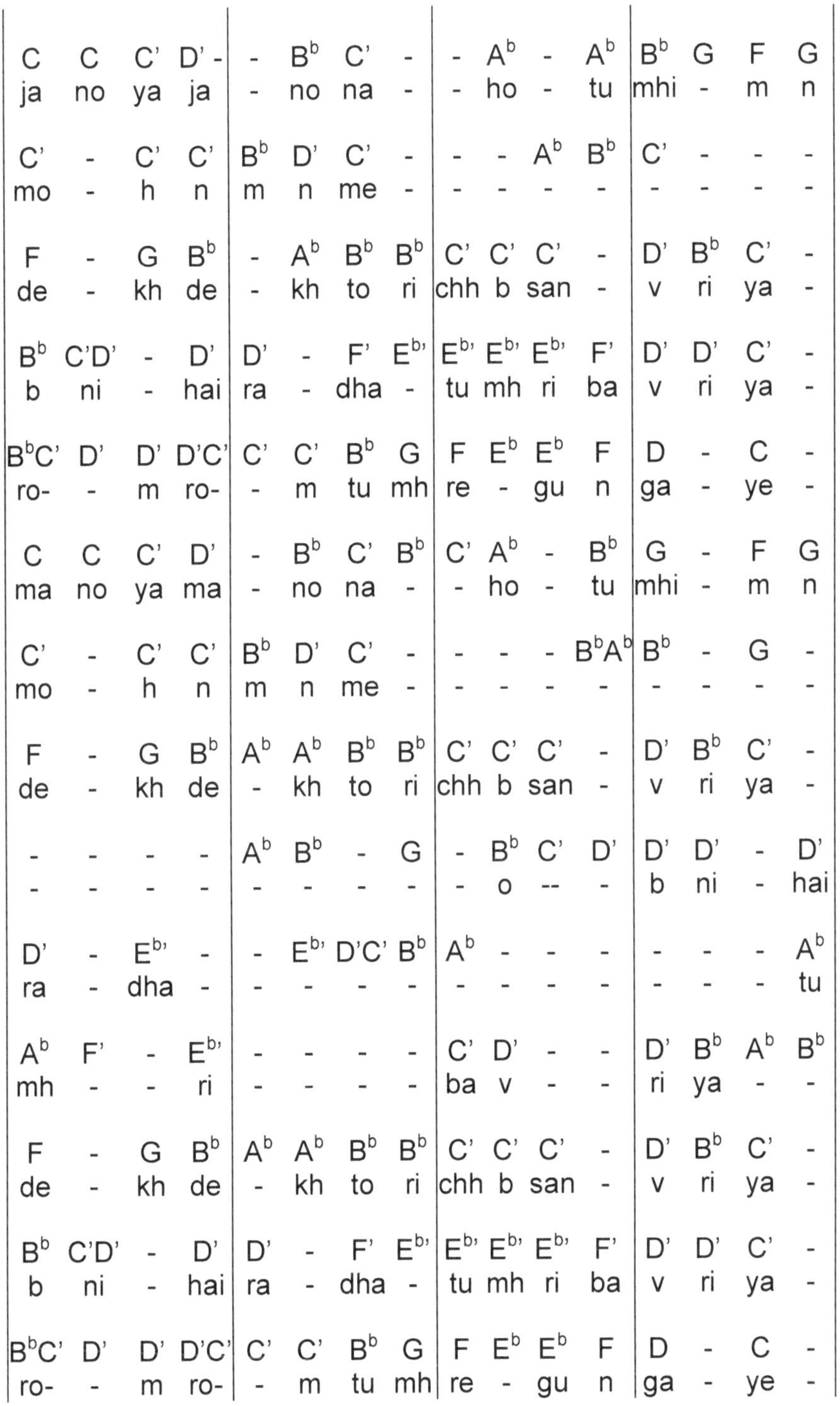

C	C	C'	D' -	-	B♭	C'	-	-	A♭	-	A♭	B♭	G	F	G
ja	no	ya	ja	-	no	na	-	-	ho	-	tu	mhi	-	m	n
C'	-	C'	C'	B♭	D'	C'	-	-	-	A♭	B♭	C'	-	-	-
mo	-	h	n	m	n	me	-	-	-	-	-	-	-	-	-
F	-	G	B♭	-	A♭	B♭	B♭	C'	C'	C'	-	D'	B♭	C'	-
de	-	kh	de	-	kh	to	ri	chh	b	san	-	v	ri	ya	-
B♭	C'D'	-	D'	D'	-	F'	E♭'	E♭'	E♭'	E♭'	F'	D'	D'	C'	-
b	ni	-	hai	ra	-	dha	-	tu	mh	ri	ba	v	ri	ya	-
B♭C'	D'	D'	D'C'	C'	C'	B♭	G	F	E♭	E♭	F	D	-	C	-
ro-	-	m	ro-	-	m	tu	mh	re	-	gu	n	ga	-	ye	-
C	C	C'	D'	-	B♭	C'	B♭	C'	A♭	-	B♭	G	-	F	G
ma	no	ya	ma	-	no	na	-	-	ho	-	tu	mhi	-	m	n
C'	-	C'	C'	B♭	D'	C'	-	-	-	-	B♭A♭	B♭	-	G	-
mo	-	h	n	m	n	me	-	-	-	-	-	-	-	-	-
F	-	G	B♭	A♭	A♭	B♭	B♭	C'	C'	C'	-	D'	B♭	C'	-
de	-	kh	de	-	kh	to	ri	chh	b	san	-	v	ri	ya	-
-	-	-	-	A♭	B♭	-	G	-	B♭	C'	D'	D'	D'	-	D'
-	-	-	-	-	-	-	-	-	o	--	-	b	ni	-	hai
D'	-	E♭'	-	-	E♭'	D'C'	B♭	A♭	-	-	-	-	-	-	A♭
ra	-	dha	-	-	-	-	-	-	-	-	-	-	-	-	tu
A♭	F'	-	E♭'	-	-	-	-	C'	D'	-	-	D'	B♭	A♭	B♭
mh	-	-	ri	-	-	-	-	ba	v	-	-	ri	ya	-	-
F	-	G	B♭	A♭	A♭	B♭	B♭	C'	C'	C'	-	D'	B♭	C'	-
de	-	kh	de	-	kh	to	ri	chh	b	san	-	v	ri	ya	-
B♭	C'D'	-	D'	D'	-	F'	E♭'	E♭'	E♭'	E♭'	F'	D'	D'	C'	-
b	ni	-	hai	ra	-	dha	-	tu	mh	ri	ba	v	ri	ya	-
B♭C'	D'	D'	D'C'	C'	C'	B♭	G	F	E♭	E♭	F	D	-	C	-
ro-	-	m	ro-	-	m	tu	mh	re	-	gu	n	ga	-	ye	-

C	C	C'	D'	-	B^b	C'	B^b	C'	A^b	-	A^b	B^b	G	F	G
ma	no	ya	ma	-	no	na	-	-	ho	-	tu	mhi	-	m	n
C'	-	C'	C'	B^b	D'	C'	-	D'	-	C'	B^b	A^b	B^b	G	-
mo	-	h	n	m	n	me	-	-	-	-	-	-	-	-	-

D'------- ^{C}B^b--- A^b B^{b}C'D'---- ^{C}B^b--- A^b ---
aa------------------------------------

D'--- D'F'--- D'--- ^{C}B^b--- A^b --- D'--- ^{C}B^b--- A^b --- B^b D'---
aa---

F'---- D'---- F'D'C'B^{b}A^b---- B^b F'--- D'C'B^b D' C' C'D' D'F' F'G'---
aa---

32.   MERA PYAR BHI TU HAI

Film: Sathi (1968)   Music: Naushad Ali
Lyrics: Majrooh Sultanpuri   Singer: Mukesh, Suman K.
Taal: Kaharwa   Chord: DFA   S=C#
Transpose +1 and play from C Scale

mera pyar bhi tu hai ye bahar bhi tu hai
tu hi nazro me jaan e tamanna
tu hi nazaro me nazaro me

tu hi to mera neel gagan hai
pyar se raoshan aankh uthae
aur ghata ke rup me tu hai
kandhe pe mere sar ko jhukaae
mujh pe late bhikhrae
mera pyar bhi tu hai…

manzil mere dil ki vahi hai
saya jaha dildar hai tera
parbat parbat teri bahein
gulshan gulshan pyar hai tera
mahke hai aanchal mera
mera pyar bhi tu hai…

jaagi nazar ka khvaab hai jaese
dekh milan ka din ye suhana
aankh to tere jalvo me gum hai
dekhu tujhe ya dekhu zamana
bekhud hai divana
mera pyar bhi tu hai….

MERA PYAR BHI TU HAI

dha	ge	n	ti	n	ke	dhi	n	dha	ge	n	ti	n	ke	dhi	n
1	2	3	4	5	6	7	8	1	2	3	4	5	6	7	8
prelude:															
B	-	-	-	-	-	-	-	E'	D'	C'	B	Bb	-	-	-
A	B	D'	E'	F'	-	-	-	-	-	-	-	-	E'	D'	B
D'	-	-	-	-	-									F	F
														me	ra
E	-	-	D	D	D	F	F	E	-	-	D	D	D	-	BB
pya	-	-r	bhi	tu	hai	ye	b	ha	-	-r	bhi	tu	hai	-	tuhi
AA	-B	-	A	G	-E	-	D	EG	F	E	-	-	D	D	D
nz	-ro	-	me	ja	-ne	-	t	mn-	-	na	-	-	tu	hi	n
EG	F#	E	D	D	-	-	D	EG	F#	E	D	D	-	-	-
za-	-	ro	-	me	-	-	n	za-	-	ro	-	me	-	-	-
E	-	-	A	F#	-	-	-	F	-	-	E	D	-	-	-
hu	-	-	-	-	-	-	-	-	-	-	-	-	-	-	-
interlude: A E' E' – E' E' E' B A , F B – B B F A – F D --															
													A	A	A
													tu	-hi	-to
B	-	B	-	-	A	-A	-A	C'	B	B	-	-	A	-B	B
me	-	ra	-	-	ni	-l	-g	gn	-	hai	-	-	pya	-r	-se
D'	C'	C'	-	-	D'	-C'	-B	A	-	A	-	-	A	-B	D'B
rau	-	shn	-	-	aan	-kh	-u	tha	-	ye	-	-	au	-r	-gh
D'	-	D'	-	-	D'	-B	-A	Bb	-	A	-	B	-B	-	B
ta	-	ke	-	-	ru	-p	-me	tu	-	hai	-	kan	-dhe	-	pe
B	-	-C'	B	AB	-A	C'	B	G	F#	G	-	-	EE	-G	-A
me	-	-re	-	sr	-ko	-	jhu	ka	-	ye	-	-	mukh	-pe	-l
C'	B	A	G	GF	-	E	F	E	D						
ten	-	bi	kh	ra-	-	ye	-	-	-						

interlude: DF BA BA DF -2
        EG BA BA EG -2
        B—ABC'E'D'C'B
        C' B--- A B C'
        A B C' B A B C' –

  AAA BB   A A AC'B B AB BD'C' C'-D'C' B AA
mnzil mere dil ki vhin- hai, saya jha- dildar hai tera

ABD'B D'D'D'D' D'BA B♭A B-BB BC'B   ABAC' B GF#G
prbt   prbt   te-ri bahe, gulshn gulshn pya--r hai te-ra

EEG   A C'BAG GFEFED   FF E--
mhke hai aan-chl me-ra-----, mera pyar...

33.   MERE MAHBOOB NA JA

Film: Noor Mahal (1965)   Music: Jaani Babu Kawwal
Lyrics: Saba Afgani   Singer: Suman K.
Taal: Daadra   Actor: Chitra,   Chord: DF#A   S=C
Jagdip

aa….aa…..
mere mehboob na ja, na ja na ja
mere mehboob na ja, aaj ki rat na ja
hone wali hai sahar,
thodi der aur thahar
mere mehboob na jaa

dekh kitana hasin mausam hai
har taraf ik ajib aalam hai
zarre is tarah aaj nikhare hai
jaise taare zami pe bikhare hai
jaise taare zami pe bikhare hai
mere mehboob…

maine kaate hai intazaar ke din
tab kahin aaye hain bahaar ke din
yun naa jaa dil ki shamaa gul kar ke
abhi dekha nahi hai ji bhar ke

abhi dekha nahi hai ji bhar ke
mere mehboob.....

jab se zulfon ki chhaon paayi hai
beqaraari ko nind aayi hai
is qayamat ko yun hi sone de
raat dhalne de subaha hone de
raat dhalne de subaha hone de
mere mehboob....

is tarah fer kar nazar mujh se
dur jaayega tu agar mujh se
chandani se bhi aag barsegi
shammaa bhi roshani ko tarsegi
shammaa bhi roshani ko tarsegi
mere mehboob...

dhadkanon me yahi taraane hain
tere rukne ke sau bahaane hain
mere dil ki zara sadaa sun le
pyaasi nazaron ki iltija sun le
pyaasi nazaron ki iltija sun le
mere mehboob...

MERE MAHBOOB NA JA

dhi	na	ti	na	dhi	na	dhi	na	ti	na	dhi	na
1	2	3	4	5	6	1	2	3	4	5	6

prelude:
EF# DE- EF# DE- EF# DE-
F' E' D' C' B A F# E D

AD' C'D' C'D' C'D' F# E' D' C' A, F# E' D' C' A
aa- aa- aa- aa-

AC' BC' BC' BC' F# E' F#', F# E' F#', F# E' F#',
aa- aa- aa- aa-

F' E' D' C' B A F#E D

A C'   D' F#' E' F#' --- E' D' C' C' C'D'
me   re m h bu ----------b na ja-

B C'D'BC'D'B ---------A   B A F# E F# D
na----------------------ja   na---------ja

F#'E' F#'E' F#'E' F#'E' F#'E' F#'E' F#'E' F#'E'
F#EF# GF#A--   F#ED

F#	-	D	D	E	-D	AF#	A	F#	F#	G	G
								me	re	m	h
F#	-	D	D	E	-D	AF#	A	F#	-	G	-
bu	-	b	n	ja	-	-	-	aa	-j	ki	-
F#	-	D	D	E	-	F#	-	F#	A	B	D'
ra	-	t	n	ja	-	-	-	ho	ne	va	-
C'	-	A	A	B	-	F#	-	F#	A	B	D'
li	-	hai	s	hr	-	-	-	tho	di	de	-r
C'	-	A	A	B	-	F#	-	F#	F#	G	G
au	-	r	th	hr	-	-	-	me	re	m	h
F#	-	D	D	E	-	-	-				
bu	-	b	n	ja	-	-	-				

interlude: G'F'E'D' D'C'BA
F#'E'F#'E'F#'---A'F#'A'F#'A'---
F#' –G'F'G'A' B'A'G'F#'E'D'
B' A' E'F#'E'F#' –E'F#'E'F#'- E'F#'E'F#'-

F#	-	F#	F#	-	F#	F#	E	D	D	E	E
								de	kh	ki	t
F#	-	F#	F#	-	F#	F#	E	E	G	F#	-
na	-	h	sii	-	n	mau	-	s	m	hai	-
E	D	D	D	E	E	F#	F#	F#	F#	-	F#
-	-	hr	t	r	f	i	k	a	ji	-	b

F#	E	E	G	F#	-	C'D'	E'F#'	F#'	F#'	F#'	F#'
aa	-	l	m	hai	-	-	-	z	rre	i	s
E'	E'	E'	D'	-	C'	C'	D'	D'	-	D'	-
t	r	h	aa	-	j	ni	kh	re	-	hain	-
C'	F#'	F#'	F#'	F#'	-	E'	-	E'	D'	-	C'
-	-	jai	se	ta	-	re	-	z	mi	-	pe
C'	D'	D'	-	D'	-	-	-	C'	C'	C'	B
bi	kh	re	-	hain	-	-	-	jai	se	ta	-
C'	-	B	C'	-	B	B	A	A	-	A	-
re	-	z	mi	-	pe	bi	kh	re	-	hain	-
F#	-	F#	F#	G	G	F#	-	D	D	E	-
-	-	me	re	m	h	bu	-	b	n	ja	-
D	-	F#	-	G	-	F#	-	D	D	E	-
-	-	aa	-j	ki	-	ra	-	t	n	ja	-
F#	-										
aa	-										

interlude:
G'F'E'D' D'C'BA
F#'E'F#'E'F#'---A'F#'A'F#'A'---
F#' –G'F'G'A' B'A'G'F#'E'D'
B' A' E'F#'E'F#' – E'F#'E'F#'- E'F#'E'F#'-

```
        DD        EF#   F#    F#F#F#EE   G    F#- ED
 2) mainne  kate  hain  intzar         ke   din

 D   DE   F#F#   F#-F#F#EE   G   F#-     C'D'E'F#'
 tb  khin aaye   hain bha-r  ke  din         music

 F#'  F#'  F#'  E'  E'  D'-C'  C'D'  D'  D' – F#'
 yu   na   ja   dil ki  shmma  gul   kr  ke

 F#'F#'   F#'E'    E'D' C'  C'D'   D'   D'
 abhi     dekha    nhin hai ji     bhr  ke
```

C'C' C'BC'   BC' B BA A A –F#
abhi de-kha   nhin hai ji- bhr ke,

F#F#   GGF#-D D E D
mere mhbu-b n ja –

    D D EF# F# F#F#   F#EEG F# - ED
3) jb se zulfo ki   chhanv pa-ii-   hai

DD EF# F# F#-F# F#EEG F#- E D
beqrari ko nin-d aa-ii-   hai

F#' F#'F#'E'   E' D'-C' D'D' D' –C' F#'
is qyamt   ko yu   hi   sone de

F#'F#' F#' E' E' D' C' D'D'   D'
rat   dhlne de subh hone de

C'C' C'BC'   B C'B   BA   A –F#
rat   dhlne   de subh hone de,

F#F#   GGF#-D D E F#
mere mhbu-b n ja –

    D   DE F#-F#   F#   F#F#E EG F# - ED
4) is   trh fe-r   kr   nzr   mujh se

DD EF#AF#F#   F#- F#F#E EG   F#- C'D'E'F#'
dur ja--ega   tu agr   mujh se

F#'F#'F#'   E' E' D'-C' C'D'D'D' –
chandni   se bhi aag   brsegi

F#'F#'   F#' E'E'D' C' C'D'D'D'
shmma   bhi roshni   ko trsegi

C'C'   C'B C'BC' B BAAA –F#
shmma   bhi- roshni ko trsegi

F#F#   GGF#-D D E –D
mere   mhbu-b n ja –

   DDE   F#   F#F# F#F#EEG F# - ED
5) dhdkno me   yhi   tra-ne-   hain

DD EAGF# F#   F#- F#F#EEG F#- BC'D'E'F#'-
tere rukne- ke   sau baha-ne-   hain

F#'F#'   F#'   E' D'D' C'C'D'   D'   D' – F#'
mere   dil   ki zra sda   sun le

F#'F#'   F#'F#'E' E' D'C'C'D'   D'D'   D'
pyasii nzro   ki   iltja-   sun   le

C'C'   C'BC' B C'BBA A A –F#D
pyasii nzro   ki iltja-   sun le

F#F#   GGF#-D D E D
mere   mhbu-b n ja –

34. MERE SANG GA GUNGUNA

Film: Jaanvar (1965) Music: Jaikishan
Lyrics: Hasrat Jaipuri Singer: Suman K.
Taal: Teen Taal Chord: FAC' S=D
Transpose +2 and play from C Scale

aa…aa…aa..aa…aa…
mere sang ga gunguna koi giit suhana -2
mere sang ga gunguna

mai bhi tumhari, dil bhi tumahara, mai bhi tumhari
mai bhi tumhari, dil bhi tumahara
sang sath jug jug se hamara -2
tere hi kadmo me sar mera
mere sang ga gunguna koi giit suhana -2
mere sang ga gunguna

shisha e dil me teri suratiya, shisha e dil me
shishaye dil me teri suratiya
dekhun raat din teri muratiya -2
tu mere pyar ka devta
mere sang ga gunguna koi giit suhana -2
mere sang ga gunguna

pahali nazar me apna banaya, pahali nazar me
pahali nazar me apna banaya
tumne pyar se jeena sikhaaya
chhote munh ab tera shukariya
mere sang ga gunguna koi giit suhana -2
mere sang ga gunguna

MERE SANG GA GUNGUNA

dha	dhin	dhin	dha	dha	dhin	dhin	dha	dha	tin	tin	ta	ta	dhin	dhin	dha
1	2	3	4	5	6	7	8	9	10	11	12	13	14	15	16

```
.F .A---------- .Bb .A .AC----
aa----------------- ---------

C      C E------- E F -----
aa------------------------

F F Bb A C' -----   C'---- Bb A ---- FE ----
aa---------------- aa--------------------

E --- D --- C--- .A C---
aa--------------------
```

1	2	3	4	5	6	7	8	9	10	11	12	13	14	15	16
								.A	-	C	-	-	F	-	A
								me	-	re	-	-	sn	-	g
C'	-	-	-	-	C'	-	Bb	A	-	-	-	-	-	A	A
ga	-	-	-	-	gun	-	gu	na	-	-	-	-	-	ko	ii
A	Bb	A	F	F	-	D	C								
gi	-	t	su	ha	-	na	-								
A	G	A	F	G	F	A	-	C'	B	C'	A	Bb	G	A	-
main	-	bhi	tu	mha	-	ri	-	dil	-	bhi	tu	mha	-	ra	-
-	AG	A	G	A	F	A	-	-	-	-	-	-	-	-	-
-	main-	bhi	tu	mha	-	ri	-	-	-	-	-	-	-	-	-
A	G	A	F	G	F	A	-	C'	B	C'	A	Bb	G	A	-
main	-	bhi	tu	mha	-	ri	-	dil	-	bhi	tu	mha	-	ra	-
AEb'	-	D'	C'	-	C'	A	G	C'	B	C'	A	Bb	G	A	-
sn-	-	g	sa	-	th	ju	g	ju	g	se	h	ma	-	ra	-
-	C	.A	C	F	-	-	F	D	F	A	-	-	A	F	A
-	te	-	re	hi	-	-	k	d	mo	me	-	-	s	r	me
F'	-	-	-	-	-	D'	C'	Eb'	-	-	-	D'	-	C'	-
ra	-	-	-	-	-	-	-	-	-	-	-	-	-	-	-

A	G	A	F	G	F	A	-	C'	B	C'	A	B^{b}	G	A	-
shi	-	sha	e	dil	-	me	-	te	-	ri	su	r	ti	ya	-
-	AG	A	F	G	F	A	-	-	-	-	-	-	-	-	-
-	shi-	sha	e	dil	-	me	-	-	-	-	-	-	-	-	-
AE^{b}'	-	D'	C'	-	C'	A	G	C'	B	C'	A	B^{b}	G	A	-
de-	-	khu	ra	-	t	di	n	te	-	ri	mu	r	ti	ya	-
-	C	.A	C	F	-	-	F	D	F	A	-	-	A	F	A
-	tu	-	me	re	-	-	pya	-	r	ka	-	-	de	-	v
F'	-	-	-	-	-	D'	C'	E^{b}'	-	-	-	D'	-	C'	-
ta	-	-	-	-	-	-	-	-	-	-	-	-	-	-	-
A	G	A	F	G	F	A	-	C'	B	C'	A	B^{b}	G	A	-
p	h	li	n	z	r	me	-	a	p	na	b	na	-	ya	-
-	AG	A	F	G	F	A	-	-	-	-	-	-	-	-	-
-	ph	li	n	z	r	me	-	-	-	-	-	-	-	-	-
AE^{b}'	-	D'	C'	-	C'	A	G	C'	B	C'	A	B^{b}	G	A	-
tum	-	ne	pya	-	r	se	-	ji	-	na	si	kha	-	ya	-
-	C	.A	C	F	-	-	F	D	F	A	-	-	A	F	A
-	chho	-	te	muh	-	-	a	b	te	ra	-	-	shu	k	ri
F'	-	-	-	-	-	D'	C'	E^{b}'	-	-	-	D'	-	C'	-
ya	-	-	-	-	-	-	-	-	-	-	-	-	-	-	-

35. NA TUM HAME JAANO

Film: Baat Ek Raat Ki (1962) Music: Hemant Kumar
Lyrics: Majrooh Sultanpuri Singer: Hemant Kumar, Suman K.
Taal: Kaharwa
Chord: DFB^b DFA S=C

na tum hamen jaano, na ham tumhen jaane
magar lagata, hai kuchh aisa, mera hamadam, mil gaya

ye mausam ye raat chup hai
wo honthon ki baat chup hai
khaamoshi sunaane lagi hai daastaan
nazar ban gayi hai dil ki zabaan

mohabbat ke mod pe ham
mile sabako chhodke ham
dhadkate dilon ka leke ye kaarawaan
chale aaj donon jaane kahaan

NA TUM HAME JAANO

dha	ge	n	ti	n	ke	dhi	n	dha	ge	n	ti	n	ke	dhi	n
1	2	3	4	5	6	7	8	1	2	3	4	5	6	7	8
prelude: F'- $E^{b'}$- C'- A- B^b- FGF- AC'B^b-															
											F	A	C'	B^b	A
											n	tu	m	h	me
B^b	A	G	A	B^b	-	-	-	-	-	-	A	B^b	C'	B^b	A
ja	-	-	-	no	-	-	-	-	-	-	n	h	m	tu	mhe
B^b	A	G	F	A	-	-	-	-	-	-	A	A	A	A	B^b
ja	-	-	-	ne	-	-	-	-	-	-	m	g	r	l	g
A	G	-	A	A	A	A	B^b	A	F	-	F	A	-	A	-
ta	-	-	hai	ku	chh	ae	-	sa	-	-	me	ra	-	hm	-
C'	-	-	-	-	$E^{b'}$	-	D'	D'	-	-	-	-	-	-	-
dm	-	-	-	-	mi	l	g	ya	-	-	-	-	-	-	-
interlude:															
D' C' D' C' B^bA G $F^{\#}$- A- A G $F^{\#}$ G- A- B^b-															
G B^b D' C' B^b G $F^{\#}$- A C' F' $E^{b'}$ D' C' B^b-															
										B^b	C'	-	D'	-	C'
										ye	mau	-	sm	-	ye
D'	-	-	C'	D'	$E^{b'}$	B^b	-	-	-	B^b	C'	-	D'	-	C'
ra	-	-	t	chu	p	hai	-	-	-	vo	ho	-	tho	-	ki
D'	-	-	C'	D'	$E^{b'}$	B^b	-	-	-	B^b	C'	$E^{b'}$	$E^{b'}$	-	D'
ba	-	-	t	chu	p	hai	-	-	-	kha	mo	-	shi	-	su
C'	D'	B	-	-	B	B	-	-	-	D'	-	-	C'	-	C'
na	-	ne	-	-	l	gi	-	-	-	hai	-	-	da	-	s
C'	-	-	-	-	D'	B^b	-	-	-	A	A	-	A	-	A
ta	-	-	-	-	-	-	-	-	-	n	zr	-	bn	-	g
B^b	A	G	B^b	-	B^b	-	-	-	-	C'	B^b	-	C'	B^b	B^b
yi	-	-	-	-	hai	-	-	-	-	dil	-	-	ki	-	z
B^b	-	-	-	A^{Bb}	-	G^{A}	-	F	-	-	F	A	C'	B^b	A
ba	-	-	-	-	-	-	-	-	-	-	n	tu	m	h	me

B♭	A	G	A	B♭	-	-	-	-	-	-	A	B♭	C'	B♭	A
ja	-	-	-	no	-	-	-	-	-	-	n	h	m	tu	mhe
B♭	A	G	F	A	-	-	-	-	-	-	A	A	A	A	B♭
ja	-	-	-	ne	-	-	-	-	-	-	m	g	r	l	g
A	G	-	A	A	A	A	B♭	A	F	-	F	A	-	A	-
ta	-	-	hai	ku	chh	ae	-	sa	-	-	me	ra	-	hm	-
C'	-	-	-	-	E♭'	-	D'	D'	-	-	-	-	-	-	-
dm	-	-	-	-	mi	l	g	ya	-	-	-	-	-	-	-

interlude:
D' C' D' C' B♭A G F#-   A- A G F# G- A- B♭-
G B♭ D' C' B♭ G F#-   A C' F' E♭' D' C' B♭-

										B♭	C'	-	D'	-	C'
										mo	ho	-	b	t	ke
D'	-	-	C'	D'	-	B♭	-	-	-	B♭	C'	-	D'	-	C'
mo	-	-	d	pe	-	hm	-	-	-	mi	le	-	s	b	ko
D'	-	-	C'	D'	-	B♭	-	-	-	B♭	C'	E♭'	E♭'	-	D'
chho	-	-	d	ke	-	hm	-	-	-	dh	d	k	te	-	di
C'	D'	B	-	-	B	-	B	-	-	D'	-	-	C'	-	C'
lo	-	ka	-	-	le	-	ke	-	-	ye	-	-	ka	-	r
C'	-	-	-	-	D'	B♭	-	-	-	A	A	-	A	-	A
va	-	-	-	-	-	-	-	-	-	ch	le	-	aa	-	j
B♭	A	G	B♭	-	B♭	-	-	-	-	C'	B♭	-	C'	-	B♭
do	-	-	-	-	no	-	-	-	-	ja	-	-	ne	-	k
B♭	-	-	-	A B♭	-	G A	-	F	-	-	F	A	C'	B♭	A
ha	-	-	-	-	-	-	-	-	-	-	n	tum	-	h	me
B♭	A	G	A	B♭	-	-	-	-	-	-					
ja	-	-	-	no	-	-	-	-	-	-					

36. NA JAANE KAISE PAL ME BADAL

Film: Badalte Rishte (1978)   Music: Laxmikant Pyarelal
Lyrics: Anjaan   Singer: Suman K. Kishore, Md. Rafi
Taal: Daadra   Chord: FA^{b}C' E^{b}GB^b S=C#
Transpose +1 and play from C
Scale

Suman:
na jaane kaise pal me badal jaate hain -2
ye duniya ke badalte rishte
kya jaane kaise rangon me dhal jaate hain
ye duniya ke badalte rishte
na jaane kaise pal me badal jaate hain

Kishore:
judkar kahin dil jod dein toote to dil tod jaate hain ye -2
ye phool bankar hain khilte kahin
kahin dil me kaante chubhaate hain ye
jaane kahan kis mod pe de ke daga dil ko chhal jaate hain
ye duniya ke badalte rishte
na jaane kaise pal me badal jaate hain
ye duniya ke badalte rishte

Suman:
(apnon se yoon bichde hain jo
unhen kya bichhadne ka kuch gham nahin) -2
magar haar kar kyun dukhon se koi
jahar ghol de zindagi me kahin
sab khel hai taqdeer ka
taqdeer se hi badal jaate hain
ye duniya ke badalte rishte
na jaane kaise pal me badal jaate hain
ye duniya ke badalte rishte

Md. Rafi

rishte kabhi toote kahan jo toot jaaye wo rishte nahin -2

chhupi hai udaasi ke peeche hansi

dabi dard me bhi khushi hai kahin

sach to hai ye bas pyar se jeewan hamare badal jaate hain

ye duniya ke badalte rishte

na jaane kaise pal me badal jaate hain

ye duniya ke badalte rishte

NA JAANE KAISE PAL ME BADAL

dha 1	dhi 2	na 3	dha 4	tun 5	na 6	dha 1	dhi 2	na 3	dha 4	tun 5	na 6
F	-	-	G	A^b	C'	B^b	-	-	-	-	-
na	-	-	ja	ne	kai	se	-	-	-	-	-
GF	E^b	$-E^b$	F	G	B^b	A^b	-	-	-	-	-
pl	me	-b	dl	ja	te	hain	-	-	-	-	-
$E^{b'}$	-	-	$D^{b'}$	C'	B^b	B^b	G	-G	G	A^b	-
ye	-	-	duni	ya	-	ke	-	-b	dl	te	-
F	F	-	-	-	-	F	-	-	G	A^b	C'
rish	te	-	-	-	-	kya	-	-	ja	ne	kai
B^b	-	-	-	-	-	GF	E^b	E^b	F	G	B^b
se	-	-	-	-	-	rn-	go	me	dhl	ja	te
A^b	-	-	-	-	-	$E^{b'}$	-	-	$D^{b'}$	C'	B^b
hain	-	-	-	-	-	ye	-	-	duni	ya	-
B^b	G	-G	G	A^b	-	F	F	-	-	-	-
ke	-	-b	dl	te	-	rish	te	-	-	-	-
$E^{b'}$	$E^{b'}$	-D'	$E^{b'}$	-	-	$C'D^{b'}$	$E^{b'}$	$-D^{b'}$	C'	-	-
jud	kr	-k	hin	-	-	dil	jo	-d	de	-	-

B^b	B^b	$-B^b$	C'	C'	$-C'$	$C'D^{b'}$	$E^{b'}$	$-D^{b'}$	C'	-	-
tu	te	-to	dil	to	-d	ja-	te	-hain	ye	-	-
$E^{b'}$	$E^{b'}$	$-D'$	$E^{b'}$	$E^{b'}$	$-C'$	C'	$D^{b'}$	$-C'$	B^b	-	$-A^b$
ye	fu	-l	bn	kr	-hain	khil	te	-k	hin	-	-k
B^b	C'	$-B^b$	A^b	B^b	$-G$	G	A^b	$-G$	F	-	-
hin	dil	-ye	kan	te	-chu	bha	te	-hain	ye	-	-
E^b	F	$-E^b$	F	-	-	FF	G	$-F$	G	-	-
ja	ne	-k	ha	-	-	kis	mo	-d	pe	-	-
G	G	$-A^b$	B^b	B^b	B^b	$C'D^{b'}$	$E^{b'}$	$-D^{b'}$	C'	-	-
de	ke	-d	ga	dil	ko	chhl	ja	-te	hain	-	-
$E^{b'}$	-	-	$D^{b'}D^{b'}$	C'	-	B^b	-	$-G$	G	A^b	-
ye	-	-	duni	ya	-	ke	-	-b	dl	te	-
F	F	-	-	-	-	F	-	-	G	A^b	C'
rish	te	-	-	-	-	na	-	-	ja	ne	kai
B^b	-	-	-	-	-						
se	-	-	-	-	-						
$E^{b'}E^{b'}$	$E^{b'}$	$-D'$	$E^{b'}$	-	-	$C'D^{b'}$	$E^{b'}$	$-D^{b'}$	C'	-	$-A^b$
ap	no	-se	yu	-	-	bichh	de	-hain	jo	-	-u
B^b	B^b	$-B^b$	B^bC'	C'	$-C'$	$C'D^{b'}$	$E^{b'}$	$-D^{b'}$	C'	-	$-E^{b'}$
nhe	kya	-bi	chhd	ne	-ka	kuchh	gm	-n	hin	-	-m
$E^{b'}E^{b'}$	$E^{b'}$	$-D'$	$E^{b'}$	$E^{b'}$	$-C'$	C'	$D^{b'}$	$-C'$	B^b	-	$-A^b$
gr	ha	-r	kr	kyu	-du	khon	se	-ko	ii	-	-z
B^b	C'	$-B^b$	A^b	B^b	G	G	A^b	$-G$	F	-	-
hr	gho	-l	de	zin	-d	gi	me	-k	hin	-	-
E^bE^b	F	$-E^b$	F	-	-	FF	G	$-F$	G	-	-
sb	khe	-l	hai	-	-	tq	di	-r	ka	-	-
GG	G	$-A^b$	B^b	B^b	$-B^b$	$C'D^{b'}$	$E^{b'}$	$-D^{b'}$	C'	-	-
tq	di	-r	se	bhi	-b	dl	ja	-te	hain	-	-

$E^{b'}$	-	-	$D^{b'}D^{b'}$	C'	-	B^b	-	-G	G	A^b	-
ye	-	-	duni	ya	-	ke	-	-b	dl	te	-
F	F	-	-	-	-	F	-	-	G	A^b	C'
rish	te	-	-	-	-	na	-	-	ja	ne	kai
B^b	-	-	-	-	-						
se	-	-	-	-	-						
$E^{b'}$	$E^{b'}$	-D'	$E^{b'}$	-	-	$C'D^{b'}$	$E^{b'}$	$-D^{b'}$	C'	-	-
rish	te	-k	bhi	-	-	tu	te	-k	ha	-	-
B^b	B^b	$-B^b$	C'	C'	$-C'$	$C'D^{b'}$	$E^{b'}$	$-D^{b'}$	C'	-	$-E^{b'}$
jo	tu	-t	ja	ye	-vo	rish	te	-n	hin	-	chhu
$E^{b'}$	$E^{b'}$	-D'	$E^{b'}$	$E^{b'}$	$-C'$	C'	$D^{b'}$	$-C'$	B^b	-	$-A^b$
pi	hai	-u	da	sii	-ke	pi	chhe	-hn	sii	-	-d
B^b	C'	$-B^b$	A^b	B^b	G	G	A^b	-G	F	-	-
bi	d	-rd	me	bhi	-khu	shi	hai	-k	hin	-	-
E^b	F	$-E^b$	F	-	-	FF	G	-F	G	-	-
sch	to	hai	ye	-	-	bs	pya	-r	se	-	-
G	G	$-A^b$	B^b	C'	$-C'$	$C'D^{b'}$	$E^{b'}$	$-D^{b'}$	C'	-	-
ji	vn	-h	ma	re	-b	dl	ja	-te	hain	-	-
$E^{b'}$	-	-	$D^{b'}D^{b'}$	C'	-	B^b	-	-G	G	A^b	-
ye	-	-	duni	ya	-	ke	-	-b	dl	te	-
F	F	-	-	-	-	F	-	-	G	A^b	C'
rish	te	-	-	-	-	na	-	-	ja	ne	kai
B^b	-	-	-	-	-						
se	-	-	-	-	-						

37. NA NA KARTE PYAR TUMHIN SE

Film: Jab Jab Phool Khile (1965)   Music: Kalyanji Anandji
Lyrics: Anand Bakshi   Singer: Suman K., Md. Rafi
Taal: Kaharwa dugun   Chord: DFA FAC'   S=D
Transpose +2 and play from C Scale

na na karate,
na na karate pyaar tumhin se kar baithe -2
karna tha inkaar magar iqaraar tumhin se kar baithe
na na karate pyaar tumhin se kar baithe -2

dekho ji bhari hain hazaaro tumne aahen
tab kahin hum ne, achaa,
tab kahin hum ne milaai hai nigahen
tum se bhi hasin hai tumhara ye bahana
tumne hi to humko sikhayaa dil lagaana
sikha hai dildaar tumhi se pyaar tumhi se kar bethe
na na karate aaha na na karate pyaar tumhin se kar baithe
karna tha inkaar magar iqaraar tumhin se kar baithe
na na karate pyaar tumhin se kar baithe

ham ko hai pataa jo tumhaari daastaan thi
honthon pe to na thi
honthon pe to na thi jaa juthe
honthon pe to na thi magar dil mein haan thi
koi dil na degaa anaadi anajaan ko
hamane de diyaa hai to maano ehasaan ko
ham bhuule ik baar ki aankhen chaar tumhin se kar baithe
na na karate
na na karate pyaar tumhin se kar baithe
karna tha inkaar magar iqaraar tumhin se kar baithe
na na karate pyaar tumhin se kar baithe
chhodo rahane bhi do ye jhuuthe afasaane
aisa kya hai tum mein chal jhuuthi
aisa kya hai tum mein ki ham hon deewane
phir bhi tumane khwabo mein aanaa nahin chhoda

tir nazaron ke chalana nahin chhoda
ye shiqavaa sarkaar hazaaron baar tumhin se kar baithe
na na karate haan
na na karate pyaar tumhin se kar baithe
karna tha inkaar magar iqaraar tumhin se kar baithe
na na karate pyaar tumhin se kar baithe -2

NA NA KARTE PYAR TUMHIN SE

dhage nti nke dhin	dhage nti nke dhin	dhage nti nke dhin	dhage nti nke dhin
12 34 56 78	12 34 56 78	12 34 56 78	12 34 56 78
prelude: F- AGFEDE F- FF- F-			
F F AG G FAGAFGF-			
na na krte -----------			
			F F AG G
			na na kr te
F -E D E	A G F -	FA GA FG F-	F F AG G
pya r,tumhin se	kr bai the -	- - - -	na na kr te
F -E D E	A G F -	AB^b AGAB^{b}C'-	C' C' C' C'
pya r,tumhin se	kr bai the -	- - - -	kr na tha in
C' C' C' C'	C' -G G G	C' B^b A -	F F AG G
ka r,m gr ik	ra r,tumhin se	kr bai the -	na na kr te
F -E D E	A G F -		
pya r,tumhin se	kr bai the -		
interlude:			
F F F G A A A - A GAB^{b}A GFDC C- C- C-			
D- DD-E F F F FGAG FEDE F- F- F-			
F F F G A A A - A GAB^{b}A GFDC C- C- C-			
D- DD-E F F F A-G FEDC D- E- F-			
			B^b B^b D' D'
			de kho ji bh

D'	-	D'	D'	D'	E^b	D'	C'	C'	-	C'	-	B^b	B^b	D'	-
ri	-	hain	h	za	ro	tum	ne	aa	-	he	-	tb	k	hin	-

D'	-	D'	D'	D'	E^b	D'	C'	C'	-	C'	-	B^b	B^b	B^b	B^b
hm	-	ne	mi	la	ii	hain	ni	ga	-	hen	-	tum	se	bhi	hn

A	-	A	A	B^b	B^b	B^b	B^b	A	-	A	-	B^b	B^b	B^b	B^b
sii	-	hain	tum	ha	ra	ye	b	ha	-	na	-	tum	ne	hi	to

A	-	A	A	B^b	D'	C'	B^b	A	-	A	C'	C'	C'	C'	C'
hm	-	ko	l	ga	ya	dil	l	ga	-	na	-	sii	kha	hai	dil

C'	-C'	C'	C'	C'	-G	G	G	C'	B^b	A	-	G	-	F	-
dar	-tu	mhin	se	pya	r,tumhin	se		kr	bai	the	-	e	-	e	-

F	F	AG	G	FA	GA	FG	F-	F	F	AG	G	F	-E	D	E
na	na	kr	te	-	-	-	-	na	na	kr	te	pya	r,tumhin	se	

A	G	F	-
kr	bai	the	-

interlude: C' B^b A G F E C -
C- E------ DEDEDE--- 2
E- G------- GAGAG--- 2
D'- C'—A—G B^b- A—GAF--- 2

												B^b	B^b	D'	D'
												hm	ko	hai	p

D'	-	D'	D'	D'	E^b	D'	C'	C'	-	C'	-	B^b	B^b	D'	D'
ta	-	jo	tum	ha	ri	da	s	ta	-	thi	-	ho	to	pe	to

D'	-D'	-	-	A	-	-	A	D'	-	-	-	B^b	B^b	D'	D'
na	thi	-	-	ja	-	-	jhu	te	-	-	-	ho	to	pe	to

D'	-D'	-	D'	D'	E^b	D'	C'	C'	-	C'	-	B^b	B^b	B^b	B^b
na	thi	-	m	g	r	dil	me	ha	-	thi	-	ko	ii	dil	na

A	-	A	A	B^b	B^b	B^b	-	A	-	A	-	B^b	B^b	B^b	B^b
de	-	ta	a	na	di	an	-	ja	-n	ko	-	hm	ne	de	di

A	-	A	A	B^b	D'	C'	B^b	A	-	A	C'	C'	C'	C'	C'
ya	-	hai	to	ma	no	e	h	sa	-n	ko	-	hm	bhu	le	ik

C' -C' C' C'	C' -G G G	C' B^b A -
ba r,ki aan khe	chhar,tumhin se	kr bai the -

38.   PARBATON KE PEDON PAR

Film: Shagun (1964)
Lyrics: Sahir Ludhiyanvi
Taal: Daadra
Transpose +1 and play from C Scale

Music: khaiyyam
Singer: Md. Rafi, Suman K.
Chord: FAD'   S=C#

R: parbaton ke pedon par shaam ka basera hai -2
       suramayi ujala hai champayi andhera hai -2

S: dono waqt milate hai do dilo ki surat se -2
       aasma ne khush hoke rang saa bikheraa hai -2

R: thahare thahare paani me git sar saraate hai -2
       bhige bhige jhokon me khushbuon ka dera hai -2
       parbaton ke pedon par

S: kyo na jazb ho jaayein is haseen nazaare me -2
       roshani ka jhuramat hai mastiyo ka ghera hai -2
       parbaton ke pedon par

R: ab kisi nazaare ki dil ko aarzu kyon ho -2
       jab se pa liya tum ko sab jahaan mera hai -2

B: jab se pa liya tum ko sab jahaan mera hai
       parbaton ke pedon par shaam ka basera hai
       parbaton ke pedon par.

PARBATON KE PEDON PAR

dhin	dhin	na	ti	dhin	na	dhin	dhin	na	ti	dhin	na	dhin	dhin	na	ti	dhin	na
1	2	3	4	5	6	1	2	3	4	5	6	1	2	3	4	5	6
												A	A	A	A		
												p	rb	to	ke		
G	-	F	-	F	-	-	-	F	-G	G	G	^{A}G	-	G	A	A	-
pe	-	do	-	pr	-	-	-	sha	-m	ka	b	se	-	ra	-	hai	-
G^F	-	A	A	A	A	G	-	F	-	F	-	-	-	F	-G	G	G
-	-	p	rb	to	ke	pe	-	do	-	pr	-	-	-	sha	-m	ka	b
^{A}G	-	G	A	A	-	G	-	A	A	A	A	G	-	F	-	F	-
se	-	ra	-	hai	-	-	-	sur	m	yi	u	ja	-	la	-	hai	-
-	-	F	G	G	G	G	-	G	A	A	-	-	-	A	A	A	A
-	-	chn	p	yi	an	dhe	-	ra	-	hai	-	-	-	sur	m	yi	u
G	-	F	-	F	-	-	-							A	A	A	A
ja	-	la	-	hai	-	-	-							do	no	v	qt
G	-	F	-	F	-	-	-	F	G	G	G	^{A}G	-	G	A	A	-
mil	-	te	-	hain	-	-	-	do	di	lo	ki	su	-	r	t	se	-
G^F	-	A	A	A	A	G	-	F	-	F	-	-	-	F	G	G	G
-	-	do	no	v	qt	mil	-	te	-	hain	-	-	-	do	di	lo	ki
^{A}G	-	G	A	A	-	-	-	A	-A	A	A	G	G	F	-	F	-
su	-	r	t	se	-	-	-	aa	-s	ma	ne	khu	sh	ho	-	kr	-
-	-	F	G	G	G	^{A}G	-	G	A	A	-	G^F	-	A	-A	A	A
-	-	rn	g	sa	bi	khe	-	ra	-	hai	-	-	-	aa	-s	ma	ne
G	G	F	-	F	-	-	-										
khu	sh	ho	-	kr	-	-	-										
								A	A	A	A^b	A	-	A	-	B^b	-
								thh	re	thh	re	pa	-	ni	-	me	-
-	-	D'	-	C'	B^b	A	-	G	-	A	-	-	-	A	A	A	A^b
-	-	gi	-t	sr	s	ra	-	te	-	hain	-	-	-	thh	re	thh	re

A	-	A	-	B♭	-	-	-	D'	-	C'	B♭	A	-	G	-	A	-
pa	-	ni	-	me	-	-	-	gi	-t	sr	s	ra	-	te	-	hain	-
-	-	A	A	A	A	G	-	F	-	F	-	-	-	F	G	G	G
-	-	bhi	ge	bhi	ge	jho	-	ko	-	me	-	-	-	khush	bu	on	ka
ᴬG	-	G	A	A	-	Gᶠ	-	A	A	A	A	G	-	F	-	F	-
de	-	ra	-	hai	-	-	-	bhi	ge	bhi	ge	jho	-	ko	-	me	-
-	-	F	G	G	G	ᴬG	-	G	A	A	-	Gᶠ	-	A	A	A	A
-	-	khush	bu	on	ka	de	-	ra	-	hai	-	-	-	p	rb	to	ke
G	-	F	-	F	-	-	-										
pe	-	do	-	pr	-	-	-										

```
A   A    AAᵇ   A    ABᵇBᵇ    A    D'C'   BᵇAG   A-G
kyu n    jzb   ho   ja-en    is   hsi    nzare  me

AAA    A  GGFF   F    FGG        G  G-  GA      A
roshni ka jhurmt hai  mstiyon ka ghe-ra-        hai

A   AA    AᵇABᵇ  Bᵇ   A   D'   C'BᵇA   G    A-G
ab  kisii nzare  ki   dil ko   aarzu   kyu  ho

G   A   A   AG   F    F    F    GGG    G-  GA   A-G
jb  se  pa  liya tum  ko   sb   jahan  me-ra-   hai

A   A   A   AG   F    F    F    GGG    G-  GA   A-G
jb  se  pa  liya tum  ko   sb   jahan  me-ra-   hai
```

39.   PAHLA PAHLA PYAR HAI YE

Film: Badtameez (1966)   Music: Shanker Jaikishan
Lyrics: Shailendra   Singer: Suman K.
Taal: Kaharwa   Chord: CEG   S=C#
Transpose +1 and play from C Scale

ho pahla pahla pyaar hai ye pahla pahla pyaar -2
kya jaane kya ho gaya hai dil hai beqaraar-2
ho pahla pahla pyaar hai ye pahla pahla pyaar -2

(kaate jaise bichhua kuchh aisa mera haal
dil mera bole ke khud ko sambhal) -2
aaj mujhe khud par nahin hai ikhtiyaar -2
pahla pahla pyaar hai ye pahla pahla pyaar

(sharmo haya se hua hai mukh laal
pyaar ne kisi ke ye kar diya kamaal) -2
ang mora sulge ke jaise ho bukhaar -2
pahla pahla pyaar hai ye pahla pahla pyaar

(ghadi ghadi toote ye phool sa badan
rom rom phadke hai kaisi ye chubhan) -2
haay mera aanchal ude hai baar baar -2
pahla pahla pyaar hai ye pahla pahla pyaar

PAHLA PAHLA PYAR HAI YE

dha	ge	n	ti	n	ke	dhi	n	dha	ge	n	ti	n	ke	dhi	n
1	2	3	4	5	6	7	8	1	2	3	4	5	6	7	8

prelude:
GGC'C' B- B- A- A- G-
GGAA G- G- E- F- G-
GGC'C' B- B- A- A- G-
GGAA G- G- E- E- C-

dha	ge	n	ti	n	ke	dhi	n	dha	ge	n	ti	n	ke	dhi	n
														C'	-
														ha	-
C'	-	C'	-	B	-	B	-	G	-	-	-	G	-	A	-
p	h	la	-	p	h	la	-	pya	-	-	r	hai	-	ye	-
F	-	F	-	E	-	E	-	G	-	-	-	-	-	-	-
p	h	la	-	p	h	la	-	pya	-	-	r	-	-	-	-
C	-	E	-	C	-	C	-	G	-	-	F	E	-	E	-
kya	-	ja	-	ne	-	kya	-	ho	-	-	g	ya	-	hai	-
F	A	A	-	A	-	G	-	G	-	-	-	-	A	C'	-
di	l	hai	-	be	-	q	-	ra	-	-	r	-	ho	o	-

interlude:
G'F#' G'F#' G'A'G'F' E'D' E'D' E'F'E'D' D'C' D'C' D'E'D'C'
D'C'E'F'G'---
G- C'- BC' BC' BC' BC'
G- E'- D'E' D'E' D'E' D'E'
G'F'E'D'C'BAGABC'- GFEC-

dha	ge	n	ti	n	ke	dhi	n	dha	ge	n	ti	n	ke	dhi	n
		C	-	C	E	-	F	G	-	G	G	-	-	G	-
		ka	-	te	jai	-	se	bi	-	chhu	va	-	-	ku	chh
G	-	G	-	F	-	F	-	E	-	-	-	-	-	-	-
ae	-	sa	-	me	-	ra	-	ha	-	-	-	-	l	-	-
-	-	F	-	-	A	A	-	A	-	-	A	-	-	B	-
-	-	di	l	-	me	ra	-	bo	-	-	le	-	-	ke	-
C'	-	B	-	C'	-	A	-	G	-	-	-	-	-	-	-
khu	-	d	-	ko	-	sn	-	bha	-	-	-	-	-l	-	-

```
-   -   G   -  | G   B   C'  -  | D'  -   -   D'  | -   -   D'  -
-   -   aa  -  | j   mu  jhe -  | khu d   -   pr  | -   -   n   -

B   -   G   -  | B   -   C'  -  | D'  -   -   -   | -   -   -   -
hin -   hai -  | i   kh  ti  -  | ya  -   -   -   | -   -r  -   -

-   -   C'  -  | C'  D'  E'  -  | D'  E'  -   D'  | -   -   C'  -
-   -   aa  -  | j   mu  jhe -  | khu d   -   pr  | -   -   n   -

C'  -   C'  -  | C'  -   C'  -  | D'  -   C'  -   | B   -   G   -
hin -   hai -  | i   kh  ti  -  | ya  -   -   -   | -   -   -   -r
    CCE       FG  G   GG      G   FF      E
   (shrmo  hya se  huaa  hai  mukh  lal

 F     A   AA    A   B   C'   BC'  AG
 pyar  ne  kisii ke  ye  kr   diya kmal) -2

GG   BC'   D'D'   D'  BG   B    C'D'
ang  mora  sulge  ke jaise ho  bukhar

C'C'  D'E'   D'E'D'  C'  C'C'   C'  C'D' C' B G
ang   mora   sulge   ke  jaise  ho  bukha------r

C'C'  BB   G   G   A   FF   EE   G
phla  phla pyar hai ye, phla phla pyar
```

40.   PAANI ME JALE MERA GORA

Film: Muneem Ji (1955)
Lyrics: Neeraj, Hasrat Jaipuri
Taal: Kaharwa
Transpose +1 and play from C Scale

Music: Usha Khanna
Singer: Suman K.
Chord: GB^{b}D'   S=C#

pani mein jale, pani mein jale mera gora badan pani mein
mere badan ki jwala se lahro mein dekho kaisi lagi agan
lagi agan pani mein
pani mein jale, pani mein jale mera gora badan pani mein

dekho-- thandi thandi aag ye sataye
aaye-- aake koi aag ye bujhaye
jalun main jale dil jale jaan haye re
pani mein jale, pani mein jale mera gora badan pani mein

aaya-- kal koi sapno mein aaya
aake-- aake mujhe usne jagaya
bola main, tere liye aaya hun haye re
pani mein jale, pani mein jale mera gora badan pani mein

PAANI ME JALE MERA GORA

dha	-	-	te	dhin	-	dhin	dhin	dha	-	-	te	dhin	-	dhin	dhin
1	2	3	4	5	6	7	8	1	2	3	4	5	6	7	8
G	A	A	G	F	-	-	-	G	A	A	G	C'	-	A	A
pa	ni	me	j	le	-	-	-	pa	ni	me	j	le	-	me	ra
G	A	-	A	G	-	G	-	F	-	G	-	-	-	-	-
go	ra	-	b	d	n	pa	-	ni	-	me	-	-	-	-	-
C'	D'	-	C'	D'	-	E^b'	-	C'	D'	C'	B^b	C'	-	-	-
me	re	-	b	d	n	ki	-	jwa	-	la	-	me	-	-	-
C'	C'	C'	B^b	C'	D'	D'	C'	B^b	-C'	-	A	B^b	-	-	-
l	h	ro	me	de	kho	kai	sii	la	-gi	-	a	gn	-	-	-

A	-G	-	A	A	-	G	-	F	-	G	-	-	-	-	-
la	-gi	-	a	gn	-	pa	-	ni	-	me	-	-	-	-	-
G	-	B^b	-	-	-	-	-	D’	D’	C’	C’	B^b	B^b	A	G
de	-	kho	-	-	-	-	-	thn	di	thn	di	aa	-g	ye	s
A	B^b	-	-	-	-	-	-	F	-	A	-	-	-	-	-
ta	ye	-	-	-	-	-	-	aa	-	ye	-	-	-	-	-
D’	D’	C’	C’	B^b	-B^b	A	G	F	G						
aa	ke	ko	ii	aa	-g	ye	bu	jha	ye	-	-	-	-	-	-
B^b	A	B^b	-	B^b	A	B^b	-	B^b	A	B^b	-	G	-	G	F
j	lu	main	-	j	le	dil	-	j	le	jan	-	ha	-	ye	re
G	A	A	G	F	-	-	-	G	A	A	G	C’	-	A	A
pa	ni	me	j	le	-	-	-	pa	ni	me	j	le	-	me	ra
G	A	-	A	G	-	G	-	F	-	G	-	-	-	-	-
go	ra	-	b	d	n	pa	-	ni	-	me	-	-	-	-	-

GB^b-- D’D’ C’C’ B^bB^bA G AB^b
aaya-- kl koii spno me aaya

FA-- D’D’ C’C’ B^bB^bA GFG
aake – aake mujhe usne jgaya

B^bA B^b B^bA B^bB^b B^bA B^b GG F
bola main, tere lie aaya hu hay re

41. RAHE N RAHE HAM MAHKA

Film: Mamta (1966)   Music: Raushan
Lyrics: Majrooh Sultanpuri   Singer: Lata, Suman K.
Taal: Kaharwa   Chord: DGB   S=C#
Transpose +1 and play from C Scale
Lata:
rahein na rahein hum, mahaka karenge
ban ke kali, ban ke saba, baag e wafaa mein
rahein na rahein hum

mausam koi ho is chaman me rang banke rahenge ham khirama
chahat ki khushabu, yu hi zulfo se udegi, khiza hon ya baharaan
yuhi jhumate, yuhi jhumate aur khilate rahenge
ban ke kali, ban ke saba, baag e wafaa mein, rahe na rahein…..

khoye ham aise kya hai milna kya bichhadna nahi hai, yad hamko
kunche me dil ke jab se aaye sirf dil ki zami hai, yad hamko
isi sarzami, isi sarzami pe ham to rahenge
ban ke kali, ban ke saba, bage wafaa mein, rahe na rahe hum…

jab ham na hoge tab hamari khak pe tum rukoge chalte chalte
ashqon se bhigi chadani mein ik sada si sunoge chalte chalte
vahi pe kahi, vahi pe kahi ham tumse milenge
ban ke kali, ban ke saba, bage wafaa mein
rahe na rahe hum, mahaka karenge
ban ke kali, ban ke saba, bage wafaa mein, rahe na rahe hum….
Duet Version:
Suman: hai khubsurat ye nazaare, yo bahaarein
             hamare dam qadam se
Md. Rafi: zinda hui hai fir jahaan mein,
             aaj ishq aur vafa ki rasm ham se
Both: yun hi is chaman, yun hi is chaman ki
             zeenat raheinge ban ke kali ban ke saba
             baag e vafa mein,
             rahein na rahein ham…..

RAHE N RAHE HAM MAHKA

dha	ge	n	ti	n	ke	dhi	n	dha	ge	n	ti	n	ke	dhi	n
1	2	3	4	5	6	7	8	1	2	3	4	5	6	7	8
											D	D	E	.B	C
											r	he	-	n	r
D	-	-	B	-	-	-	-	-	-	-	B	-	C'	-	D'
he	-	-	hm	-	-	-	-	-	-	-	m	h	ka	-	k
D'	E'	-	C'	B	-	A	-	-	-	-	A	-	B	-	C'
ren	-	-	-	ge	-	-	-	-	-	-	b	n	ke	-	k
B	-	-	G	-	A	-	B	A	-	-	F#	-	G	-	A
li	-	-	bn	-	ke	-	s	ba	-	-	ba	-	ge	-	v
G	-	-	F#	A	G	F#	E	D	-	-	D	D	E	.B	C
fa	-	-	-	me	-	-	-	-	-	-	r	he	-	n	r
D	-	-	B								B	-	C'	-	B
he	-	-	hm								mau	-	sm	-	ko
A	B	B	-	-	B	-	A	G	A	A	-	-	A	-	G
ii	-	ho	-	-	i	s	ch	mn	-	me	-	-	rn	-	g
E	G	G	-	-	A	B	-	A	-	-	-	-	A	-	B
bn	-	ke	-	-	r	hen	-	ge	-	-	-	-	hm	-	khi
B	-	G	-	G	-	-	-	-	-	-	B	-	C'	-	B
ra	-	-	-	ma	-	-	-	-	-	-	chha	-	ht	-	ki
A	B	B	-	-	B	-	A	G	A	A	-	-	A	-	G
khu	sh	bu	-	-	yu	-	hi	zu	l	fo	-	-	se	-	u
E	G	G	-	-	A	B	-	A	-	A	-	-	A	-	B
de	-	gi	-	-	khi	za	-	ho	-	ya	-	-	ho	-	b
B	-	G	-	G	-	-	-	-	-	G	A	-	B	D'	B
ha	-	-	-	ra	-	-	-	-	-	yu	hi	-	jhu	-	m

D'	-	-	-	-	-	-	-	-	-	F'	E'	-	D'	-	B
te	-	-	-	-	-	-	-	-	-	yu	hi	-	jhu	-	m
D'	-	-	A	C'	-	B	B	-	-	-	B	-	C'	-	D'
te	-	-	-	aa	-	-	j	-	-	-	khi	l	te	-	r
D'	E'	-	C'	B	-	A	-	-	-	-	A	-	B	-	C'
he	-	-	-	ge	-	-	-	-	-	-	b	n	ke	-	k
B	-	-	G	-	A	-	B	A	-	-	F#	-	G	-	A
li	-	-	bn	-	ke	-	s	ba	-	-	ba	-	ge	-	v
G	-	-	F#	A	G	F#	E	D	-	-	D	D	E	.B	C
fa	-	-	-	me	-	-	-	-	-	-	r	he	-	n	r
D	-	-	B												
he	-	-	hm												

```
                  B   C'BABB      B   AGAA
        suman:  hai khubsu-rt   ye  nza-re

                A   GEGG     AB-A    A  BBG  G
                ye  bharen   hma-re dm-qdm se

                  BC'  BAB       B   B  AGA  A
        md. rafi:  zinda huii-   hai fir jha-  me

                AG  EG  G AB A   AB  BG  G
                aaj ishq-o-vfa ki  rsm hm  se

                  G  A  B  BD'   F' E'  D' BD'A C'B
        dono:  yu hi is chmn,  yu hi  is chmn ki-

                BC'   D' D'E'C'BA
                zint  rhe-----ge-


                A  B  C'B G  A  BA  F# G AGF# AGF#ED
                bn ke kli bn ke sba bag-e-vfa    me-----

                DD E  .BCD    B
                rhe na rhe-   hm ...
```

42. THAHARIYE HOSH ME AA LU

Film: Mohobbat isko kahte hain (1965) Music: Khaiyyam
Lyrics: Majrooh Sultanpuri Singer: Md. Rafi Suman
Taal: Kaharwa K.
Transpose +2 and play from C Scale Chord: CEG S=D

R: thahariye hosh mein aa loo, to chale jaaiyega
S: uun huun
R: aap ko dil mein bithhaa loo to chale jaaiyega
S: uun huun
R: aap ko dil mein bithhaa loo to chale jaaiyega
R: kab talak rahiyega yoon door kee chaahat ban ke -2
   dil mein aa jaaeeye, iqaraar-e-mohabbat ban ke
   apanee taqadeer banaa loo, to chale jaaiyega
S: uun huun
R: aap ko dil mein bithhaa loo to chale jaaiyega

S: mujh ko iqaraar-e-mohabbat pe hayaa aatee hai -2
   baat kahate huye gardn meree jhuk jaatee hai
   dekhiye sar ko jhukaa loon, to chale jaaiyega
R: uun huun
S: dekhiye sar ko jhuka lun to chale jaaiyega
R: aap ko dil mein bithhaa loo to chale jaaiyega

R: aesee kyaa sharm zaraa, paas to aane dije -2
   rukh se bikharee huyee julfein to hataane dije
   pyaas aankhon kee bujhaa loo, to chale jaaiyega
Both: thahariye hosh mein aa loo, to chale jaaiyega

THAHARIYE HOSH ME AA LUN

dha	ge	n	ti	n	ke	dhi	n	dha	ge	n	ti	n	ke	dhi	n
1	2	3	4	5	6	7	8	1	2	3	4	5	6	7	8
prelude: C'BC'D'C'B BABC'BA AGABAG G-															
											G	G	B	A	B
											th	h	ri	ye	-
G	-	-	-	E	E	D	-	E	-	-	-	E	G	AB	C'
ho	-	-	-	sh	me	aa	-	lu	-	-	-	to	ch	le-	-
A	-	A	G	^{G}A	-	A	G	B	-	-	G	-	B	A	B
ja	ii	ye	-	ga	-	un	-	hu	-	-	aa	-	p	ko	-
G	-	G	E	-	E	D	-	E	-	-	-	E	G	AB	C'
dil	-	me	-	-	bi	tha	-	lu	-	-	-	to	ch	le-	-
A	-	A	G	^{G}A	-	A	G	B	-	-	G	-	B	A	B
ja	ii	ye	-	ga	-	un	-	hu	-	-	aa	-	p	ko	-
G	-	G	E	-	E	D	-	E	-	-	-				
dil	-	me	-	-	bi	tha	-	lu	-	-	-				
interlude: DEGABC' A-A^{b}A- AABAGAE E-DE DEGEDEC															
sarangi: BA AG EA^b															
											A^b	A^b	A^b	A^b	A^b
											k	b	t	l	k
A	A	A	-	-	A^b	A	-	AB	C'	-	-	A	A	A	A^b
r	hi	ye	-	-	ga	yu	-	du-	-	-	-	r	ki	chha	-
A	A	A	A^b	B	G	E	-	-	-	-	A^b	-	A^b	A^b	-
h	t	b	n	ke	-	-	-	-	-	-	dil	-	me	aa	-
A	-	-	A	A	-	A	A	AB	C'	-	-	A	A	A	
ja	-	-	ii	ye	-	i	q	ra-	-	-	-	re	mo	ho	
A	A	A	A	B	G	E	-	-	-	-	G	G	B	A	B
b	t	b	n	ke	-	-	-	-	-	-	a	p	ni	t	q
G	-	-	-	E	E	D	-	E	-	-	-	E	G	AB	C'
di	-	-	-	r	b	na	-	lu	-	-	-	to	ch	le	-

A	-	A	G	^{G}A	-	A	G	B	-	-	G	-	B	A	B
ja	ii	ye	-	ga	-	un	-	hu	-	-	aa	-	p	ko	-
G	-	G	E	-	E	D	-	E	-	-	-				
dil	-	me	-	-	bi	tha	-	lu	-	-	-				

interlude: DEGABC' A-A^{b}A- AABAGAE E-DE DEGEDEC
BA AG EA^b

											A^b	A^b	A^b	A^b	A^b
											mu	jh	ko	i	q
A	-	A	-	-	A	A	-	AB	C'	-	-	A	A	A	-
ra	-	re	-	-	mo	ho	-	b-	-	-	t	se	h	ya	-
A	-	A	-	B	G	E	-	-	-	-	A^b	-	A^b	A^b	A^b
aa	-	ti	-	hai	-	-	-	-	-	-	ba	-	t	k	h
A	-	-	A	A	-	A	A	AB	C'	-	-	A	A	A	A
te	-	-	hu	e	-	g	r	dn-	-	-	-	me	ri	jhu	k
A	-	A	-	B	G	E	-	-	-	-	G	-	B	A	B
ja	-	ti	-	hai	-	-	-	-	-	-	de	-	khi	ye	-
G	-	-	-	E	E	D	-	E	-	-	-	E	G	AB	C'
sr	-	-	-	ko	jhu	ka	-	lu	-	-	-	to	ch	le	-
A	-	A	G	^{G}A	-										
ja	i	ye	-	ga	-										

43. TUJHE PYAR KARTE HAIN

Film: April Phool (1964) Music: Shanker Jaikishan
Lyrics: Hasrat Jaipuri Singer: Md. Rafi, Suman K.
Taal: Kaharwa Chord: DF#A F#ADb, S=C#
Transpose +1 and play from C Scale

R: tujhe pyaar karte hain karte rahenge
ke dil banke dil me dhadakte rahenge
S: tera naam le le ke jeete rahenge
tera naam le le ke marte rahenge
R: tujhe pyaar karte hain karte rahenge
ke dil banke dil mein dhadakte rahenge

R: tujhe bhool jaaun ye mumkin nahin hai
kahin bhi rahoon mera dil to yahin hain
ghate chand lekin mujhe gham na hoga
tera pyaar dil se kabhi kam na hoga
guzarne ko ye din guzarte rahenge
ke dil ban ke di me dhadakte rahenge
S: tera naam le le ke jeete rahenge
tera naam le le ke marte rahenge
R: tujhe pyaar karte hain karte rahenge
ke dil banke dil me dhadakte rahenge

S: haseen phool ki zindgaani bhi kya hai
abhi hans raha tha abhi ro raha hai
jo guzre khushi me wahi zindagi hai
nahin to ye duniya badi besuri hai
teri dhun me bante swarte rahenge
ke dil banke dil me dhadakte rahenge
S: tera naam le le ke jeete rahenge
tera naam le le ke marte rahenge
R: tujhe pyaar karte hain karte rahenge
ke dil banke dil me dhadakte rahenge

R: agar mar gaya rooh aaya karegi
        tujhe dekh kar geet gaaya karegi
        mujhe dekh kar tum na aansoo bahaana
        bas itni guzaarish hai tum muskuraana
        tere pyar me rang bharte rahenge
        ke dil banke dil me dhadakte rahenge
S: tera naam le le ke jeete rahenge
        tera naam le le ke marte rahenge
R: tujhe pyar karte hain karte rahenge
        ke dil banke dil me dhadakte rahenge

TUJHE PYAR KARTE HAIN

dha	ge	n	ti	n	ke	dhi	n	dha	ge	n	ti	n	ke	dhi	n
1	2	3	4	5	6	7	8	1	2	3	4	5	6	7	8
prelude: sitar:															
E'- D'E' D'E'F#'E' D' B -2															
E'- D'- B- Db' D' Db' A D' B Db' Ab A -2															
flute: Ab Ab A --- F# F# Ab F# Ab – E EF# EF#- D- E- -2															
synthe: ABDb'D' F#' E' D' -2 F#AbAB D'- B- A- -2															
DEF#Ab A- Ab F#- E															
A Ab F#- E- E-															
														E	-
														tu	-
E	-	-	F#	-	-	E	-	E	-	-	F#	-	-	E	-
jhe	-	-	pya	-	-	r	-	k	r	-	te	-	-	hain	-
E	-	-	F#	-	-	E	-	F#	A	-	A	-	-	A	-
k	r	-	te	-	-	r	-	hen	-	-	ge	-	-	ke	-
B	A	-	A	-	-	F#	-	F#	E	-	E	-	-	D	-
dil	-	-	bn	-	-	ke	-	dil	-	-	me	-	-	dh	-
F#	F#	-	F#	-	-	E	-	E	-	-	E	-	-	E'	-
d	k	-	te	-	-	r	-	hen	-	-	ge	-	-	te	-

E'	-	-	D'	B	-	B	-	B	D'	-	D'	-	-	D'	-
ra	-	-	na	-	-	m	-	le	-	-	le	-	-	ke	-

D^{b}'	-	-	B	-	-	A	-	B	-	-	A	-	-	A	-
ji	-	-	te	-	-	r	-	hen	-	-	ge	-	-	te	-

A	B	-	A	-	-	F$^{\#}$	-	F$^{\#}$	-	-	E	-	-	D	-
ra	-	-	na	-	-	m	-	le	-	-	le	-	-	ke	-

D	F$^{\#}$	-	F$^{\#}$	-	-	E	-	E	-	-	E	-	-
m	r	-	te	-	-	r	-	hen	-	-	ge	-	-

interlude: flute:

D^{b}' D^{b}' D^{b}' D^{b}' D'F$^{\#}$' F$^{\#}$'-   E'- E'D'- D' D^{b}'-

D^{b}' D^{b}'F$^{\#}$' F$^{\#}$' E'- E'D'- D' D^{b}'-

D^{b}' D' F$^{\#}$'- E'F$^{\#}$'- E'F$^{\#}$'-

F$^{\#}$' F$^{\#}$'A' A' G'- G'F$^{\#}$'- F$^{\#}$'E'-   F$^{\#}$' F$^{\#}$'A' A' G'- G'F$^{\#}$'- F$^{\#}$'E'-

A'G'F$^{\#}$'E'-

synthe: D^{b}'- D'E' D^{b}'B D^{b}'B D^{b}' A-   D^{b}'B D^{b}'B D^{b}' A D^{b}'-

														A	-
														tu	-

D^{b}'	-	-	D^{b}'	-	-	D^{b}'	-	D^{b}'	-	-	D'	-	-	D'	-
jhe	-	-	bhu	-	-	l	-	ja	-	-	un	-	-	ye	-

D^{b}'	-	-	D'	-	-	D^{b}'	-	B	D^{b}'	-	D^{b}'	A	-	A	-
mu	m	-	kin	-	-	n	-	hin	-	-	hai	-	-	k	-

D'	-	-	D'	-	-	D'	-	D'	-	-	D'	-	-	D'	-
hin	-	-	bhi	-	-	r	-	hu	-	-	me	-	-	ra	-

D^{b}'	-	-	B	-	-	A	-	D^{b}'	-	-	D^{b}'	-	-	E'	-
dil	-	-	to	-	-	y	-	hin	-	-	hai	-	-	gh	-

E'	-	-	D^{b}'	-	-	B	-	D'	-	-	D'	-	-	D'	-
te	-	-	chan	-	-	d	-	le	-	-	kin	-	-	mu	-

D^{b}'	-	-	B	-	-	A	-	B	-	-	A	-	-	A	-
jhe	-	-	gm	-	-	n	-	ho	-	-	ga	-	-	te	-

B	-	-	A	-	-	F#	-	F#	-	-	E	-	-	D	-
ra	-	-	pya	-	-	r	-	dil	-	-	se	-	-	k	-
F#	-	-	F#	-	-	E	-	E	-	-	E	-	-	E	-
bhi	-	-	km	-	-	n	-	ho	-	-	ga	-	-	gu	-
E	-	-	F#	-	-	E	-	E	-	-	F#	-	-	E	-
z	r	-	ne	-	-	ko	-	ye	-	-	din	-	-	gu	-
E	-	-	F#	-	-	E	-	F#	A	-	A	-	-	A	-
z	r	-	te	-	-	r	-	hen	-	-	ge	-	-	ke	-
B	-	-	A	-	-	F#	-	F#	-	-	E	-	-	D	-
dil	-	-	bn	-	-	ke	-	dil	-	-	me	-	-	dh	-
D	F#	-	F#	-	-	E	-	E	-	-	E	-	-		
d	k	-	te	-	-	r	-	hen	-	-	ge	-	-		

interlude: sitar

F# A♭ A B D♭' D'   E' E' D' B D♭'
F# A♭ A B D♭' D'   E' E' D' B D' D' D♭'
B D♭' D'   F#' E' D'   A B D♭'   D' D♭' B
A♭ A B D♭' B A   D♭' B A♭ A –

														A	-
														hn	-
D♭'	-	-	D♭'	-	-	D♭'	-	D♭'	-	-	D'	-	-	E'	-
sii	-	-	fu	-	-	l	-	ki	-	-	zin	-	-	d	-
D♭'	-	-	D'	-	-	D♭'	-	B	D♭'	-	D♭'	A	-	A	-
ga	-	-	ni	-	-	bhi	-	kya	-	-	hai	-	-	a	-
D'	-	-	D'	-	-	D'	-	D'	-	-	D'	-	-	D'	-
bhi	-	-	hn	-	s	r	-	ha	-	-	tha	-	-	a	-
D♭'	-	-	B	-	-	A	-	D♭'	-	-	D♭'	-	-	E'	-
bhi	-	-	ro	-	-	r	-	ha	-	-	hai	-	-	jo	-
E'	-	-	D♭'	-	-	B	-	D'	-	-	D'	-	-	D'	-
gu	z	-	re	-	-	khu	-	shi	-	-	me	-	-	v	-
D♭'	-	-	B	-	-	A	-	B	-	-	A	-	-	A	-
hi	-	-	zin	-	-	d	-	gi	-	-	hai	-	-	n	-

B	-	-	A	-	-	F$^{\#}$	-	F$^{\#}$	E	-	E	-	-	D	-
hin	-	-	to	-	-	ye	-	du	ni	-	ya	-	-	b	-
F$^{\#}$	-	-	F$^{\#}$	-	-	E	-	E	-	-	E	-	-	E	-
di	-	-	be	-	-	su	-	ri	-	-	hai	-	-	te	-
E	-	-	F$^{\#}$	-	-	E	-	E	-	-	F$^{\#}$	-	-	E	-
ri	-	-	dhun	-	-	me	-	bn	-	-	te	-	-	sn	-
E	-	-	F$^{\#}$	-	-	E	-	F$^{\#}$	A	-	A	-	-	A	-
v	r	-	te	-	-	r	-	hen	-	-	ge	-	-	ke	-
B	A	-	A	-	-	F$^{\#}$	-	F$^{\#}$	E	-	E	-	-	D	-
dil	-	-	bn	-	-	ke	-	dil	-	-	me	-	-	dh	-
F$^{\#}$	F$^{\#}$	-	F$^{\#}$	-	-	E	-	E	-	-	E	-	-		
d	k	-	te	-	-	r	-	hen	-	-	ge	-	-		

interlude: flute:
D^{b}' D^{b}' D^{b}' D^{b}' D'F$^{\#}$' F$^{\#}$'-   E'- E'D'- D' D^{b}'-
D^{b}' D^{b}'F$^{\#}$' F$^{\#}$' E'- E'D'- D' D^{b}'-
D^{b}' D' F$^{\#}$'- E'F$^{\#}$'- E'F$^{\#}$'-
F$^{\#}$' F$^{\#}$'A' A' G'- G'F$^{\#}$'- F$^{\#}$'E'- F$^{\#}$' F$^{\#}$'A' A' G'- G'F$^{\#}$'- F$^{\#}$'E'-
A'G'F$^{\#}$'E'-
synthe: D^{b}'- D'E' D^{b}'B D^{b}'B D^{b}' A- D^{b}'B D^{b}'B D^{b}' A D^{b}'-

   D^{b}'D^{b}' D^{b}' D^{b}'D^{b}' D'E' D^{b}'D' D^{b}'BD^{b}'D^{b}'A
(agr   mr gya ruh   aaya   kare-gi-

AD'   D'D' D' D'E' D^{b}'B AD^{b}'D^{b}'
tujhe dekh kr git   gaya karegi) -2

E'E'   D^{b}'B D' D' D' D^{b}'B ABA
mujhe dekh   kr tum n aansu bahana

A BAF$^{\#}$ EF$^{\#}$ED D F$^{\#}$ F$^{\#}$EEE
bs itni   gujarish hai tum   muskurana

EE F$^{\#}$E E F$^{\#}$E EF$^{\#}$ EF$^{\#}$AA
tere pyar men rng   bhrte rhen-ge

A B A F$^{\#}$ F$^{\#}$E E
ke dil bnke   dil me …

44.   TUM NE PUKARA AUR HAM

Film: Rajkumar (1964)
Lyrics: Shailendra
Taal: Kaharwa
Transpose +1 and play from C Scale

Music: Shanker Jaikishan
Singer: Md. Rafi, Suman K.
Chord: GB^{b}D' DF$^#$A DFA
S=C#

R: tum ne pukaaraa aaur hum chale aaye
       dil hathelee par le aaye re
S: tum ne pukaaraa aaur hum chale aaye
       jaan hathelee par le aaye re

R: aao baithho humaare pahaloo mein panaah le lo
       meree jalatee huyee aakhon pe ye aankhe rakh do
       aye mere pyaar ke khwaabon kee hasiin shahajaadi
       honthh kyo kaanp rahe hai, zaraa kuchh to bolo
R: tum ne pukaaraa aaur hum chale aaye
       jaan hathelee par le aaye re
S: aaj khelo meree zulfon se, ijaazat hai tumhe
       muz ko chhoo lo, meri nas nas mein sharaare bhar do
       mere diladaar, meri aakhon mein rahane waale
       mai tumhaari hoo, meri maang mein taare bhar do
R: tum ne pukaaraa aaur hum chale aaye
       dil hathelee par le aaye re

R: naam raushan hain tum hee se mere afasaane kaa
       zindagee naam hai ulafat mein jiye jaane kaa
       tum agar hum ko na milate to ye soorat hoti
       log le jaate janaazaa tere diwaane kaa
S: tum ne pukaaraa aaur hum chale aaye
       jaan hathelee par le aaye re

TUM NE PUKARA AUR HAM

dha	ge	n	ti	n	ke	dhi	n	dha	ge	n	ti	n	ke	dhi	n
1	2	3	4	5	6	7	8	1	2	3	4	5	6	7	8

prelude:
D′------- C′ D′ E♭′ --------- D′------
aa-------aa aa aa ------ aa -----

music: G′F′E♭′D′C′B♭ E♭′D′C′B♭AG D′ C′ E♭′ ---- C′ B♭ G ---

dha	ge	n	ti	n	ke	dhi	n	dha	ge	n	ti	n	ke	dhi	n
										D	-	-	F♯	-	G
										tum	-	-	ne	-	pu
A	-	A	-	A	-	A	-	-	-	B♭	C′	-	B♭	A	-
ka	-	ra	-	au	-	r	-	-	-	hm	-	-	ch	le	-
G	-	G	-	-	-	-	-	-	-	D′	-	-	-	B♭	-
aa	-	ye	-	-	-	-	-	-	-	dil	-	-	-	h	-
C′	-	C′	-	B♭	-	A	-	G	-	A	C′	B♭	-	-	-
the	-	li	-	p	r	le	-	aa	-	ye	-	re	-	-	-
C′	-	-	-	B♭	A	G	-	-	-	D	-	-	F♯	-	G
-	-	-	-	-	-	-	-	-	-	tum	-	-	ne	-	pu
A	-	A	-	A	-	A	-	-	-	B♭	C′	-	B♭	A	-
ka	-	ra	-	au	-	r	-	-	-	hm	-	-	ch	le	-
G	-	G	-	-	-	-	-	-	-	D′	-	-	-	B♭	-
aa	-	ye	-	-	-	-	-	-	-	jan	-	-	-	h	-
C′	-	C′	-	B♭	-	A	-	G	-	A	C′	B♭	-	-	-
the	-	li	-	p	r	le	-	aa	-	ye	-	re	-	-	-
C′	-	-	-	B♭	A	G	-	-	-	D	-	-	F♯	-	G
-	-	-	-	-	-	-	-	-	-	tum	-	-	ne	-	pu
A	-	A	-	A	-	A	-	-	-	B♭	C′	-	B♭	A	-
ka	-	ra	-	au	-	r	-	-	-	hm	-	-	ch	le	-
G	-	G	-	-	-	-	-	-	-						
aa	-	ye	-	-	-	-	-	-	-						

interlude: saxophone
C' D' ---- C' E$^{b'}$ ---- E$^{b'}$ D' ---- x2
D A ---- G B^{b} A G---
synthe: A'G' G'F' F'E$^{b'}$ E$^{b'}$D' F'—E$^{b'}$ D' F'--- E$^{b'}$ D' D'—
D'C' C'B^{b} B^{b}A AG GAB^{b}—A G B^{b} A G G-- D E^{b} F G

FF   FG   GFF   FGG G   FFG G G
aao baitho hmare phlu me pnah le lo

AA   AA AA   AB^{b} A   G   FG   G   G
meri jlti huii aankhon pe ye aankhe   rkh do

C'   C'C'   C'C' C'   C'D'   C' B^{b}AG B^{b} B^{b}B^{b}
ae   mere   pyar ke khwabo ki hnsi- shahzadi

D'D'   C'D'   E^{b}'D'   C'B^{b}C' D'   AG FF   FG GG
hoth   kyu   kanp   rhe-   hain, zra kuchh to- bolo

45. TUM SE O HASEENA KABHI

Film: Farz (1967)
Lyrics: Anand Bakshi
Taal: Kaharwa

Music: Laxmikant Pyarelal
Singer: Md. Rafi, Suman K.
Chord: GBD' S=C

tumse o haseena kabhi mohabbat na maine karni thi -2
magar mere dil ne mujhe dhokha de diya -2

tumse o deewane kabhi mohabbat na maine karni thi -2
magar mere dil ne mujhe dhokha de diya -2

aag sulag gayi nas nas mein neend rahi na raha chain bas mein
todi jaaye na ab mujhse pyaar ki ye rasmein kasmein
a gayi bulbul kafas mein
tauba meri tauba ye apni haalat na maine karni thi -2
magar mere dil ne mujhe dhokha de diya ha-2

log ye mujhko hain samjhaate beet rahi thi hanste gaate
maine tumhein kisaliye chheda raahon mein aate jaate
mujhe sab hain sataate
tauba meri tauba ke ye sharaarat na maine karni thi -2
magar mere dil ne mujhe dhokha de diya ha -2

shaam savere dil ghabraaye
raaz e dil na khul jaaye
raat hamaare sapanon mein chhup ke
roz koi aaye jaaye kaahe neha lagaaye
tauba meri tauba ke ye qayaamat na maine karni thi -2
magar mere dil ne mujhe dhokha de diya ha -2

TUM SE O HASEENA KABHI

dha	-	-	ti	na	-	ghe	na	dha	-	-	ti	na	-	ghe	na
1	2	3	4	5	6	7	8	1	2	3	4	5	6	7	8

prelude:

DD GG x 8

D'D' G'G' F'F' E'E' D'D' C'C' BB AA

G- A- G- A- G- A- G-

D'D'D' F' D'D'D' F' D'D'D' F' D'D'D' F'

C'C'C'E'- BBBD'- AAAC'- GGGB-

GGGA x 4 G-

D- G- DGB- x 3 D- G-G-G- D- G- DGB- x 3 D- G-G-G-

1	2	3	4	5	6	7	8	1	2	3	4	5	6	7	8
		D'	-	B	B	-	B	B	-	D'	-	B	B	-	B
		tum	-	se	o	-	h	sii	-	na	-	k	bhi	-	mo
B	-	D'	-	B	B	-	B	B	A	A	B	B	-	A	-
ho	-	bt	-	na	main	-	ne	k	r	ni	-	thi	-	-	-
-	-	A	A	-	A	A	-	A	-	B^b	-	-	A	G	-
-	-	m	gr	-	me	re	-	dil	-	ne	-	-	mu	jhe	-
G	-	B	-	-	A	-	G	G	-	-	-	-	-	A	-
dho	-	kha	-	-	de	-	di	ya	-	-	-	-	-	aa	-
		D'	-	B	B	-	B	B	-	D'	-	B	B	-	B
-	-	tum	-	se	o	-	di	va	-	ne	-	k	bhi	-	mo
B	-	D'	-	B	B	-	B	B	A	A	B	B	-	A	-
ho	-	bt	-	na	main	-	ne	k	r	ni	-	thi	-	-	-
-	-	A	A	-	A	A	-	A	-	B^b	-	-	A	G	-
-	-	m	gr	-	me	re	-	dil	-	ne	-	-	mu	jhe	-
G	-	B	-	-	A	-	G	G	-	-	-	-	-	A	-
dho	-	kha	-	-	de	-	di	ya	-	-	-	-	-	ha	-

interlude: play sthayi and then play

G'- A'- D'E'- G'- A'- D'E'-

G- A- BD' GB x 4 BD'G

G- A- BD' GB x 4 BD'G

C'- C'D'C'BAB---

Each cell below is notated as *note / syllable*; the four measure groups are separated by the column bars in the original.

1	2	3	4	5	6	7	8	9	10	11	12	13	14	15	16
		B / aa	D' / -	B / -	- / -g	G / su	- / -	G / l	- / -	A / g	- / -	B / g	- / -	C' / yi	- / -
D' / n	- / -	C' / s	- / -	C' / n	- / -	D' / s	- / -	D' / me	- / -	C' / -	- / -	- / -	- / -	- / -	- / -
- / -	- / -	AB / nin	- / -	- / -	- / -d	F# / r	- / -	F# / hi	- / -	G / n	- / -	A / r	- / -	B / ha	- / -
B / chai	- / -	- / -	- / -n	C' / b	- / -	B / s	- / -	B / me	- / -	- / -	- / -	A / -	- / -	- / -	- / -
- / -	- / -	B / to	C' / -	B / di	- / -	G / ja	- / -	G / ye	- / -	A / -	- / -	B / na	- / -	C' / -	- / -
D' / a	- / -	C' / b	- / -	C' / mu	- / -	C' / jh	- / -	D' / se	- / -	C' / -	- / -	- / -	- / -	- / -	- / -
- / -	- / -	B / pya	- / -	- / -	- / -	F# / r	- / -	F# / ki	- / -	G / -	- / -	A / r	- / -	B / s	- / -
B / me	- / -	A / -	- / -	C' / k	- / -	B / s	- / -	B / me	- / -	- / -	- / -	B / aa	- / -	B / g	- / yi
A / bul	- / -	- / -	A / bul	- / -	- / -	G / k	- / -	G / f	- / -	G / s	- / -	G / me	- / -	- / -	- / -
- / -	- / -	D' / tau	- / -	B / ba	B / me	- / -	B / ri	B / tau	- / -	D' / ba	- / -	B / ye	B / a	- / p	B / ni
B / ha	- / -	D' / l	- / t	B / n	B / main	- / -	B / ne	B / k	A / r	A / ni	B /	B / thi	- / -	A / -	- / -
- / -	- / -	A / m	A / gr	- / -	A / me	A / re	- / -	A / dil	- / -	B♭ / ne	- / -	- / -	A / mu	G / jhe	- / -
G / dho	- / -	B / kha	- / -	- / -	A / de	- / -	G / di	G / ya	- / -	- / -	- / -	- / -	- / -	A / ha	- / -

interlude:

AG x 8 GAEFABGABC'AB

B B C'D'D' BC'— A A BC'C' AB- x2

		B	D'	B	-	G	-	G	G	-	A		-	B	-
-	-	lo	-	-	-g	ye	-	mu	jh	-	ko	-	-	hain	-
D'	-	C'	-	C'	-	-	-	D'	-	C'	-	-	-	-	-
s	-	m	-	jha	-	-	-	te	-	-	-	-	-	-	-
-	-	B	-	-	-	F#	-	F#	-	G	-	A	-	B	-
-	-	bi	-	-	-t	r	-	hi	-	thi	-	hn	-	s	-
B	-	A	-	C'	-	B	-	B	-	-	-	-	-	-	-
te	-	-	-	ga	-	-	-	te	-	-	-	-	-	-	-
-	-	B	-	B	-	G	-	G	-	A	-	B	-	C'	-
-	-	main	-	ne	-	tu	-	mhe	-	-	-	kis	-	li	-
D'	-	C'	-	C'	-	-	-	D'	-	C'	-	-	-	-	-
ye	-	-	-	chhe	-	-	-	da	-	-	-	-	-	-	-
-	-	A	B	-	-	F#	-	F#	-	G	-	A	-	B	-
-	-	ra	-	-	-	ho	-	me	-	-	-	aa	-	-	-
B	-	A	-	C'	-	B	-	B	-	-	-	B	-	B	-
te	-	-	-	ja	-	-	-	te	-	-	-	mu	-	jhe	-
B	A	-	A	-	-	G	-	G	-	-	-	G	-	-	-
s	b	-	hain	-	-	s	-	ta	-	-	-	te	-	-	-
-	-	D'	-	B	B	-	B	B	-	D'	-	B	B	-	B
-	-	tau	-	ba	me	-	ri	tau	-	ba	-	ke	ye	-	sh
B	-	D'	-	B	B	-	B	B	A	A	B	B	-	A	-
ra	-	r	t	n	main	-	ne	k	r	ni	-	thi	-	-	-
-	-	A	A	-	A	A	-	A	-	B♭	-	-	A	G	-
-	-	m	gr	-	me	re	-	dil	-	ne	-	-	mu	jhe	-
G	-	B	-	-	A	-	G	G	-	-	-	-	-	A	-
dho	-	kha	-	-	de	-	di	ya	-	-	-	-	-	ha	-

interlude:

DDG- DEF- FFA- FF

G A G A G C'BAG G A G A G C'BAG

G A G A E ABFG ABFG ABFG G-

BD'B   GGA   BC' D'C'C' D'C' ^{A}B F$^{\#}$ F$^{\#}$G A BA C'B
sha-m svere dil ghbra- ye--, raz e dil   na khul jae

BC'B GGA   BC'D' C' C'C'   D'C' B F$^{\#}$F$^{\#}$G ABBA C'B
ra-t   hmare spno me chhup ke-, roz koii-   aa-ye- jae

BB   AA   GGG
kaahe neha lgaye

D'B   BB   BD' B B   BB D' B   BB   BAAB BA
tauba meri tauba ke ye, qyamt n   mainne krni-   thi- -2

AA   AA   A B^{b} AG   GB   A   GG   A
mgr mere dil ne mujhe   dhokha de diya ha -2

46. TUMHI MERE MEET HO

Film: Pyase Panchhi (1961)   Music: Kalyanji Anandji
Lyrics: Qamar Jalalabadi   Singer: Suman K. , Hemant Kumar
Taal: Kaharwa   Chord: EGB   S=C

S: tumhi mere meet ho tumhi meri priit ho -2
      tumhi meri aarzu ka pahala pahala giit ho
H: tumhi mere meet ho tumhi meri prit ho -2
      tumhi meri zindagi ki pahali pahali jiit ho
      tumhi mere meet ho

S: tum ho bechain sainya ham beqaraar se
      jaane naa dungi tumko naino ke dwaar se -2
H: teri nigaaho ne dekha hai pyaar se
      mila aaj pyaasa panchhi nadiya ki dhaar se
S: tumhi chitchor mere tumhi dil ki jiit ho -2
      tumhi meri aarzu ka pahela pahela giit ho
B: tumhi mere miit ho.

H: tu kisi baagbaan ke gulshan kaa phool hai
      chhup chhup ke tujhko chaaha rahi ki bhool hai
S: aa… rahi ki bhool nahi qismat ki bhool hai
      qismat ki bhool sainya hamko kubul hai
H: mere dil ke saaj ka tumhi tumhi sangiit ho -2
      tumhi meri zindagi ki pahali pahali jiit ho
B: tumhi mere meet ho tumhi meri priit ho
      tumhi meri zindagi ki pahali pahali jiit ho
      tumhi mere meet ho.

TUMHI MERE MEET HO

dha	ge	n	ti	n	ke	dhi	n	dha	ge	n	ti	n	ke	dhi	n
1	2	3	4	5	6	7	8	1	2	3	4	5	6	7	8

E'F#' E'G' E'F#' E'G' D'E' C'C' BC' B
aa--------------- tumhi mere mit ho
prelude:
    A G E D C D- F#- A G E D C D- E-
F# E F# E F# D C D- F#- A G E D C D- E-

1	2	3	4	5	6	7	8	1	2	3	4	5	6	7	8
										B	B	-	B	-	Bb
										tu	mhi	-	me	-	re
B	-	-	Bb	B	-	-	-	-	-	B	C'	-	A	-	Ab
mi	-	-	t	ho	-	-	-	-	-	tu	mhi	-	me	-	ri
A	-	-	Ab	A	-	-	-	-	-	G	G	-	G	-	F#
pri	-	-	t	ho	-	-	-	-	-	tu	mhi	-	me	-	ri
G	-	-	A	B	-	A	-	-	-	G	A	G	F#	G	F#
aa	-	-	r	zu	-	ka	-	-	-	p	h	la	p	h	la
E	-	-	Eb	E	-	-	-	-	-	B	B	-	B	-	Bb
gi	-	-	t	ho	-	-	-	-	-	tu	mhi	-	me	-	re
B	-	-	Bb	B	-	-	-	-	-	B	C'	-	A	-	Ab
mi	-	-	t	ho	-	-	-	-	-	tu	mhi	-	me	-	ri
A	-	-	Ab	A	-	-	-	-	-	G	G	-	G	-	F#
pri	-	-	t	ho	-	-	-	-	-	tu	mhi	-	me	-	ri
G	-	-	A	B	-	A	-	-	-	G	A	G	F#	G	F#
zin	-	-	d	gi	-	ki	-	-	-	p	h	li	p	h	li
E	-	-	Eb	E	-	-	-	-	-	B	B	-	B	-	Bb
ji	-	-	t	ho	-	-	-	-	-	tu	mhi	-	me	-	re
B	-	-	D'	C'	-	B	-	-	-						
mi	-	-	t	ho	-	o	-	-	-						

interlude: EG – C'- B- G- D'C'B-
             D'- C' BA AG GF#-
             F#'----E'D'C'BAGF#E--

```
                                    B   C' | -   E'  -   E'b
                                    tu  m  | -   ho  -   be

 E'  -   -   E'b| F#' -   E'  -  | -   -   E'  F#'| -   D'  -   D'b
 chai -  -   n  | sai -   ya  -  | -   -   hm  -  | -   be  -   q

 D'  -   -   D'b| D'  -   -   -  | -   -   C'  -  | C'  -   C'  -
 ra  -   -   r  | se  -   -   -  | -   -   ja  -  | ne  -   na  -

 B   C'  C'  -  | B   C'  C'  -  | -   -   D'  E' | -   C'  -   B
 dun -   gi  -  | tu  m   ko  -  | -   -   nai -  | -   no  -   ke

 B   -   -   Bb | B   -   -   -  | -   -   B   C' | -   E'  -   E'b
 dwa -   -   r  | se  -   -   -  | -   -   te  -  | -   ri  -   ni

 E'  -   -   -  | F#' -   E'  -  | -   -   E'  F#'| -   D'  -   D'b
 ga  -   -   -  | ho  -   ne  -  | -   -   de  -  | -   kha -   hai

 D'  -   -   D'b| D'  -   -   -  | -   -   C'  C' | -   C'  -   C'
 pya -   -   r  | se  -   -   -  | -   -   mi  la | -   aa  -   j

 B   -   C'  -  | B   -   C'  -  | -   -   C'  D' | -   C'  -   B
 pya -   sa  -  | pn  -   chhi - | -   -   n   di | -   ya  -   ki

 B   -   -   Bb | B   -   G   -  | E   -   B   B  | -   B   -   Bb
 dha -   -   r  | se  -   -   -  | -   -   tu  mhi| -   chi -   t

 B   -   -   Bb | B   -   B   -  | -   -   B   C' | -   A   -   Ab
 cho -   -   r  | me  -   re  -  | -   -   tu  mhi| -   di  -   l

 A   -   -   Ab | A   -   -   -  | -   -   G   G  | -   G   -   F#
 ji  -   -   t  | ho  -   -   -  | -   -   tu  mhi| -   me  -   ri

 G   -   -   A  | B   -   A   -  | -   -   G   A  | G   F#  G   F#
 aa  -   -   r  | zu  -   ka  -  | -   -   p   h  | la  p   h   la

 E   -   -   Eb | E   -   -   -  | -   -   B   B  | -   B   -   Bb
 gi  -   -   t  | ho  -   -   -  | -   -   tu  mhi| -   me  -   re

 B   -   -   D' | C'  -   B   -  | -   -
 mi  -   -   t  | ho  -   o   -  | -   -
```

BC' E' E^{b}' E' E^{b}' F$^{#}$' E' E'F$^{#}$'D'- D^{b}' D' D^{b}' D'
hemant:tu- kisii bagba   ki gulshn ka ful   hai

C' C' C' BC'C'   B-C' D'E'-C' B   BB^{b} B
chhupchhup ke tujhko chha-ha ra--hi ki bhul hai

suman:
 F$^{#}$' E' BC'E' E^{b}' E'E^{b}' F$^{#}$'E' E'F$^{#}$' D' D^{b}' D'D^{b}'D'
aa.. aa... ra-hi ki bhul nhin kismt ki bhul hai

C' C' C' BC'C' BC'C' C' D' C' BBB^{b} B G E
kismt ki bhu-l sai-ya hme to qubul hai o—

BB B B^{b} BB^{b} B B C' AA^{b}AA^{b} A -
hemant:mere dil ke saj ka tumhi sn-git   ho -2

GG GF$^{#}$ G A B A GAG F$^{#}$GF$^{#}$ EE^{b} E
tumhi meri zindgi ki phli   phli   jit   ho

47. VO DEKHO DEKH RAHA THA PAPIHA

Film: Fariyad (1964)
Lyrics: Kedar Sharma
Taal: Kaharwa
Transpose +1 and play from C Scale

Music: Snehal Bhaatkar
Singer: Mahendra Kumar,
Suman K.
Chord: EGC' S=C#

wo dekho dekha dekh raha tha papiha
papiha dekho dekh raha tha papiha
papiha jaake sabase kahega papiha
papiha bhala chup kyon rahega papiha
papiha dekho dekha dekh raha

rim jhim jhim badariya barase
aise men jaiyo nahin ghar se
hamra jiya ghabraaye
aji tum bin raha na jaae

sar sar sar chale sard hawaaen
ful hanse kaliyaan muskaae
hamko ye samajhaaye
ham milkar naachein gaayein

tim tim tim karate hain sitaare
ap hue hai jab se hamaare
ham fuule nahin samaaein
ham ghadi ghadi muskaaein

VO DEKHO DEKH RAHA THA PAPIHA

dha	ge	n	ti	n	ke	dhi	n	dha	ge	n	ti	n	ke	dhi	n
1	2	3	4	5	6	7	8	1	2	3	4	5	6	7	8

prelude:
A A A GAC'A G- E- EGAG E- D- DEG DEGE A-
A A A GAC'A G- E- EGAG E- D- DEG
GE D- E- E'- D'- C'-
GA E'- D'- C'- G- E'- C'-

dha	ge	n	ti	n	ke	dhi	n	dha	ge	n	ti	n	ke	dhi	n
											C'	A	C'	G	A
											vo	de	kho	de	kha
E'	-	D'	E'	C'	-	C'	D'	A	A	-	C'	A	C'	G	A
de	-	kh	r	ha	-	tha	p	pi	ha	-	p	pi	ha	de	kho
E'	-	D'	E'	C'	-	C'	D'	A	A	-	C'	A	C'	G	A
de	-	kh	r	ha	-	tha	p	pi	ha	-	p	pi	ha	ja	ke
E'	E'	D'	E'	C'	-	C'	D'	A	A	-	C'	A	C'	G	A
s	b	se	k	he	-	ga	p	pi	ha	-	p	pi	ha	bh	la
E'	E'	D'	E'	C'	-	C'	D'	A	A	-	C'	A	C'	G	A
chu	p	kyu	r	he	-	ga	p	pi	ha	-	p	pi	ha	de	kho
E'	-	D'	E'	C'	-	-	D'	A	-	-	-	-	-	-	-
de	-	kh	r	ha	-	-	-	tha	-	-	-	-	-	-	-
C'	-	E'	-	C'	-	-	C'	C'	C'	B	A	B	B	G	-
rim	-	jhim	-	jhim	-	-	b	d	ri	ya	-	b	r	se	-
A	-	E'	-	C'	-	C'	-	C'	-	B	A	B	B	G	-
ae	-	se	-	me	-	ja	i	yo	-	n	hin	gh	r	se	-
G	G	G	-	A	A	D'	D'	C'	-	-	B	-	-	A	G
h	m	ro	-	ji	ya	gh	b	ra	-	-	y	-	-	a	ji
G	G	G	-	A	B	-	D'	C'	-	-	C'	-	-	-	-
tu	m	bi	n	r	ha	-	n	ja	-	-	y	-	-	-	-
C'	-	E'	-	C'	-	C'	C'	C'	-	B	A	B	-	G	-
s	r	s	r	s	r	ch	le	s	r	d	h	va	-	yen	-

A	-	E'	E'	C'	-	C'	C'	C'	-	B	A	B	-	G	-
fu	-	l	hn	se	-	k	li	ya	-	mu	s	ka	-	yen	-

G	G	G	-	A	-	D'	D'	C'	-	-	-	B	-	A	G
h	m	ko	-	ye	-	s	m	jha	-	-	-	yen	-	h	m

G	G	G	-	A	-	D'	-	C'	-	-	-	C'	-	-	-
mi	l	k	r	na	-	chen	-	ga	-	-	-	yen	-	-	-

C'	E'	C'	C'C'C'	B	ABG
tim	tim	tim	krte	hain	sitare,

A	E'	E'C'	C'	C'C'	B	ABG
aap	hue	hain	jb	se	hmare	-2

GG	GG	AB	D'C' B
hm	fule	nhin	sma e,

AG	GG	GA	D'D'C'	C'
hm	ghdi	ghdi	muska	yen

48. VO PARI KAHAAN SE LAAUN

Film: Pahchan (1970)
Lyrics: Verma Malik
Taal: Kaharwa
Transpose +1 and play from C Scale

Music: Shanker Jaikishan
Singer: Mukesh, Suman K.
Chord: $DF^\#B$ $S=C\#$

S: (vo pari kahaan se laaun teri dulhan jise banaaun
      ki gori koi pasand na aaye tujhako
      ki chhori koi pasand na aaye tujhako) -3

S: ye to meri hai saheli, dilavaali alabeli
      jaise motiyaa chameli, jaise pyaar ki paheli
      solah saal ki umar, kokaa-kolaa si kamar
      ratti bhar bhi qasar kahi aaye na nazar
      kuchh huaa hai asar?

M: gol jude me ye veni, aur veni me ye tahani
      kaise judiyo se ped ugaaye
      ye gagaaraam ke samajh me na aaye -2

S: vo pari kahaan se laaun teri dulhan jise banaaun

ki gori koi pasand na aaye tujhako
ki chhori koi pasand na aaye tujhako

S: aankh jisaki hai billi naam iskaa hai lilli
        aise kajare ki dhaar, jaise tikhi talavaar
        dekh hotho kaa ye rang dekh chalane kaa dhang
        kate angrezi baal, baandhaa reshami rumaal
        bolo kyaa hai khayaal?
M: ise jab liyaa taq meraa rang huaa faq
        chhori ho ke hajaamat karaaye
        ye gagaaraam ke samajh me na aaye
S: vo pari kahaan se laaun teri dulhan jise banaaun
        ki gori koi pasand na aaye tujhako
        ki chhori koi pasand na aaye tujhako

S: nam iska kamal jaise ganne ki fasal
        jaise khila hai gulab dekh phura hai panjab
        dekh rup ki umang jaise hirni ka ang
        jaise milti ho khajur aisa mukhde pe nur
        bol hai manzur?
M: ye to nache chham chham mera nikale hai dam
        ise bhangda kon nachaye?
        ye gagaaraam ke samajh me na aaye
S: vo pari kahaan se laaun teri dulhan jise banaaun
        ki gori koi pasand na aaye tujhako
        ki chhori koi pasand na aaye tujhako

S: ye to sindh se hai aayi kare bee ae ki padhaayi
        tang kurta paijama ye to chhokari hangama
        jaise titli ke ang jaise udti patang
        jaise koyal ki ku jaise khile khushbu
        kahti hai i love u
M: he prabhu he prabhu tu hi tu tu hi tu
        aise nakhare kaun uthaaye?
        ye gagaaraam ke samajh me na aaye
S: vo pari kahaan se laaun teri dulhan jise banaaun
        ki gori koi pasand na aaye tujhako

ki chhori koi pasand na aaye tujhako

S: na ye dil ki hai chhoti na ye pyar ki hai khoti
zara ho gayi hai moti tabhi lagti hai chhoti
dekh iske masal ghi khati hai asal
tere kheton me jaye tere hal bhi chalaaye
tere bade kam aaye

M: mujhe karo na hairan ye to lage pahalvan
ise kasarat kon karaye?
ye gagaaraam ke samajh me na aaye

S: vo pari kahaan se laaun teri dulhan jise banaaun
ki gori koi pasand na aaye tujhako
ki chhori koi pasand na aaye tujhako

S: chhodo ye to hai naadaan, kare sabko hairaan
nahin samjhega pyar bilkul hai ganwar
ise rahne do kanwara firne do mara mara
aao ham sab jaayein maza isko chakhaayein
hosh iske udaayein

M: ye hont jab khole baar baar yahi bole
gangaraam ki samajh mein n aaye
ye gangaraam ki samajh mein n aaye

VO PARI KAHAAN SE LAAUN

dha	ge	n	ti	n	ke	dhi	n	dha	ge	n	ti	n	ke	dhi	n
1	2	3	4	5	6	7	8	1	2	3	4	5	6	7	8

prelude:
BBBB BBBB AAAA AAAA
GGGG GGGG $F^\#F^\#F^\#F^\#$ $F^\#F^\#F^\#F^\#$
BD'C'BAGF$^\#$EF$^\#$-

      B BD' D'D' C' BA AA AC'C' BA GAG
suman: vo pri kha   se laun teri dulhn jise bnaun

    F$^\#$ EF$^\#$ ED DD G G- GF$^\#$F$^\#$
    ki gori koii psnd n aaye tujhko

F#   EF#   ED   DD   A   AG   GF#F#
ki   chhori koii psnd   n   aaye tujhko

interlude: F# D' Db' Db'Db' Db'Db'_ Db'Db'_Db'Db' Db'Db'
           F# Db' B BB BB BB BB BB
           F#F#GA F#Db'BA F#F#GA F#Db'BA
           BB BB BB BB Db' B A G F#

     F#   F F#F#   F#   FF#F#   F#FF#F#   F#FF#F#
suman: ye to meri hai sheli,   dilvali   albeli

     F#F# GGG   F#GG   F#F#   G-   G F#GG
     jaise motiya chmeli, jaise   pyar ki pheli

     GF# G- G F#G   GF# GG   G F#G
     solh sal ki umr, koka-kola   sii kmr

     F#A A   A   AbA   ADb'   Db'   B BB
     rtti bhr bhi qsr   khin   aaye n nzr

     Glay Chord (DF#B)
     kuchh huaa hai asr?

        D'   D'D'   D'   Db' D'D'   D'   D'D'   D'   Db'   D'D'
mukesh: gol jude me ye veni, aur veni me ye tahni

     D'D'   BD'D'   D' D'C'C' BBA
     kaise judiyon se pe-d   ugaye

     A AAAC'   C' BBA A   G GF#
     ye qngaram ki smjh me n aaye

        B BD' D'D' C' BA
suman: vo pri kaha se laun   ...

play rest of the song as above.

49.   YUN HI DIL NE CHAHA THA

Film: Dil Hi To Hai (1963)   Music: Raushan
Lyrics: Sahir Ludhiyanvi   Singer: Suman K.
Taal: Kaharwa   Chord: CFA^{b} S=C#
Transpose +1 and play from C Scale

yunhi dil ne chaahaa thaa ronaa rulaanaa
teri yaad to ban gayi ik bahaanaa

hame bhi nahi ilm, ham jis pe roye
vo biti rute hai ke aataa zamaanaa
vo biti rute hai ke aataa zamaanaa
teri yaad to ban gayi ik bahaanaa

gam-e-dil bhi hai aur gam-e-zindagi bhi
na isakaa thikaanaa na usakaa thikaanaa
na isakaa thikaanaa na usakaa thikaanaa
teri yaad to ban gayi ik bahaanaa

koi kis pe tadape, koi kisape roye
idhar dil jalaa hai, udhar aashiyaanaa
idhar dil jalaa hai, udhar aashiyaanaa
teri yaad to ban gayi ik bahaanaa

yunhi dil ne chaahaa thaa ronaa rulaanaa
teri yaad to ban gayi ik bahaanaa

(on this tune you can play many similar songs like:
-chura le na tumko ye mausam suhana khuli wadiyon me)

YUN HI DIL NE CHAHA THA

dha	ge	n	ti	n	ke	dhi	n	dha	ge	n	ti	n	ke	dhi	n
1	2	3	4	5	6	7	8	1	2	3	4	5	6	7	8

prelude: sitar: E♭ A♭ G A♭ F

dha	ge	n	ti	n	ke	dhi	n	dha	ge	n	ti	n	ke	dhi	n
														F	-
														yu	-
G	-	E♭	-	-	F	-	G	B♭	-	-	-	B♭	-	B♭	-
hi	-	-	-	-	dil	-	ne	chha	-	-	-	ha	-	tha	-
-	-	B♭	C'	-	C'	-	B♭	B♭	-	-	-	A♭	-	G	-
-	-	ro	-	-	na	-	ru	la	-	-	-	na	-	-	-
F	-	F	F	-	F	-	F	F	G	-	-	F	-	E♭	-
-	-	te	ri	-	ya	-	d	to	-	-	-	bn	-	-	-
-	-	G	G	-	A♭	-	G	F	-	-	-	F			
-	-	g	yi	-	i	k	b	ha	-	-	-	na	-		

interlude:

Cynthe: F E♭ F A♭ G A♭ C' B♭ D' C' F' –

sitar: B♭ A♭ G B♭ C' D' – D' – B♭ A♭ A♭ B♭

flute: FA♭GFE♭ CFE♭A♭ FE♭ CFEF

dha	ge	n	ti	n	ke	dhi	n	dha	ge	n	ti	n	ke	dhi	n
														F	-
														h	-
G	B♭	A♭	B♭	-	G	-	F	F	-	-	-	F	-	F	-
me	-	-	-	-	bhi	-	n	hin	-	-	-	il	-	m	-
-	-	E	-	-	F	-	G	E	-	F	-	D	-	C	-
-	-	hm	-	-	jis	-	pe	ro	-	-	-	ye	-	-	-
-	-	G	G	-	G	-	G	G	-	A♭	-	F	-	F	-
-	-	vo	bi	-	ti	-	ru	te	-	-	-	hain	-	ke	-
-	-	A	-	-	A	-	B♭	G	-	-	-	F	-	F	-
-	-	aa	-	-	ta	-	z	ma	-	-	-	na	-	vo	-
G	-	E♭	-	-	F	-	G	B♭	-	-	-	B♭	-	B♭	-
bi	-	-	-	-	ti	-	ru	te	-	-	-	hain	-	ke	-
-	-	B♭	C'	-	C'	-	B♭	B♭	-	-	-	A♭	-	G	-
-	-	aa	-	-	ta	-	z	ma	-	-	-	na	-	-	-

```
F  -  F  F | -  F  -  F | F  G  -  - | F  -  Eᵇ  -
-  -  te ri| -  ya -  d | to -  -  - | bn -  -  -

-  -  G  G | -  Aᵇ -  G | F  -  -  - | F  -
-  -  g  yi| -  i  k  b | ha -  -  - | na -
 D’ D’   C’ D’   D’Bᵇ   BᵇBᵇ  D’  D’ C’D’ D’Bᵇ  Bᵇ-
 gm e   dil bhi hai-   aur  gm e  zindgi-  bhi-
```

```
Bᵇ  BᵇBᵇF  GC’C’   C’  BᵇBᵇF  GBᵇBᵇ
n   iska  thikana  n   uska  thikana
```

```
F  GEᵇF  GBᵇBᵇ    Bᵇ  BᵇC’C’  BᵇBᵇ  AᵇGF
n  iska  thikana  n   uska    thikana—
```

```
FF   FF  FG  F  Eᵇ  GG  Aᵇ  GFF
teri yad to- bn-- gayi ik  bahana
```

```
FGBᵇAᵇBᵇ   G  F  FFF  EE  F  G  FEF D C
koii       kis pe tdpe koii kis pe ro----ye—
```

```
GG  G  G G Aᵇ F  AA  A Bᵇ G F
idhr dil jla--   hai udhr aashiyana
```

```
FGEᵇ   F  GBᵇ  Bᵇ   BᵇBᵇC’ C’BᵇBᵇ  AᵇGF
idhr   dil jla hai  udhr   aashiyana---
```

```
FF   FF  FG  F  Eᵇ  GG  Aᵇ  GFF
teri yad to- bn-- gayi ik  bahana
```

50. YE KISNE GEET CHHEDA

Film: Meri Surat Teri Aankhein (1963)
Lyrics: Shailendra
Taal: Daadra
Transpose +4 and play from C Scale

Music: Sachindev Burman
Singer: Mukesh, Suman K.
Chord: CEG   S=E

ye kisane giit chheda -2
dil mera naache, thirak, thirak, ye kisane giit chheda
ye kisaki zulf bikhari -2
jag saara gaya, mahak, mahak, ye kisaki zulf bikhari

chori chori, hole hole, thhndi thhndi, hawa aye -2
kaliyon ke, mukh chume, bagiya ko, dularaaye
daali daali, jaaye lachak lachak kisaki zulf bikhari
ye kisane giit chheda -2
dil mera naache, thirak, thirak, ye kisane giit chheda

tumane hi, kiya tona, tumane hi, jaadu fera
anjaani, dagari pe, chala dekho man mera
matawaala, gaya bahak bahak kisane giit chheda
ye kisaki zulf bikhari -2
jag saara gaya, mahak, mahak, ye kisaki zulf bikhari

ek baazi, maine jiti, ek baaji, dil haara -2
mere saajan, tere kaaran, maine chhoda, jag saara
sng tere chali runak jhunak kisane giit chheda
ye kisaki zulf bikhari -2
jag saara gaya, mahak, mahak, ye kisaki zulf bikhari
ye kisane giit chheda -2
dil mera naache, thirak, thirak, ye kisane giit chheda -2

Vinod Kumar

YE KISNE GEET CHHEDA

dhi	na	ti	na	dhi	na	dhi	na	ti	na	dhi	na
1	2	3	4	5	6	1	2	3	4	5	6

prelude:
GA^{b}GFG -2 GA^{b}GFG -2 GC'   G- A^{b}GF
hu-------- aa------   aa--- aa------

flute: FG FEF -2 AGAFG-
guitar: E'D'C'BA^b GA^{b}B^b C'D'E' -2 G E G E' C'-

1	2	3	4	5	6	1	2	3	4	5	6
										C	-
										ye	-
D	E	C	D	.B^b	C	C	-	C	-	E	E
ki	s	ne	gi	-	t	chhe	-	da	-	di	l
E	F	-	-	E	D	E	D	C	D	C	.B^b
me	ra	-	-	na	che	thi	r	k	thi	r	k
C	E	C	D	.B^b	C	C	-	C	-	C	-
ki	s	ne	gi	-	t	chhe	-	da	-	ye	-
D	E	C	D	.B^b	C	C	C	C	-	E	E
ki	s	ki	zu	-	lf	bi	kh	ri	-	j	g
E	F	-	-	E	D	E	D	C	D	C	.B^b
sa	ra	-	-	g	ya	m	h	k	m	h	k
C	E	C	D	.B^b	C	C	C	C	-		
ki	s	ki	zu	-	lf	bi	kh	ri	-		

interlude: G—AC'A AC'AGE—EFG—A--- AG-

1	2	3	4	5	6	1	2	3	4	5	6
										E	E
										cho	ri
F	G	-	-	A	B^b	G	A	-	-	B^b	A
cho	ri	-	-	hau	le	hau	le	-	-	thn	di
A	G	F	-	G	A	G	G	-$^{\#}$	-	F	E
thn	di	-	-	h	va	aa	ye	-	-	k	li
F	G	-	-	A	B^b	A	A	-	-	B^b	A
yon	ke	-	-	mu	kh	chu	me	-	-	b	gi

A	G	F	-	G	A	G	G	E	G	E	E
ya	ko	-	-	du	l	ra	ye	-	-	da	li
E	F	-	-	E	D	E	D	C	D	C	.B^b
da	li	-	-	ja	ye	l	ch	k	l	ch	k
C	E	C	D	.B^b	C	C	C	C	-	C	-
ki	s	ki	zu	-	lf	bi	kh	ri	-	ye	-
D	E	C	D	.B^b	C	C	-	C	-	E	E
ki	s	ne	gi	-	t	chhe	-	da	-	di	l
E	F	-	-	E	D	E	D	C	D	C	.B^b
me	ra	-	-	na	che	thi	r	k	thi	r	k
C	E	C	D	.B^b	C	C	-	C	-		
ki	s	ne	gi	-	t	chhe	-	da	-		

interlude: GG GG G- E^{b}E^b E^{b}E^b E^b- EE EE E- C.B^b C E C-

										E	E
										tu	m
F	G	-	-	A	B^b	A	A	-	-	A	B^b
ne	hi	-	-	ki	ya	to	na	-	-	tu	m
A	G	F	-	G	A	G	G	-$^\#$	-	F	E
ne	hi	-	-	ja	du	fe	ra	-	-	a	n
F	G	-	-	A	B^b	A	A	-	-	B^b	A
ja	ni	-	-	d	g	ri	pe	-	-	ch	la
A	G	F	-	G	A	G	G	E	G	E	E
de	kho	-	-	m	n	me	ra	-	-	m	t
E	F	-	-	E	D	E	D	C	D	C	.B^b
va	la	-	-	g	ya	b	h	k	b	h	k
C	E	C	D	.B^b	C	C	-	C	-	C	-
ki	s	ne	gi	-	t	chhe	-	da	-	ye	-
C	E	C	D	.B^b	C	C	C	C	-	E	E
ki	s	ki	zu	-	lf	bi	kh	ri	-	j	g

E	F	-	-	E	D	E	D	C	D	C	.B♭
sa	ra	-	-	g	ya	m	h	k	m	h	k
C	E	C	D	.B♭	C	C	C	C	-		
ki	s	ki	zu	-	lf	bi	kh	ri	-		

interlude: G—AC'A AC'AGE—EFG—A--- AG-interlude:

										E	E
										e	k
F	G	-	-	A	B♭	A	A	-	-	A	B♭
ba	zi	-	-	main	ne	ji	ti	-	-	e	k
A	G	F	-	G	A	G	G	-*	-	F	E
ba	zi	-	-	di	l	ha	ra	-	-	me	re
F	G	-	-	A	B♭	A	A	-	-	B♭	A
sa	jn	-	-	te	re	ka	rn	-	-	main	ne
A	G	F	-	G	A	G	G	E	G	E	E
chho	da	-	-	j	g	sa	ra	-	-	sn	g
E	F	-	-	E	D	E	D	C	D	C	.B♭
te	re	-	-	ch	li	ru	n	k	jhu	n	k
C	E	C	D	.B♭	C	C	-	C	-		
ki	s	ne	gi	-	t	chhe	-	da	-		

-* music: C' A C'--- G E G --- (for repeating the line)

51. YE MAUSAM RANGEEN SAMAA

Film: Modern Girl (1961)
Lyrics: Gulshan Bawra
Taal: Kaharwa
Transpose -1 and play from C Scale

Music: Ravi
Singer: Mukesh, Suman K.
Chord: CEG   S=B

ye mausam rangin sama, thahar zra o jaan-e-jaan
tera mera, mera tera pyaar hai, to fir kaisa sharamaana
ruk to main jaaun jaan-e-jaan, mujhako hai inkaar kahaan
tera mera, mera tera pyaar sanam na ban jaaye afsaana

ye chaand ye sitaare, kahate hain mil ke saare, aaja pyaar karein
ye chnda bairi dekhe, aise men bolo kaise iqraar karein
dil men hai kuchh, kuchh kahe zubaan pyaar yahi hai jaan-e-jaan
tera mera, mera tera pyaar hai, to fir kaisa sharamaana

ye pyar ki lambi rahen, kahati hain ye nigahen kahin dur chalein
baithe hain ghera daale, ye zaalim duniya waale, hamen dekh jale
jalata hai to jale jahaan thhahar jra o jaan-e-jaan
tera mera, mera tera pyaar sanam na ban jaaye afsaana

Vinod Kumar

YE MAUSAM RANGEEN SAMAA

dha	ge	n	ti	n	ke	dhi	n	dha	ge	n	ti	n	ke	dhi	n
1	2	3	4	5	6	7	8	1	2	3	4	5	6	7	8
C'	-	C'	B	C'	-	C'	B	C'	B	A	G	F	-	-	-
ye	-	mau	-	sm	-	rn	-	gi	-	n	s	ma	-	-	-
B	B	B	A	B	-	B	A	B	A	G	F	E	-	-	-
th	h	r	z	ra	-	o	-	ja	-	ne	-	ja	-	-	-
C	C	C	D	E	E	E	F	G	-	-	A	B	-	B	-
te	ra	me	ra	me	ra	te	ra	pya	-	-	r	hai	-	to	-
B	C'	C'	E'	D'	-	C'	C'	B	-	C'	-	-	-	-	-
fi	r	kai	-	sa	-	sh	r	ma	-	na	-	-	-	-	-

music: G- E'- D'- C'BA BD'C'

dha	ge	n	ti	n	ke	dhi	n	dha	ge	n	ti	n	ke	dhi	n
C'	-	C'	B	C'	-	C'	B	C'	B	A	G	F	-	-	-
ru	k	to	main	ja	-	un	-	ja	-	ne	-	ja	-	-	-
B	B	B	A	B	-	B	A	B	A	G	F	E	-	-	-
mu	jh	ko	-	hai	-	i	n	ka	-	r	k	ha	-	-	-
C	C	C	D	E	E	E	F	G	-	-	A	B	-	B	-
te	ra	me	ra	me	ra	te	ra	pya	-	r	s	nm	-	na	-
B	C'	C'	E'	D'	-	C'	C'	B	-	C'	-	-	-	-	-
b	n	ja	-	e	-	a	f	sa	-	na	-	-	-	-	-

interlude: G G A – GAGAGE G G A –
            G' G' A' – G'A'G'A'G'E' G' G' A'-
            E' --- G' --- E'G'E'D'C'- E' --- G' --- E' D' C'
            G G A GAGAGE GGA BD'E'-

dha	ge	n	ti	n	ke	dhi	n	dha	ge	n	ti	n	ke	dhi	n
															E'
															ye
Eb'	-E'	Eb'	E'	C'	A	-	E'	Eb'	E'	Eb'	E'	C'	A	A	D'
chan	-d	ye	si	ta	re	-	kh	te	hain	mil	ke	sa	re	aa	ja
C'	-	C'C'	C'	-	-	G	A	D'	-	-	C'	D'	C'	-	E'
pya	-	r,k	ren	-	-	-	-	-	-	-	-	-	-	-	ye
Eb'	-E'	Eb'	E'	C'	A	-	E'	Eb'	E'	Eb'	E'	C'	A	A	D'
chan	-d	ye	si	ta	re	-	kh	te	hain	mil	ke	sa	re	aa	ja

C'	-	C'C'	C'	-	-	-	E'	E'ᵇ	-E'	E'ᵇ	E'	C'	A	-	E'
pya	-	r,k	ren	-	-	-	ye	chn	da	bai	ri	de	khe	-	ae

Eᵇ	E'	E'ᵇ	E'	C'	A	A	D'	C'	-C'	C'	C'	-	-	-	-
se	me	bo	lo	kai	se	i	q	ra	-r	k	ren	-	-	-	-

C'	-	C'	B	C'	-	C'	B	C'	B	A	G	F	-	-	-
di	l	me	hai	ku	chh	ku	chh	k	he	-	zu	ba	-	-	-

B	-	B	A	B	-	B	A	B	A	G	F	E	-	-	-
pya	-	r	y	hi	-	hai	-	ja	-	ne	-	ja	-	-	-

C	C	C	D	E	E	E	F	G	-	-	A	B	-	B	-
te	ra	me	ra	me	ra	te	ra	pya	-	-	r	hai	-	to	-

B	C'	C'	E'	D'	-	C'	C'	B	-	C'	-	-	-	-	-
fi	r	kai	-	sa	-	sh	r	ma	-	na	-	-	-	-	-

interlude: C' D' E' D' A – A B C' B G ---
            C' D' E' D' A – A B C' B G ---
            E'D'C'AG- BA D'C' E'D' G'E' A'G' C'D'E'-

E' Eᵇ' E' E'ᵇE' C'A E'Eᵇ' E' Eᵇ' E'C'A AD' C'C' C'C'
ye pyar ki lmbi rahe kahti hain ye nigahe, khin dur chle

E'Eᵇ' E' Eᵇ'E' C'A E' Eᵇ'E' Eᵇ'E' C'A AD' C'C' C'C'
baithe hain ghera dale ye zalim duniya vale, hme dekh jle

C' C'B C' C'B C'BA GF BB AB BA BAG F E
jlata- hai to- jle- jhan, thhr zra o- ja-n-e-jan

tera mera ...

52.   SARGAM OR ALANKAR OR PALTE

C D E F G A B C'
C' B A G F E D C

CC DD EE FF GG AA BB C'C'
C'C' BB AA GG FF EE DD CC

CCC DDD EEE FFF GGG AAA BBB C'C'C'
C'C'C' BBB AAA GGG FFF EEE DDD CCC

CD DE EF FG GA AB BC'
C'B BA AG GF FE ED DC

CDE- DEF- EFG- FGA GAB- ABC'-
C'BA- BAG- AGF- GFE- FED- EDC-

CDEF DEFG EFGA FGAB GABC'
C'BAG BAGF AGFE GFED FEDC

CDEFG DEFGA EFGAB FGABC'
C'BAGF BAGFE AGFED GFEDC

CE DF EG FA GB AC'
C'A BG AF GE FD EC

CF DG EA FB GC'
C'G BF AE GD FC

CG DA EB FC'
C'F BE AD GC

CA DB EC'
C'E BD AC

CDCDE– DEDEF– EFEFG- FGFGA– GAGAB– ABABC'-
C'BC'BA- BABAG– AGAGF– GFGFE–FEFED– EDEDC-

CDECDCDE DEFDEDEF EFGEFEFG
FGAFGFG GABGAGA ABC'ABABC'

C'BAC'BC'BA BAGBABAG AGFAGAGF
GFEGFGFE FEFEFED EDCEDEDC

C
C D C
C D E D C
C D E F E D C
C D E F G F E D C
C D E F G A G F E D C
C D E F G A B A G F E D C
C D E F G A B C' C' B A G F E D C

C'
C' B C'
C' B A B C'
C' B A G A B C'
C' B A G F G A B C'
C' B A G F E F G A B C'
C' B A G F E D E F G A B C'
C' B A G F E D C D E F G A B C'

C-CDE- D-DEF- E-EFG- F-FGA- G-GAB- A-ABC'-
C'-C'BA- B-BAG- A-AGF- G-GFE- F-FED- E-EDC-

DC ED FE GF AG BA C'B D'C'
BC' AB GA FG EF DE CD .BC

CED DFE EGF FAG GBA AC'B BD'C'
C'AB BGA AFG GEF FDE ECD D.BC

.G G .A A .B B C C' D D' E E' F F'
F' F E' E D' D C' C B.B A.A G.G

C D^b E^b F G A^b B^b C'
C' B^b A^b G F E^b D^b C

C D^b E F G A^b B C'
C' B A^b G F E D^b C

53.   Other books of Vinod Kumar

Mukesh Songs' Western Notes, Part-1, 2

Lata Songs' Western Notes

Kishore Songs' Western Notes, Part-1, 2

Md. Rafi Songs' Western Notes, Part-1,2,3,4

Asha Songs' Western Notes

SD Burman and Yesudas Songs' Western Notes

Manna Dey Songs' Western Notes

Kumar Shanu Songs' Western Notes

Composer SD Burman Songs' Western Notes

Suman Kalyanpur Songs' Western Notes

Superhit Gazals' Western Notes

Bhajan Western Notes, Part-1,2,3

Sloan Duployan Shorthand book

These Books are also available in English SRGM and Western CDEFG style at notionpress.com and amazon.in and at Flipkart.com

For English SRGM books search… (Singer name) 51 Songs' Sargam, book.

For Western CDEFG books search… (Singer name) Songs' Western Notes, book.

If you like the books, pl. tell others.

vinod kumar (vinod66vk@gmail.com)

Enquiry may be made at mob: 9452904656
These books are available online only.
Whats app to Kavita Prakashan at 9452904656
Scan to Purchase from flipkart.com
Scan to Purchase from amazon.in

Scan below QR Code from your mobile to get Vinod Kumar's (Singer name) 51 Songs' Sargam books from Flipkart.com site . (Hindi, English, Western all)

Scan below QR Code from your mobile to get Vinod Kumar's (Singer name) 51 Songs' Sargam books from Amazon.in site . (Hindi, English, Western all)

ASHA
SONGS' WESTERN NOTES
Love Songs
Sad Songs
CDEFGABC
VINOD KUMAR

LATA
SONGS' WESTERN NOTES
Love Songs
Sad Songs
CDEFGABC'
VINOD KUMAR

SUPERHIT 51
GAZALS'
WESTERN NOTES
Gazals and Nazams in English and Western Notes
CDEFGABC'
VINOD KUMAR

Composer
S.D. Burman
Songs' Western Notes Part-1
Saiiya dil me aana re, Aake fir na jana re...
CDEFGABC
VINOD KUMAR

KISHORE
SONGS WESTERN NOTES
Part-2
CDEFGABC'
VINOD KUMAR

KISHORE
SONGS' WESTERN NOTES
CDEFGABC
VINOD KUMAR

KUMAR SHANU
SONGS' WESTERN NOTES
Songs' Lyrics in English and Notations in CDEF
CDEFGABC'
VINOD KUMAR

MANNA DEY
Songs' Western Notes
CDEFGABC
VINOD KUMAR

MD RAFI
SONGS' WESTERN NOTES Part-4
Mujhe ishq hai tujhi se....
Songs' Lyrics in English and Notations in CDEF
CDEFGABC'
VINOD KUMAR

Md RAFI
SONGS' WESTERN NOTES Part-3
Songs' Lyrics in English and Notations in CDEF
CDEFGABC
VINOD KUMAR

SONGS' WESTERN NOTES Part-2
Chal ud ja re panchhi
ke ab ye desh hua begana
CDEFGABC'
VINOD KUMAR

MD RAFI
SONGS' WESTERN NOTES
Songs' Lyrics in English and Notations in CDEF
CDEFGABC
VINOD KUMAR

SONGS' WESTERN NOTES
Songs' Lyrics in English and Notations in CDEF
CDEFGABC
VINOD KUMAR

MUKESH
SONGS' WESTERN NOTES Part-2
CDEFGABC
VINOD KUMAR

MUKESH
SONGS' WESTERN NOTES
Sad Songs
Love Songs
Songs' Lyrics in English and Notations in CDEF
CDEFGABC'
VINOD KUMAR

Hindi सा रे ग म
English SRGM
And
Western CDEF
All type books